Praise

'Absolutely heartbreaking' *Guardian*

'In her brave new memoir, Ruby's daughter Shari Franke opens up about the abuse she and her siblings experienced, and her own path toward survival' **People**

'Shari reveals the disturbing truth behind 8 Passengers for the first time' ***Variety***

'[A] bombshell new memoir' ***Page Six***

'Heart-wrenchingly personal . . . dizzying' ***Rolling Stone***

the house of my mother

A Daughter's Quest for Freedom

SHARI FRANKE

GALLERY BOOKS UK

London · New York · Amsterdam/Antwerp · Sydney/Melbourne · Toronto · New Delhi

First published in the United States by Gallery Books,
an imprint of Simon & Schuster, LLC, 2025
First published in Great Britain by Gallery Books,
an imprint of Simon & Schuster UK Ltd, 2025
This edition published in Great Britain by Gallery Books, an
imprint of Simon & Schuster UK Ltd, 2026

Copyright © Shari Franke, 2025

The right of Shari Franke to be identified as the author of this work has been asserted in accordance with the Copyright, Designs and Patents Act, 1988.

Some names and identifying characteristics have been changed,
and some dialogue has been recreated.

1 3 5 7 9 10 8 6 4 2

Simon & Schuster UK Ltd
1st Floor
222 Gray's Inn Road
London WC1X 8HB

For more than 100 years, Simon & Schuster has championed authors and the stories they create. By respecting the copyright of an author's intellectual property, you enable Simon & Schuster and the author to continue publishing exceptional books for years to come. We thank you for supporting the author's copyright by purchasing an authorised edition of this book.

No amount of this book may be reproduced or stored in any format, nor may it be uploaded to any website, database, language-learning model, or other repository, retrieval, or artificial intelligence system without express permission. All rights reserved. Enquiries may be directed to Simon & Schuster, 222 Gray's Inn Road, London WC1X 8HB or RightsMailbox@simonandschuster.co.uk

Simon & Schuster strongly believes in freedom of expression and stands against censorship in all its forms. For more information, visit BooksBelong.com.

www.simonandschuster.co.uk
www.simonandschuster.com.au
www.simonandschuster.co.in

Simon & Schuster Australia, Sydney
Simon & Schuster India, New Delhi

The authorised representative in the EEA is Simon & Schuster Netherlands BV, Herculesplein 96, 3584 AA Utrecht, Netherlands. info@simonandschuster.nl

The author and publishers have made all reasonable efforts to contact copyright-holders for permission, and apologise for any omissions or errors in the form of credits given. Corrections may be made to future printings.

A CIP catalogue record for this book is available from the British Library

Paperback ISBN: 978-1-3985-4787-2
eBook ISBN: 978-1-3985-4785-8
Interior design by Jaime Putorti

Printed and Bound in the UK using 100% Renewable Electricity at CPI Group (UK) Ltd

To anybody who has been silenced, gaslit, abused, or lonely.

You are stronger than you know.

May earthly and heavenly angels lift you up.

CONTENTS

INTRODUCTION: Finally — *xv*

PART ONE:
The Garden of Earthly Delights

CHAPTER 1: Sealed — 3
CHAPTER 2: Teardrops — 9
CHAPTER 3: Mommy Isn't Very Nice to Me — 12
CHAPTER 4: The Rage Inside — 18
CHAPTER 5: Pioneers — 22
CHAPTER 6: Ruby's Rage — 28
CHAPTER 7: Refuge — 32

PART TWO:
Ship of Fools

CHAPTER 8: A Star Is Born — 41
CHAPTER 9: Baby Climbs Out of Crib — 45
CHAPTER 10: Remodeling Reality — 50
CHAPTER 11: Teenage Influencer — 54
CHAPTER 12: I Don't Think My Mother Loves Me — 63
CHAPTER 13: Busted — 69
CHAPTER 14: Mommy's Little Drama Queen — 74
CHAPTER 15: One Million Followers — 82

PART THREE:
The Conjurer

CHAPTER 16:	Snake in the Garden	*95*
CHAPTER 17:	The Cult of ConneXions	*103*
CHAPTER 18:	Isolation Tactics	*111*
CHAPTER 19:	Winning the Self-Loathing Olympics	*115*
CHAPTER 20:	Dirty Laundry	*118*
CHAPTER 21:	Jodi Says	*124*
CHAPTER 22:	Burn It and Be Damned	*130*
CHAPTER 23:	Obedient Little Drone	*138*
CHAPTER 24:	The Demon in My Room	*145*

PART FOUR:
Mankind Beset by Devils

CHAPTER 25:	Ninth Passenger	*153*
CHAPTER 26:	In Spirit and in Truth	*156*
CHAPTER 27:	Dirty. Shameful. Ruined.	*164*
CHAPTER 28:	Grateful	*168*
CHAPTER 29:	Jingle Hell	*175*
CHAPTER 30:	Children Are Not Entitled to a Magical Childhood	*179*
CHAPTER 31:	Poisoned Well	*185*
CHAPTER 32:	Seeds of Healing	*190*
CHAPTER 33:	Puppets and Puppeteers	*194*
CHAPTER 34:	Facsimile Father	*198*
CHAPTER 35:	Care Package	*206*
CHAPTER 36:	Fawn	*213*
CHAPTER 37:	Showdown	*217*

PART FIVE:
Fall of the Damned

CHAPTER 38: The Echo Chamber	229
CHAPTER 39: Abandoned by Justice	233
CHAPTER 40: Mommy's Mausoleum	236
CHAPTER 41: True Crimes	252
CHAPTER 42: The House of My Mother	260
CHAPTER 43: Rings of Remembrance	263
CHAPTER 44: Evidence in Plain Sight	269
CHAPTER 45: Home Sweet Home	275
CHAPTER 46: Judgment Day	278
CHAPTER 47: Ruby's Journal	284
CHAPTER 48: It Ends Here	288
EPILOGUE: Seven Passengers	295
Acknowledgments	299

the

house

of my

mother

I would lead you and bring you into the house of my mother—she who used to teach me.

SONG OF SOLOMON 8.2,
NEW AMERICAN STANDARD BIBLE

INTRODUCTION

finally

August 30, 2023

It was a Wednesday, the start of a new college year, and I was slumped at my cramped desk, drowning in a sea of syllabi and first-week reading assignments. I skimmed the pages, but my mind refused to engage, thoughts always circling back to my five siblings.

A year had passed since I'd heard their voices, seen their faces, and the thought of them trapped in that house was eating me alive. Despite all my efforts—the countless phone calls, the desperate pleas to anyone who would listen—it seemed like there was nothing we could do to remove them from harm's way.

My phone rang, our neighbor's name flashing on the screen. My heart skipped a beat—each call from this neighbor represented a lifeline. It meant an update about the kids. It meant that they were still alive.

"Shari, the police are at your mother's house!" The words exploded through the speaker, no time for hello. "They've got guns out, they're about to bust down the door!"

My heart seized in my chest as vivid, horrifying images flooded my mind. Tiny body bags being carried out of my mother's home by faceless figures in uniforms.

It's happened, came the thought. *They're dead.*

In a daze, I grabbed my car keys and bolted. The drive from my student apartment to my mother's house in Springville usually took twenty minutes, but today it was an eternity compressed into moments of blind panic.

I hadn't been back to that house since Ruby had disowned me a year prior. Ruby, the self-anointed saint of motherhood. Ruby, who had turned my life into a surreal version of *The Truman Show* for her social media disciples. Ruby, who had subjected me and my siblings to her twisted interpretation of crime and punishment all our lives—until Jodi came along, adding terrifying new flavors of sadism to the regime.

Jodi. Our family's very own cult leader, a false prophet who swept into our lives like a hurricane, turning my mother into a fawning, starstruck acolyte who lapped up her every demented word like it was holy water. My father, once our anchor, had been banished, leaving Ruby and Jodi to rule unchallenged over my four youngest siblings who were still there with them.

I drove through the familiar streets of Springville, a dull, all-too-familiar anger simmering within me as I navigated the quiet of suburbia. Why did no one have any information on the children? Why had they been pulled out of school? Why couldn't anyone shield them from harm?

Countless warnings had already been sent to the Division of Child and Family Services (DCFS), to law enforcement by me and by concerned neighbors. I'd been shouting from the rooftops for a year. Yet, despite the glaring signs of trouble, no action had been taken. The red flags we'd raised might as well have been invisible, and the system that was supposed to protect my siblings had left them at the mercy of two women drunk on delusion and unchecked power.

I turned onto our sleepy cul-de-sac and encountered a war zone. Police cruisers formed a barricade of flashing lights. SWAT teams prowled our front lawn. Neighbors huddled on the sidewalks, fear and fascination on their faces.

I got out of my car and an officer blocked my path, his face a tombstone. "I can't let you go past this point, miss."

"But that's my house!" I pleaded. "My siblings—are they safe? Where are they?"

Snippets of radio chatter teased me. Was that my brother's name I heard?

"Please," I begged. "Will someone tell me what's happening?"

An officer approached, his tone urgent.

"Miss, can you provide us with the layout of the house? Any safes? Guns?"

Through my tears, I gave him the information he needed: seven bedrooms, six bathrooms where we once jostled for mirror space, some guns locked away, a pantry that could outlast an apocalypse. Each room echoing with the ghosts of who we once were.

Then, chaos erupted. The front door splintered under the battering ram's assault. Officers swarmed in like angry hornets. I stood, rooted to the spot, watching.

God, please. Let them be alive, I prayed.

A surreal thought bubbled up. This moment, this climax of my family's descent into madness, needed to be documented, preserved, and shared on social media. Just like every forced smile, every staged perfection had been, too.

I pulled out my phone, my hands steady despite the madness around me.

Frame shot. Snap.

The caption crystallized in my mind, a single word that carried the weight of years:

FINALLY.

Upload to Instagram. Share.

This nightmare was born on social media—it should die there, too.

PART ONE

the
garden
of
earthly
delights

CHAPTER 1

sealed

I have a recurring dream. It always starts so beautifully.

Ethereal light bathes rolling fields as far as the eye can see. A sense of profound peace washes over me as I realize this must be heaven. My earthly journey has ended.

The landscape shifts, familiar yet otherworldly. Loved ones I've lost appear in the distance, their faces radiant. I move toward them, weightless, unburdened, embracing them with tears of joy. *This is paradise*, I think. *This is peace.*

Then I see those eyes. Cold and unyielding, boring into me with a power as ancient as the stars. It's her. Ruby.

Suddenly, God's voice booms around me, shaking the very foundations of heaven:

"My child, you were wrong to defy your mother!"

I jolt awake, heart pounding, and for a moment the terror lingers—even in the afterlife, will I never be free from her?

◇◇◇◇◇◇◇

My mother was born Ruby Griffiths on January 18, 1982, in Logan, Utah, the first child of five to Chad and Jennifer Griffiths, whose families had been devout members of the Church of Jesus Christ of Latter-day Saints (LDS) for generations.

When Ruby was young, her family relocated to Roy, Utah—a small city where the LDS church shaped nearly every aspect of life. In this tight-knit community, days revolved around scripture study, clean living, and, above all else, family. That is, after all, the cornerstone of our faith.

As the eldest in a strict, conservative home, Ruby's childhood was less about play and more about responsibility, and she was tasked with helping to raise her younger siblings. I can easily imagine a young Ruby, spine straight and eyes determined, navigating her family's expectations with a sense of righteous purpose, eagerly anticipating the day when she would have a family of her own, relishing the thought of finally being the one to make the rules and shape her home exactly as she saw fit. For Ruby, motherhood wasn't just a future role—it was the pinnacle of her aspirations, the one thing she had always wanted for herself above all else.

Her reverence for motherhood is not uncommon in the LDS theology I was raised with. Becoming a mother, in my faith, is a spiritual calling of the highest order, a chance to emulate the divine and participate in the grand tapestry of creation. Perhaps that's why the physical toll—the discomforts of pregnancy, the searing pain of childbirth—weren't seen as obstacles to be overcome or burdens to be endured, by Ruby. Rather they were sacred trials, opportunities to demonstrate her unwavering faith in God's plan and secure her place in the celestial afterlife alongside the hallowed ancestors who had walked this path before her.

As soon as she turned eighteen, the starting gun went off in

Ruby's race toward eternal exaltation, and my mother embarked on her mission to populate not just her earthly home but her heavenly mansion as well.

First, though, she needed a husband.

In the year 2000, when eighteen-year-old Ruby first set foot on the Utah State University campus, she had one thing on her mind: manhunting. Yes, she had chosen accounting as her major but college was never about learning for Ruby. It was about finding a mate so she could get married, start a family, and begin fulfilling her divine purpose, A.S.A.P.

On a color-coded vision board Ruby outlined the key qualities she required in a man. "Five inches taller than me." "Handsome." "Car paid off." "Engineer." (Her own father was an engineer, so perhaps she liked the idea of history repeating itself.) It goes without saying, her ideal man had to be devoted to the church.

Enter my father, Kevin Franke: a senior living on campus, four years older at twenty-two, on the brink of completing his civil engineering degree, and very much a product of his LDS faith. He stood five inches taller than Ruby (check), had a chiseled jawline (handsome—double check), and his keen intellect and ambition hinted at a promising future.

Plus, he seemed so . . . nice. Exuding genuine kindness, Kevin had a laid-back aura that was a balm to Ruby's intense spirit. Ruby had no interest in power struggles, after all; what she needed was someone relaxed enough to let her take the reins without too much resistance, a copilot content to let her navigate their shared journey, pay the bills, and give her the children she longed for.

Born on October 9, 1978, in Ogden, Utah, Kevin was the youngest of seven siblings, trailing his nearest brother by a full twelve years. Kevin's late arrival made him something of an anomaly—while his siblings were navigating high school and beyond, he was still learning to tie his shoes, and his days unfolded in a haze of neighborhood adventures and sports on TV, overseen by parents who'd done it all before.

Kevin's mom didn't like to cook or bake—life revolved around premade meals, TV, and talk of faith. The household was generally relaxed, without a lot of rules; an easygoing environment that sculpted Kevin into a gentle, even-keeled sort of guy.

Like Ruby, Kevin was devoted to finding his spiritual partner; a future mother to the children he hoped to raise in the gospel. But he had come to college to learn, secure his future, and had been in no hurry to meet his wife. Until he laid eyes on Ruby, that is.

He saw her first, working the room at a welcome week hot dog social on campus. The undisputed queen bee, Ruby flitted from man to man, her flirtatious confidence unlike anything he'd ever seen before. It helped that she was naturally beautiful, blond, with a huge dazzling smile and a svelte figure—Ruby was just his type.

As she methodically auditioned potential husbands, like a director casting her leading man, Kevin sensed the clock was ticking. Ruby was a prize catch, and if he didn't somehow distinguish himself in the crowd, he'd wind up just another also-ran in Ruby's race to the altar.

One evening, Kevin was sitting next to Ruby, holding her hand under a blanket as they watched a movie with some friends. Kevin couldn't care less about what was happening on the screen—all he could think about was the softness of her skin, the gentle pressure of her grip, the occasional brush of her thumb across his knuckles. Each sensation was electric, sending shivers up his arm and straight to his core.

Then Kevin glanced over and noticed another guy—one of Ruby's admirers—sitting way too close on her other side. His stomach dropped as he realized Ruby was holding this guy's hand under the blanket, too. Usually so levelheaded, Kevin jumped up, his face burning, heart racing. Without a word, he stormed out, leaving Ruby gaping after him.

The next day, Kevin talked to Ruby and laid down the law. No more hand-holding with other guys. Period. Ruby, attracted to his passion for her, fast-tracked Kevin to meet the Griffiths, her parents and toughest critics. They approved, and Kevin, in turn, introduced Ruby to his parents, the Frankes, who thought Ruby seemed like a lovely young lady, perfect for their son.

Two weeks after the day they met, Ruby cut to the chase. "So, are we getting married?" she asked.

Kevin, caught off-guard, uttered the most dangerous word in the dictionary: "Yes."

In just fourteen days, they had gone from strangers to engaged.

As Ruby and Kevin threw themselves into wedding planning, they got to know each other a little more. Turned out they both loved playing the piano, though their approaches to the instrument could not have been more different. Kevin had a photographic memory and could play jazz numbers and popular songs without even practicing. Ruby, on the other hand, had once poured her entire being into the piano. Throughout her teens, she'd immersed herself in the world of classical music, her dreams filled with visions of concert halls and standing ovations. She approached each piece with meticulous precision, spending hours perfecting every note, every dynamic shift. For her, playing wasn't about fun—it was about excelling, and when she fell short of perfection, it left a dent in her ego that no amount of practice seemed to fill.

Ruby's entire self-worth was built on exceptionalism, so if she couldn't be extraordinary, then what was the point? She needed a new dream, a fresh source of validation. If music wouldn't define her greatness, then motherhood would. Cherubic faces to beam up at her with the love and adoration she craved. Blank slates, ready to be inscribed with her wisdom, her values, her Rubyness.

A couple of kids would've suited Kevin fine, but Ruby craved a clan, and Kevin was happy to agree to Ruby's grand vision, vowing to move heaven and earth to support her in her dreams. Thus, the dynamic was set: Kevin, the perpetual supporting actor to Ruby's lead role in her epic production of "Ultimate Mother."

On December 28, 2000, barely three months after their first meeting, Ruby and Kevin strode toward the temple, ready to be eternally sealed in the eyes of God. Ruby was a vision in ivory, her hair a cascade of curls, a Southwestern blanket draped over her shoulders against the winter chill. Even Kevin's mismatched shoes—one black, one brown, thanks to rushed dressing in the dark—couldn't dim her smile.

This was it—Ruby's fairy-tale moment come to life. As the vows left her lips, she felt her happily-ever-after unfurling before her like a red carpet—finally, her life was about to begin.

CHAPTER 2

teardrops

"She's getting tired in there," the obstetrician said. "We'll need to do an assisted delivery."

Then, with a contraption that looked better suited to cleaning carpets than guiding new life, the doctor suctioned my head and forcibly pulled me out into the world.

It was March 3, 2003, and after nine difficult months of pregnancy filled with a slew of medical complications, twenty-one-year-old Ruby had finally evicted me, her first baby, from her womb. Somehow, through her fog of pain and exhaustion, Ruby managed a victorious smile. In her arms lay not just a baby but a woman's ultimate power. Her divine right to mold a new soul in her own image.

Cradling me in the exhausted aftermath of delivery, she looked past the squalling, writhing bundle in her arms to the exalted future I represented. In my tiny frame, Ruby saw the first brushstrokes of her magnum opus, Chapter One in the epic narrative that would be her legacy of unparalleled parenting prowess.

When I was around three months, Ruby took me to the pediatrician to find out why I was so grouchy—my constant wailing was testing her vision of motherly bliss—but the doctor said it was just colic. When I began refusing my bottles and growing lethargic, Kevin freaked out, rushing me to the emergency room, where they discovered that I had a life-threatening intestinal blockage. Without the immediate surgery I received, I most likely would have died. From the very start, it seemed, my childhood was destined to be a fight for survival.

Ruby didn't believe in comforting me when I was a baby, not in the way most parents do. Why would she? Her family's philosophy had always been that it doesn't hurt a baby to cry things out. Babies shouldn't be coddled. Tantrums should not be tolerated. It's for their own good, so they know who's boss, and when they grow up, they can learn to handle whatever life throws at them without being weak losers or crybabies.

Yet, ironically, my earliest memories are of Ruby crying. She had tears for every occasion. Joy, sorrow, boredom—it didn't matter, Ruby wept through it all, a woman perpetually at odds with her own equilibrium. Perhaps that's why she wanted so many children. A set of Russian nesting dolls, each one a slightly smaller version of the last, to absorb the tsunami of her raging emotions. For what better way to fill the gaping void within than to surround yourself with adoring little mini-mes? Interesting, though, how someone who cried so much herself seemed entirely immune to the tears of others, including mine.

I often wonder how much of my adult self was forged in those early formative years. My tendency to bottle up emotions, to present a stoic face to the world—are these echoes of an infant learning that her distress will always go unheeded? Even before I could form words or thoughts, was I learning that my pain didn't matter, that my needs were inconvenient? If my tears had been met with comfort instead of calculated indifference, would I have grown into someone more open, less guarded? Or was I always destined to retreat inward, becoming emotionally distant at a moment's notice, my feelings trapped behind a fortress that I still struggle to breach?

There's no way to know for sure—nature and nurture dance a complex tango, after all. But as I reflect on the many incongruities of my childhood, I can't help but feel sadness for the baby girl who cried for her mother. Who wanted a different kind of love than the kind she received. A love that allows for vulnerability, for tears, for the full range of human emotion. A love that allows a child the freedom to feel.

CHAPTER 3

mommy isn't very nice to me

In 2005, when I was two, the Ruby Show expanded its cast with my brother Chad's debut. Alongside him, another addition—our first dog, Nolly, a bouncing yellow Labrador puppy full of energy and love. She'd bound up to me, tail wagging furiously, showering me with sloppy kisses. Nolly, much like my little brother, would never fail to make me laugh.

In 2007, Ruby's third child, a girl, arrived on the scene. I will not be naming her in this book. Throughout this narrative, except for Chad, all my younger siblings will remain nameless. This isn't an oversight—it's my last line of defense for them.

In a kinder world, their stories would not be fodder for a book. Their private moments would be their own, known only to friends and family, not dissected by strangers on the internet. But peace and anonymity were never in the cards for us. We have Ruby to thank for that. Ruby and her insatiable hunger for attention and success.

My mother's journey into the spotlight started innocently enough—a mommy blog, titled *Good Lookin Home Cookin*. Mommy blogging was still a wild frontier then, ripe for the taking, and Ruby, like her sisters and friends, was excited to explore the possibilities of online media.

"My main goal for this blog is to journal our family's growth and experiences," Ruby proclaimed on her shiny new Blogger profile. "I want my children to have a place on the internet to go and enjoy reading about themselves and to see how they've progressed."

In my church, we're encouraged to document our lives meticulously, creating a road map for future generations to understand their roots, and it seemed as though the internet was just an extension of that, another way in which to do the Lord's work. Her little recipe-filled blog gave Ruby her first taste of online existence and the possibilities it held—as a tool for self-expression, a way to project an identity and forge a connection with people by sharing her recipes for raspberry butter, honey-lime chicken, and trail mix cookies—painting a picture of a home filled with the constant aroma of freshly baked bread and lovingly prepared meals.

The truth is, I'm not sure she ever made those dishes. Sure, Ruby was always baking something (she enjoyed trying out recipes from her Ann Romney cookbook) but most of the recipes on *Good Lookin Home Cookin* were aspirational rather than realistic, part of an image, that of the smiling, flour-smudged mama, the gaggle of cherubs gathered around the table. Even at this early stage of her online career, Ruby was showing her willingness to sacrifice authenticity on the altar of appearances.

There are some exceptions—I can confirm that her bread was legendary, a staple of every family gathering and potluck. She'd slice it thick, each piece a small loaf in itself, with uneven air pockets that spoke of hand-kneading and patience. The crust always had a slight crackle, giving way to a soft, warm interior. It was the kind of bread that demanded to be noticed, that turned a simple sandwich into a meal. One slice was often enough to fill me up, though I'd usually end up eating more.

She went on to start other blogs: *Full Suburban* and a mommy blogging group with her friends called *Yummy Mummy's*. Exercising her natural flair for marketing, she started branding our family photos, putting a logo in the corner, saying "It's A Franke Life." My three aunts, Ellie, Bonnie, and Julie, who had all settled within an hour and a half's drive of one another with their husbands and own growing broods, showed similar interests in blogging. It seemed embedded in the Griffiths' DNA, this feminine urge to take family life and turn it into something bigger.

"All my kids are going to learn how to play the piano," Ruby proclaimed, and as the firstborn, I got to be the guinea pig. From the age of five, Ruby would wake me up at 6:00 a.m. and plonk me in front of our Kawai upright to practice under her exacting gaze.

"Curve your fingers, Shari! Count it out!" she'd bark, slamming the piano with her hand, making me jump. "And for heaven's sake, don't give me that face."

I quickly learned that anything less than unbridled enthusiasm would trigger Ruby into a rage. One hint of displeasure on my face, and *whack*! A smack on my arm, a flick to my lips, or a sharp tug on my ear. I rarely cried when Ruby punished me—only one person in this house was allowed to shed tears, and it wasn't me. So I kept quiet, maintained a neutral expression. But beneath that calm exterior, a realization was taking root.

Mommy isn't very nice to me.

I was grateful for Nolly, who'd grown from an adorable puppy into a full-grown Labrador.

During those grueling piano practice sessions, when Mom's critical voice seemed to fill every corner of the room, Nolly would position herself under the piano, her warm body pressed against my feet. When Mom's tirade became too much, I'd glance down to see Nolly's gentle brown eyes gazing up at me, full of love and reassurance, as if to say, "It's okay, we're in this together."

"Mommy," I'd whimper, padding into my parents' room late at night, my stuffed horse, Bubbles, clutched to my chest. "My tummy hurts again."

Ruby would sigh heavily, her face pinched with annoyance. "Shari, we've been through this. There's nothing wrong with you. Go back to bed."

Even then, at five years old, my body was beginning to rebel, as if my very cells were crying out in protest against the environment in which they found themselves. I know now, of course, that the pain in my stomach was more than just a childish complaint—it was a physical response to my anxiety.

At night, that constant sense of unease would transform into something frightening. I would lie in bed, feeling the darkness press on me, utterly convinced that at any moment, a real-life demon would materialize beside me in my bed, ready to steal my soul. The fear was so real, I would plead with Ruby to leave the light on when I went to bed. But she had no time for my antics.

"No, Shari, you need to learn to sleep in the dark. There are no demons in my house." She was wrong, of course. There was certainly one.

And as soon as the lights went out, others would appear, grotesque figures straight out of a medieval hellscape, demonic entities leering with twisted grins. Their contorted faces haunted my sleepless nights, their agonized stories playing out in my dreams.

Why might a little girl harbor such tangible fears of demonic possession? I'm sure the deeply religious paradigm I was steeped in played a role. We firmly believe in Satan's power and the ability of his legion of fallen spirits to possess individuals. We believe that evil can inhabit physical forms, sometimes fleetingly, sometimes for extended periods. Having been raised to believe the very air I breathed was thick with unseen forces battling for dominion over my soul, it was a small step for my young mind to imagine that battle raging in my own bedroom.

Perhaps, too, my constant sense of dread around my emotionally volatile mother had primed me for such fears—as if my subconscious, unable to make sense of the chaos at home, had conjured supernatural terrors to give shape to the formless anxiety that seemed to permeate our home.

One week, I practiced a new song my piano teacher had assigned, drilling each note and chord until I could practically play it in my sleep. Ruby seemed pleased with my progress and decided it was time to move on to another piece of music. But then came my piano lesson.

"Not quite there yet, sweetie," said the teacher, after hearing me play. "Let's work on it for one more week."

One more week before she'd give me a sticker, passing it off as complete. Which doubtless seemed like a small thing to her. What she didn't realize was that little gold star represented life or death to me—how was I supposed to tell Ruby that her judgment had been overruled? Did my teacher not understand the precarious position in which she had placed me, the delicate balance of power she had just upset?

Hot tears pricked the corners of my eyes, and I squirmed in my seat as my teacher looked at me quizzically, unused to seeing such intense reactions from a five-year-old.

"What's the matter, Shari?" she asked.

"It's just, my mom thinks it's ready," I said, voice quavering.

How could I possibly explain to my teacher the minefield I was navigating daily, the eggshells upon eggshells that I was forced to tread?

My teacher, sensing that Pandora's box had just opened, chose wisely to shut it.

"Okay, never mind, here's a sticker, well done! You're doing great. New piece next week?"

Phew. I was out of the quicksand . . . for now.

Looking back, I marvel at how quickly my young mind adapted to Ruby's moods. At five, I knew my place instinctively. Be pliable. Be obedient. Shape and mold myself into whatever form would earn Ruby's conditional affection. I was a plant straining toward the sun, contorting myself into unnatural shapes just to catch a ray of her approval. But no matter how much I twisted and turned, no matter how much I achieved or accomplished, it would never be enough. There would always be some new hoop to jump through, some new standard to meet.

No child should ever have to earn a parent's affection. And no amount of achievement can ever fill the void where unconditional love should be. Today, the mere thought of sitting at a piano triggers some of my earliest and deepest anxieties, all tied to my mother. It's a shame how the most beautiful things, even music, can be ruined by the shadows of our past.

CHAPTER 4

the rage inside

When I was six years old, in 2009, Ruby gave birth to baby number four, another girl. My three aunts and their husbands were all present at the delivery, and as the story went, my sister just "popped" out, very fast, as though she were excited to be a part of the party.

The day Ruby came home from the hospital, I remember hovering in the doorway of her bedroom, watching as Ruby's mother presented her with a gift—a set of beautiful silk pajamas.

As I stood there, taking in the scene, I couldn't help but feel a pang of something I couldn't quite name. Jealousy? Longing? Ruby and her mother shared a bond that seemed impenetrable, a closeness I both admired and envied. Their easy laughter and shared smiles made me feel even more aware of the distance between Ruby and me.

I blurted out, "Will you bring me silk pajamas, too, when I have a baby?"

"Absolutely!" Ruby said, her voice light. "When you have a baby, that's when we can be friends."

In that instant, everything clicked into place. The distance I'd always felt, the longing for a closer relationship with my mother—it all made sense. Ruby and I couldn't be real friends until I was a woman with a husband and a family of my own. Until I was her equal. Just as Ruby had to become a wife and mother to truly earn her own mother's respect, I, too, would have to do the same. I would have to wait to be loved.

As I watched Ruby and her mother coo over the silk pajamas, I made a silent vow to myself. *One day, I will have a baby of my own. One day, I will receive my own set of pajamas. And on that day, finally, Ruby and I will be friends.*

Ruby started trying for her next baby immediately—even though it was obvious the stress of the constant pregnancies was getting to her. There were days her eyes would narrow to slits, her lips pressed into a thin, bloodless line as she observed the chaos of a house filling up with tiny humans. She'd survey our home with the cold calculation of a general assessing a battlefield, deciding how to impose order. Her weapon of choice? Her voice, sometimes her hands. Whoever was nearest bore the brunt of her frustration. A toppled vase, a stray toy, a glass bearing the faintest smudge—all became excuses for her assaults.

As soon as her children could toddle, Ruby enlisted us as her pint-size cleaning crew. Ruby's philosophy was simple: everyone contributes, everyone stays busy. Idle hands were the devil's playground, after all. One of her favorite tactics was the cleaning blitz. She'd gather us all with a glint in her eye and announce, "All right, troops. I'm setting the timer for one hour. We're going to clean this house from top to bottom. Ready, set, go!" We'd all scatter, a whirlwind of dusting, scrubbing, and tidying. It was chaotic, exhausting, and weirdly exhilarating. I didn't mind being Mommy's little helper, taking charge of my siblings to assist in our increasingly demanding domestic life.

Money was very tight, but Kevin's career as a geotechnical engineer was on the rise. He was genuinely fascinated by plate tectonics and earth liquefaction, immersing himself in an academic world where changes happened on a geological timescale. It was a stark contrast to the daily kitchen-sink dramas that consumed Ruby's psyche; the emotional meltdowns that left us all walking on eggshells.

One day, something shifted in Ruby. Her ever-present tears took on a new weight, and even with my limited understanding, I sensed something very sad had occurred. Ruby had suffered another miscarriage—her third—at seventeen weeks. The pregnancy was far enough along that she had felt those first fluttering kicks, knew the gender—a boy—and had even chosen a name. This time, it wasn't just losing a pregnancy; it felt like losing a son, a piece of herself.

Ruby never allowed herself time to grieve—she'd been taught that when life gets tough, you pull up your bootstraps and keep going. Keep having more babies, keep baking bread, keep bustling around.

One night, she had a dream she was grocery shopping and saw a little boy standing alone by the apples. She asked him where his mommy was. He told her he didn't have one. "Would you like to come home with me?" she said. "I could be your mommy!" He nodded his head, and Ruby put him in the cart on top of the bread and bananas. A month later, she was pregnant. As soon as Ruby's belly began to swell with her fifth child, a rare, fleeting calm washed over her. Pregnancy, for her, remained the highest calling, a sacred connection to her divine purpose. In those moments of quiet contemplation, when Ruby's hand rested gently on her growing bump, I saw glimpses of her at her most peaceful and fulfilled. How I longed to taste that same sense of purpose, to embark on my own spiritual journey and discover the true meaning of life.

CHAPTER 5

pioneers

When I was eight years old, we moved into our first detached family home. Finally, a swing set in the yard! I spent countless hours on those swings, pumping my legs and imagining I could touch the sky.

Ruby, in her enthusiasm for a fresh start, immediately set about painting the walls and doors various shades of yellow—her favorite color.

"Mommy," I once asked, "why does everything have to be so . . . bright?"

The garish hue was overwhelming, making every room feel loud and chaotic.

She just beamed at me, clearly proud of her handiwork. "It's cheerful! Don't you feel happy looking at it?"

I didn't have the heart to tell her that it mostly made me feel like I was trapped inside a giant banana.

Our house was in Springville, a flat, sprawling settlement of around ten thousand people, founded in 1850 by LDS pioneers.

Springville is nestled at the foot of the Wasatch Mountains—those mountains marked the edge of the world to me, for the longest time.

If you're after fine dining and high culture, you might be disappointed by Springville's offerings. We have a Walmart, a neighborhood grocery store, a couple Taco Bells, and an IHOP. That's about it. For more interesting entertainment options, people make the fifteen-minute drive to Provo or Spanish Fork.

Springville doesn't have its own temple, so many residents drive to the Provo temple to worship. It used to look like a wedding cake spaceship—an oval with a spire that resembled a UFO—but they've since added a more conventional redbrick building. For the classic white LDS temple experience, it's an hour-and-a-half drive north to the awe-inspiring Salt Lake Temple in Salt Lake City, its tallest central eastern spire crowned by the golden statue of the angel Moroni.

I remember how the nerves fluttered in my stomach as I stepped into the baptismal font, the water lapping at my ankles through the lace of my white jumpsuit. I was eight years old and about to officially take my first significant steps into my LDS faith through baptism.

As I was submerged beneath the surface, I felt a rush of peace. I was safe now. Protected by God and my faith, no matter what else happened around me. For what were Ruby's tantrums and tirades compared to the eternal truths of the gospel? Baptism felt like safety, security, and warmth, and I clung to that feeling like a lifeline, writing in my journal how being baptized felt like a warm waffle had been laid on top of me.

Around this time, Ruby felt I was old enough to have the "talk." About the birds and the bees. The front porch of our new home was the setting, and I don't remember exactly what prompted the discussion—maybe I had asked an innocent question about babies—

but I do recall struggling to process this new and frankly disturbing information.

I asked Ruby how long "it" had to stay in for a girl to get pregnant. Her vague answer—some arbitrary number—only added to my bewilderment. In my young mind, I imagined couples setting timers, treating the act with the same clinical detachment as baking a cake. *Plug it in for thirty seconds, and voilà! A baby is on the way.*

My worldview shifted dramatically as suddenly every adult I saw became a participant in this bizarre ritual. Our neighbor, taking out his garbage, had done this strange act. When our bishop drove by with his kids, I was mortified. *Oh my gosh, my bishop too?* The idea that these respectable adults, pillars of our community, engaged in such an act was almost too much to bear. I was left with a sense of disgust and confusion, viewing sex as a weird, slightly gross thing that adults obviously did out of duty to God, rather than desire.

In my family, it's a tradition to mark a child's baptism with a gift of their first set of scriptures. Mine was bound in rich leather, my name embossed in gold on the cover. Though the language within those pages often eluded me, I spent hours poring over each verse, highlighting favorite passages in a rainbow of colors. As soon as I began to learn about the story of Joseph Smith, the prophet and founder of our church, my fascination with my religion spilled over into obsession.

I loved this swashbuckling character who dared to challenge the religious establishment of his day, back in the 1830s. I was captivated by the stories of his treasure-hunting adventures transformed into holy quests, how his trances and visions gave rise to a whole new religion. Most little girls are into Disney, dolls, and cartoons (and I liked those things, too) but for me, the story of Joseph Smith and the golden plates was right up there with *Frozen*.

It helped that he wasn't some distant figure from the pages of ancient history or an Old Testament saint from a far-off land—he was kind of like us, a regular American from regular beginnings. And I loved that his story hadn't happened all that long ago, taking place recently enough that my blood ancestors, like the Widow of Nauvoo, might have been his friend.

The Widow of Nauvoo, an early ancestor on my mother's side of the family, lived in Nauvoo, Illinois, in the 1840s, during the persecution of LDS congregations. When a mob gathered to burn her house unless she denounced her faith, she stared them down, fearless. "Burn it and be damned!" she declared. Growing up, I had heard this story countless times; it was a sacred family legend.

Some days I'd look out the window and daydream, imagining the Widow of Nauvoo walking this very same terrain as she journeyed west to start anew. She could feel the grit underfoot, the sun on her back, as she dreamed of a future where she could finally be free from the horrors of her past—

"Shari! Come set the table for dinner!"

Ugh. I hated it when Ruby interrupted my spiritual reveries to make me do chores.

As I arranged the plates and napkins with practiced precision, my mind lingered on thoughts of the Widow, standing tall before a crowd of skeptics, her eyes blazing with the fire of conviction. In my mind's eye, I was right there beside her. Sometimes those moments felt more real to me than anything in the world around me.

"No, no, the forks go on the left, how many times do I have to tell you?" Ruby tutted disapprovingly, my youngest brother, still just a baby—resting on her hip.

Kevin's eyes flickered to mine with a sympathetic glimmer. I'd always felt a strong kinship with him, like we were shipmates sailing stormy waters, side by side. There was a stoicism to him, a quiet strength that I couldn't help but admire. Kevin might not have been a visionary like Joseph Smith or an iconoclast like the Widow of Nauvoo, but in his own way, he was a hero, too; a man who had taken on the thankless task of being the "nice guy" in our family.

As my mother fussed over dessert, cursing under her breath, I sat on my father's lap, full of questions as always.

"Dad, why do we have to pay tithing?" I asked, having just learned that everyone in my faith gives 10 percent of their income to the church. "Doesn't God have enough money already?"

Kevin chuckled and tousled my hair. "It's not about God having enough money, sweetie. Tithing is an ancient principle that goes back thousands of years. We give one-tenth of what we earn back to Him as an offering, to show our gratitude and obedience."

"But what does the church do with all that money?" I pressed.

"Well, the money goes to build temples and churches, and to fund missionary work around the world. But tithing is about more than just giving money. It's a covenant, which means a special promise we make with God. By giving a portion of what we have to Him, we show that we trust Him to take care of us in return."

I thought about this for a moment, trying to wrap my young mind around the concept. "So, it's like sharing our stuff with God, and then He shares His blessings with us?"

"Exactly." Kevin smiled. "When we keep our promises to God, He blesses us in ways we can't even imagine."

I nodded, feeling a sense of pride in being part of something so important.

"I want to pay tithing, too, Dad. When I'm older and have my own money, I'm going to give one-tenth back to God, just like you do."

Ruby, who had been listening quietly, chimed in, "That's right,

Shari. A woman's first duty is to her husband and family, but if she makes money on top of that, God is especially happy when she pays her tithing. It shows that she's putting God first, even in her financial affairs."

I looked up at my mother, surprised and pleased by her approval. It felt good to know that there were so many ways a girl could be a faithful servant of the Lord, not just by being a dutiful wife and mother but by contributing financially to the church as well.

"Do you wish you could make lots of money, too, to give to God?" I asked Ruby, my eyes wide with curiosity.

Ruby rolled her eyes. "Sure, if you kids weren't so much work! Do you know how exhausting it is being your mom? But being a mother is a divine calling, and I know that by raising you in the faith, I'm doing God's work, too. And that's reward enough."

As she spoke, I couldn't help but think about my aunts, who had started filming themselves with janky cameras, putting videos on the internet and making money out of it. We'd watched some of the videos together, and I wondered what it would look like if my mom started filming herself for YouTube, too, like them.

No, I thought. *She probably wouldn't want people to see how angry she is all the time.*

CHAPTER 6

ruby's rage

Ruby was always angry with us, constantly on edge, primed to blow, no matter how small the irritation. I probably could have handled her blustering, if it weren't for the edge of cruelty that so often colored her rages.

I remember being in the bathroom, experimenting with my kid's makeup palette. I must have been around nine years old, and like many young girls testing the waters of cosmetics, my attempts were far from subtle—think bold red lipstick, metallic eyeshadow that could signal planes, and foundation that bore little relation to my actual skin tone. I was a riot of clashing colors and misplaced enthusiasm.

Ruby called me downstairs to the piano to practice a duet, one she loved to perform. This duet required a singing partner, and that role inevitably fell to me. I always dreaded these impromptu concerts, feeling like an unwilling actress thrust onto a stage I never asked to occupy.

Reluctantly, I descended the stairs, my face a wild rainbow, and grudgingly took my place at the piano. I played the notes mechanically, but I couldn't bring myself to sing.

"*Shari, why on earth aren't you singing?!*" she snapped, her fingers stabbing at the keys.

"I don't know, Mom. . . ." My voice was barely a whisper.

"Maybe you have so much makeup on your face that you've forgotten how to listen to your mother," she said, her voice dripping with disdain. "Perhaps I should smack it all off!"

Ruby's hand would often find its way to my face, a sharp sting of displeasure delivered with precision. Her slaps were calibrated—never hard enough to leave visible bruises, at least on me, but always sufficient to instill fear. In her twisted logic, she was molding obedience, sculpting compliance with each stinging blow. I also think we were just her punching bag, a way for her to release her anger. She always seemed calmer once she'd blown off steam on one of us.

One day, I was sitting cross-legged on my bedroom floor, engrossed in a book, when I felt a sharp tug at the back of my head, followed by a faint snipping sound.

Startled, I whirled around just in time to see Chad, my impish seven-year-old brother, darting past, a pair of scissors clutched in his hand and a mischievous grin on his face. My hand flew to the back of my head, where a small clump of hair was now conspicuously missing.

Uh-oh.

"*Chad!*" I yelled, leaping to my feet and chasing after him. "*What did you do?*"

But he was gone, his laughter echoing down the hallway as he made his escape. Chad was already showing a tendency for pranking and clowning behavior, as many little boys are wont to do. He seemed to delight in causing mischief and mayhem, and was always looking for new ways to get a rise out of people.

I returned to my room, assessing the damage in the mirror. I knew there would be hell to pay—Ruby was obsessed with my thick, long brown hair and had forbidden me from ever cutting or altering it in any way. She always said that one day, men would want to marry me just because of my beautiful locks.

Suddenly, Ruby stormed in, holding a small clump of my hair.

"How could you do this to yourself?"

"I didn't! Chad did it, when I wasn't looking."

Rage crackled around her like electricity.

"He was just playing a joke, you can't even tell it's gone, see?" I said, attempting to diffuse the situation. But Ruby was having none of it.

"*Chad, come here!*" Ruby yelled, her voice ringing through the house.

I winced. Chad was in for it now.

As I watched my little brother slink into the room, his eyes wide with trepidation, I felt a surge of protectiveness. Yes, he could be a little terror at times, but he was still my brother, and I hated seeing him bear the brunt of Ruby's anger.

"What were you thinking, cutting your sister's hair like that?" Ruby demanded, her voice icy.

Chad shuffled his feet, looking down at the ground. "I don't know," he shrugged, his lower lip trembling.

I stepped forward, trying to intervene. "Mom, it's not a big deal. It'll grow back."

But Ruby ignored me, her attention focused solely on Chad.

"Come on, buddy, let's go to the bathroom. Time for you to have a little haircut, too."

I watched, frozen, as Ruby marched Chad down the hallway, her hand clamped tight around his arm. A moment later, the buzz of electric clippers. I held my breath, straining to hear any hint of what was happening. Then the bathroom door swung open, and Chad shuffled out, his head hung low. Ruby had buzzed a thick, uneven stripe down the center of his head, leaving him with a harsh reverse Mohawk. Tufts of hair stuck out at odd angles, making him look like a plucked chicken.

"There," Ruby said, satisfied with her work. "Maybe next time you'll think twice before you decide to play barber."

She looked to me, her eyes hard. "And let that be a lesson to you, too, Shari. In this house, we don't make excuses for other people's bad behavior."

I nodded mutely, my throat too tight to speak.

When Ruby went downstairs, I gathered my brother into my arms, stroking his ragged hair.

"I'm sorry, Chad," I whispered, feeling a crushing sense of guilt.

CHAPTER 7

refuge

I was eleven, at the threshold of adolescence, my body and mind beginning to change in ways I didn't fully understand yet. Meanwhile Ruby was pregnant with her sixth and final child—another girl—and our already full household was adjusting to the idea of yet another sibling joining our ranks.

Our routine was fully established by now. We'd all wake up around 6:00 or 6:30 a.m., when the house came alive with the sound of piano, violin, or harp practice. Then we'd converge in the kitchen, where Ruby would whip up oatmeal or eggs. Sometimes we'd squeeze in some scripture study over breakfast, since evenings were usually busy with everyone's after-school activities.

Next, we'd pack our own school lunches, a daily exercise in responsibility and self-reliance. I remember watching my siblings standing on tiptoes, barely tall enough to reach the counter, carefully assembling sandwiches and selecting fruits. "This is how you become a capable adult," Ruby would say.

Then we'd head off to class. Ruby never drove us; getting to school was another daily exercise in independence that she insisted would build character. Because of our ages, we weren't always at the same school, so our commutes varied. Some of us took the bus, a rumbling yellow behemoth that swallowed us up each morning and spat us out again in the afternoon. For me, at that point in my life, it was a walk. About a mile, a distance that seemed to stretch endlessly before me on those bitterly cold Utah mornings when the wind cut right through my coat. I'd power walk, sometimes breaking into a run, my backpack thumping against my spine.

Birthdays were special, though—that's when Ruby would treat us with a ride home from school. The excitement of seeing her car in the pickup line, knowing I wouldn't have to make that long walk home, was better than any wrapped gift. It was a glimpse of the mother I longed for every day—attentive, interested, present.

We rarely had friends over at the house. It wasn't that we were explicitly forbidden from inviting friends into our home but rather that our house seemed to repel social gatherings by its very nature. The cramped spaces, the constant presence of siblings, and Ruby's perpetual state of stress created an atmosphere that seemed to naturally discourage visitors.

Most of my siblings found a middle ground, forming friendships with neighborhood kids and playing outside. This outdoor socializing seemed safer somehow, less intrusive than bringing outsiders into the complex dynamics of our household. For me, the very idea of inviting friends over felt foreign and uncomfortable. It wasn't that I lacked friends entirely but rather that the thought of merging my school life with my home life filled me with a sense of dread I couldn't quite articulate.

After school, family dinners were important to us, though they became more challenging to coordinate as we got older. Homework was usually done at the kitchen table in our old house since our bedrooms were too small for desks.

There wasn't much time for TV, and a lot of content wasn't deemed appropriate for us to watch. To this day, I often feel out of the loop with certain pop culture references. But I was allowed to watch *Sponge Bob Squarepants* and *The Simpsons*, both of which I loved. And we did love watching movies together, as a family. That became our family's default mode of dealing with tension or seeking comfort. We'd gather in the living room, the flickering light of the TV casting a soft glow on our faces, and for a couple of hours, we'd feel at peace.

Frozen and the Harry Potter films, in particular, were our favorites. I loved *Harry Potter and the Order of the Phoenix*, the fifth movie in the series. There was something exotic about the hidden corners of London, the secretive nature of the Order's headquarters. But it was the story of Professor Dolores Umbridge that I enjoyed most, for some reason—the tyrannical, power-hungry, condescending, sanctimonious sadist who ultimately faces her comeuppance.

Ruby, too, had her favorite Harry Potter moment, though hers came from *Harry Potter and the Half-Blood Prince*. A scene where Dumbledore, challenged about performing restricted magic within Hogwarts, simply responds, "Being me has its privileges." Ruby would quote this line often, with a glimmer in her eye. The idea of being above the rules clearly resonated with my mother.

It was during this time of awkward adolescence that I developed a new habit: picking at my lips until they bled. This nervous tic seemed to emerge from nowhere yet quickly became a constant in my daily life. I would catch sight of myself in the mirror, noticing the small scabs on my lips. I'd try to hide the marks, knowing the sight of them would trigger Ruby's anger.

"Look at your face, Shari!" she'd scold. "You *have* to stop. No man is ever going to want to marry you with a bunch of ugly scars all over your lips!"

At night I prayed for unblemished skin, a pretty face, all the things I needed to be for my future husband. Still, whether it was hormones or just the cumulative anxiety caused by living with Ruby, my anxiety seemed to be spiraling like never before. I needed an outlet, some way to express my feelings. That's when I started to really lean into my practice of nightly journaling.

Recordkeeping is deeply ingrained in the LDS faith; it's a sacred duty, a way of bearing witness to God's hand in our daily lives. We're taught that our personal histories will serve as testaments for future generations, spiritual road maps guiding our descendants through their own mortal journeys.

Every night, without fail, Ruby would make her rounds, with a reminder: "Did you write about what we did today? Don't forget to mention that funny thing your brother said!" We all responded to this nightly ritual with varying levels of enthusiasm. I was definitely the most consistent writer among my siblings.

In those quiet moments before sleep, hunched over my journal by the dim glow of a reading lamp, I could be me. On the page, I could express my anxieties and frustrations with my parents, ponder the pressures of being a tweenager, and wonder about all these new feelings I was having about boys.

JOURNAL

Mom and Dad pulled me into their room tonight. They said that all of my friend problems in school were my fault. They said I'm not a fun person to be around, and nobody gets me. Which may be true. Then they said it seems like I try on purpose to annoy my family. But the truth is, I just don't enjoy being around them. Ruby and Kevin are the ones who annoy me.

I finally got invited to a populars party. It's super hard to get invited, so I was excited, and I thought Mom and Dad would be pleased, because they're always saying I don't have enough friends. Instead, they said I can't go to the party if there are going to be boys there, which means I'll have to stay home. I'm so mad! Can't they see I'm growing up? I'm not their baby girl anymore? I can manage myself!

I am so mad at Mom sometimes. Whenever she helps me practice piano, she promises not to yell, but by the time we are done, she's screaming at the top of her lungs. She is so stressed, uptight, and strict, that it's impossible to have fun or relax when she's around. Dad on the other hand is loose, easygoing, and handles stress very well. One thing's for sure—I am a daddy's girl.

Mom has become obsessed with this place called West Point Military Academy, which means she now punishes us by making us condition, like soldiers. For example, earlier today she got mad at Chad and me for not putting away the clothes, so she punished us by making us run around the block five times. Then at dinner, Chad was hiding and refusing to help me clear the table, so Ruby made us both do pushups—Chad for shirking his responsibilities, me for not being enough of a leader.

I yearned for my mother's guidance, her support, her friendship during this insecure time of puberty. But Ruby maintained a strict emotional distance, as if affection might somehow compromise her authority. "Remember: I'm not your friend; I'm your mother," she'd say whenever I asked her why we couldn't do things like go to lunch together, like I saw my friends doing with their moms. "My job is to train you how to be ready for the world. When you're an adult, we can be friends." Eventually, I gave up on the idea of being close to Ruby, and just saved my feelings for my diary.

In this emotional desert, I did find additional solace in the worlds of literature and history—Charles Dickens, Jane Austen, and Dostoevsky. Authors became my companions, offering insights into life, family, and love that I knew I couldn't get from my mother. While fiction offered an escape, a chance to live a thousand lives between the covers of books, it was nonfiction that truly captured my heart and mind. History, in particular, became my obsession, and the Second World War. (In middle school, I read more than one hundred books on World War II, and my teacher ended up having *me* teach that section of history because I knew more than he did.)

As I delved into stories of courage and resilience during humanity's darkest hours—like Anne Frank's diary—my own struggles began to shift into perspective. The hardships faced by those who lived through the war—the fear, the loss, the unimaginable choices—made my own challenges seem more manageable, if not insignificant. And that was comforting, in a way.

One day, I walked into my history class, clutching my latest library find—a thick, worn volume on the rise and fall of the Third Reich. As I slid into my seat, my friend eyed the book with a mixture of curiosity and disbelief. She wrinkled her nose.

"Isn't that kind of a heavy topic, Shari?"

"Yeah, it is heavy," I admitted, running my hand over the book's worn spine. "But the Nazi rise in Europe is really important for us to study. Don't you want to know about the suffering and cruelty of the Holocaust? The millions of lives extinguished in the name of Aryan supremacy?"

As the words left my mouth, I realized how intense I must have sounded. My friend's expression softened, but I could see the discomfort lingering in her eyes.

"Of course, but I don't want to think about it all the time, Shari. It's sad."

"I know it's sad," I said. "But it's also inspiring. People survived. They resisted. They held on to hope in the darkest of times. I think that's something we can all learn from."

PART TWO

ship
of
fools

CHAPTER 8

a star is born

Ruby's life was about to pivot. She had approached motherhood with the intensity of an Olympic athlete training for gold, her identity singularly focused on procreation for more than a decade. But now, aged thirty, with her sixth and last baby weaned, the Franke family was finally complete, leaving her with a strange mix of accomplishment and unease, questioning what came next. She needed a fresh outlet for her energy and ambition.

Ruby's sisters, Ellie and Bonnie, were already finding success on YouTube as content creators—Ellie's channel, *Ellie and Jared*, launched in 2011, was particularly thriving. Documenting her struggles with infertility, Ellie's vlog—short for video blog—had built a following of women who saw their own longing reflected in her journey, filling her comments section with messages of support and solidarity, holding their collective breath with each new treatment cycle.

When Ellie finally got pregnant after three years of trying—and posting about it three times a week—her vlog hit a thousand subscribers. In the vlogging world, this was a significant milestone. It meant YouTube started taking her seriously, opening doors for monetization through advertising, sponsorships, and merchandise sales. From there, Ellie's subscriber base had grown exponentially, and with it, her income.

Bonnie, the bubbliest of the siblings, had started her own channel in 2013. Married to her high school sweetheart, she followed in Ellie's digital footsteps, crafting content around the universal themes of pregnancy and child-rearing. Her channel, named Bonnie Hoellein, quickly gained momentum, riding the crest of the family vlogging wave that surged across YouTube between 2012 and 2015.

This era marked a seismic shift in social media content. Ordinary people from diverse backgrounds began offering viewers an unfiltered lens into their lives—capturing everything from mundane morning routines to milestone moments. Family vlogs, in particular, struck a chord, transforming kitchen tables and living rooms into stages for a new kind of reality show.

The most adept of these digital storytellers found themselves at the helm of a peculiar new industry. They were turning bedtime stories and first steps into ad revenue and sponsorship deals, blurring the lines between intimate family moments and marketable content. It was a brave new world where a camera-ready smile and a knack for wholesome narrative could transmute domestic life into a lucrative enterprise.

As Ruby scrolled through her sisters' videos, a spark of inspiration ignited. Ellie and Bonnie were becoming vanguards of the family vlogging revolution. But wasn't Ruby the one with the largest brood of all? Six children, each a character in their own right, a ready-made cast for this new type of reality show? The potential was there, waiting to be tapped—if Ellie and Bonnie could transform the mundane into gold, surely Ruby could craft an empire and prove to the world—and perhaps to herself—that she, Ruby Franke, was not just a mother, but a matriarch worthy of widespread admiration and emulation.

In a moment of clarity, the perfect name for her YouTube channel crystallized in Ruby's mind: 8 Passengers. It was elegant in its simplicity, yet rich with meaning—encapsulating our family's journey. Ruby and Kevin at the helm, with their six children as the precious cargo.

In January 2015, Ruby's vision materialized with the official launch of 8 Passengers on YouTube. The channel would become a stage for our family drama, a curated window into the Franke household and our everyday lives. Kevin, ever supportive, claimed the honor of being the first subscriber. Ruby was the second. And I, about to turn twelve and caught up in the excitement of this new family venture, eagerly claimed the third spot. To me, it all seemed so innocent—just a fun new project, a way to share our lives with the world.

But as Ruby practiced her opening lines to an imaginary audience, I wonder if perhaps she felt a familiar flutter in her stomach—the same nervous energy that had accompanied each of her pregnancies. After all, she was, in a sense, giving birth again. This time, to a new version of herself and a new chapter in our family's story.

In many ways, family vlogging is a very LDS-aligned pursuit, a natural extension of our traditional practices. Vlogging offers a modern form of bearing testimony and keeping personal and family records, while simultaneously engaging in passive missionary work. Vlogs mean church members can share their faith, values, and daily lives with a global audience, potentially attracting interest in the church and its teachings. In a way, the synergy between YouTube and LDS families seemed almost predestined, fitting perfectly with the church's desire to be "in the world but not of the world," allowing members to engage with modern culture while maintaining our distinct values and beliefs.

Perhaps that's why Utah and the broader LDS community have become such powerhouses in the realms of family vlogging and traditional lifestyle content creation. Some of the earliest and most successful family vlogging channels have come from our communities, documenting life with multiple children, showcasing the appeal of family life to a mainstream audience while demonstrating how modern media can be harnessed to share testimonies and values in a relatable, engaging way.

Who knew that in the age of viral scandals and cancel culture, it would be the wholesome, family-centered content of LDS vloggers that would capture the world's attention? And who could have foreseen that my own family would come to embody both—the wholesome ideal and the scandalous—becoming a cautionary tale of what happens when the line between authenticity and performance becomes blurred beyond recognition?

CHAPTER 9

baby climbs out of crib

I actually don't remember the exact moment when the cameras first started rolling. All I know is that one day, we were just a regular family, going about our lives; the next, there was a janky camera constantly pointed in our direction, documenting our every move for the consumption of strangers on the internet.

Ruby posted her first video on January 8, 2015, with my youngest sister in the starring role. It began with footage from her gender reveal party in 2013. In our kitchen, the five of us children and Ruby are filmed by Kevin as we gather around a cake on the kitchen counter, Ruby's pregnancy bump clearly visible. Kevin asks a question from behind the camera.

"So, what are we doing today?" he asks.

"Cutting a cake, and inside is the color of the baby!" Chad exclaims, excited. His disappointment is palpable as Ruby slices into the cake, revealing a pink sponge interior.

The scene shifts to the hospital, where Ruby cradles our newborn sister, her sixth and youngest child, a tiny pink bow perched atop her nearly bald head. We kids fuss and coo over our new sibling, our faces alight with wonder. My youngest brother is shown cradling the tiny infant in his arms.

"Give her a kiss," Ruby gently coaxes.

He leans in, placing a soft kiss on her forehead.

"Say I love you," Ruby encourages.

"I love you," he whispers.

The video then cuts to my youngest sister, now a toddler, sprawled on the kitchen table, eyeing me and my banana with unmistakable interest. She rises, her steps wobbly but determined, and takes a hearty bite when offered the fruit. Ruby's novice editing skills become apparent in the next shot, featuring our beloved yellow Lab, Nolly—charming footage, except it was upside down.

And that was that. Ruby's entry into the world of family vlogging. Nothing Oscar-winning, by any means.

Two weeks later, Ruby dropped her second video, "Tasting Sushi for the First Time!" Picture this: Ruby, out with Kevin's academic buddies, bravely facing down her first plate of sushi. Spoiler alert: She's not a fan. The end.

A few days later, video number three: "Meet the 8 Passengers—Chad!" introducing my ten-year-old blond, blue-eyed prankster of a brother. It was cute, and people liked it. And so on.

My mom kept making videos, starring us, and posting them to 8 Passengers. Little did we know, this bizarre ritual would come to dominate our lives for the next seven and a half years.

We never chose to be internet celebrities. But that made no difference—soon, our lives now revolved around nonstop content creation—whether we liked it or not. Birthdays, barbecues, even lazy Sunday afternoons—no moment was too mundane to escape documentation. Ruby, her sisters, and her brother Beau—who had also jumped aboard the vlogging bandwagon—were now constantly filming us for their respective vlogs. You couldn't sneeze without it being immortalized from multiple angles.

My mother and her sisters seemed to operate on some unspoken biological synchronicity and had an uncanny tendency to get pregnant around the same time, as if their bodies were attuned to some shared familial rhythm—except for me and Chad, who had no cousins the same age, the cousins on my mother's side grouped neatly into age brackets, creating miniature cohorts that mirrored each other in age and development, growing up in tandem, perfect for the aunts to share their milestones and experiences on YouTube. It was a content creator's dream.

But for me, a twelve-year-old girl, this constant surveillance was excruciating. All I wanted was to grow up in peace, deal with my bodily changes and these pesky new zits without it being recorded. But my mother was omnipresent, her phone an extension of her arm, directing us like a Hollywood producer: "Do this, do that, Shari—we're filming!" "Smile, Shari! Say good morning!" I was beginning to feel like a sideshow freak: "Step right up and witness Shari, the Amazingly Awkward Adolescent, in all her cringeworthy glory!"

The worst part? The internet ate it up. Everyone seemed to love what Ruby was posting. Which, of course, encouraged her to post more. She approached YouTube with the dedication of a start-up CEO, putting in long hours, day after day. She had done her homework and knew that in the Wild West of social media, consistency is king, you have to post regularly, which meant every little moment was mined for content. First steps, lost teeth, epic tantrums—you name it, Ruby filmed it, laser-focused on building her subscriber base, knowing vlogging was a numbers game. And Ruby had always been good with numbers.

She knew the main way vloggers make money is through You-

Tube's AdSense program, but you have to hit a one-thousand-subscriber milestone and rack up four thousand hours of watch time in the last year in order to qualify. Once you've checked those boxes, you start making money every time someone watches or clicks on an ad in your videos. Ruby became hyperfocused on getting those first one thousand subscribers—it was her golden ticket to the big leagues.

"I interrupt our regular schedule to make an announcement," Ruby said on July 9, 2015, filming a special announcement video. "We have hit over a thousand subscribers! I am so excited, especially considering that last month, we only had 142."

It had taken her about six months to hit the magic number.

Not long after, the gravity of how much this YouTube thing was going to turn our lives upside down finally sank in. I was sitting at the kitchen table, feeding my youngest sister apple sauce, when Ruby burst into the kitchen, her face flushed with excitement.

"Shari, you won't believe this," Ruby announced. "Our little lady is a bona fide internet sensation!" She scooped my two-year-old sister out of her high chair and twirled her around.

"What do you mean, Mom?"

"I mean, that video of her climbing out of her crib? It's gone viral! Fifty thousand views and counting!"

"Wow, that's . . . a lot of people."

I didn't get it. My sister, in her nursery, had climbed out of her crib for the first time. What was so interesting about that?

Ruby laughed, planting a kiss on my sister's chubby cheek. "Isn't it amazing? Our little family, touching so many lives."

As I watched her practically dance out of the room, I felt a sinking sensation in my gut. Our lives were already starting to feel like a reality show; did going viral mean we were about to go prime-time?

As the weeks turned into months, that crib video continued its astonishing ascent, racking up views by the millions. Ten million. Twenty million. By year's end, an unfathomable fifty million strangers had glimpsed into our lives.

Meanwhile, our subscriber count was climbing steadily. By September, we had reached five thousand subscribers. Then 100,000 by April; 400,000 come August. Unfathomable reach, from Louisiana to Laos, Kentucky to Kenya. It was surreal.

Watching the subscriber numbers tick upward, I could barely believe each one represented a real person out there in the world who had chosen to watch videos like "Spiders Slugs and Snails OH MY!" and "DUTCH BRAID your own hair," not to mention the horror movie that was "Shari's Piano Recital," the first—but certainly not the last time—Ruby would take one of my most awkward moments and turn it into the story of the week.

As the numbers climbed, a nagging thought kept creeping into my mind: *Surely, at some point, people would get bored of this? Surely one day this would all end and our lives could go back to normal?* Little did I know then that "normal" was a luxury we had already left far behind.

CHAPTER 10

remodeling reality

As our YouTube channel evolved, so did our home. Ruby invested heavily in remodeling, every change designed to please the camera's eye. Goodbye, ugly yellow walls. Hello, stark white and board-batten. Sterile, but oh-so-photogenic. Ruby meticulously curated the porch, adding stylish patio furniture, plump pillows, and atmospheric lanterns. We even removed the house numbers to avoid the hassle of having to blur them in videos. The result was a picturesque facade, perfect for the camera but perhaps a bit too perfect for real life—a visible symbol of our transition from an ordinary family to YouTube stars.

For me, every video shoot remained a special kind of torture. I could never get used to it, or relax. It was like one of those recurring nightmares where you're suddenly naked on a stage, with a sea of eyes staring back at you, mocking. I mean, puberty is brutal enough, let alone with an audience.

Thankfully, I found a silver lining in this heinous new situation—leverage. I figured out that if I wanted something from Ruby—a later bedtime, a new outfit, or permission to hang out with friends—my best bet was to ask her while the camera was rolling. It was a "you scratch my back, I'll scratch yours" kind of deal. Ruby wanted me as her happy, smiling costar? It was going to cost her. A trip to the mall, a get-out-of-chores-free card, a shiny new gadget—whatever I needed at the time.

Ruby tried to make the whole surreal enterprise seem fun, even beneficial to us. "If you film your ice cream outing, you can pay for it with the 8 Passengers credit card," she'd say. "Just think, free food and a tax write-off!" What teen wouldn't want to flash a credit card, to feel grown-up and important?

I became fluent in the language of tax loopholes before I could even drive. Outfit hauls, trips to the mall—I learned it could all be written off as business expenses. If I filmed in the car on our way to the amusement park, even the gas could be written off as a business expense. It did start to feel like we'd hacked the system. Why wouldn't everyone want to make a living by turning their kids into content, by commodifying every moment from cradle to college?

Our first brand deal was with a slow-cooker company. They sent us one of their fancy pots and a bunch of meals to cook in it. After that, the floodgates opened. Our house became a revolving door of brand deals and swag. Clothes, tech, snacks—you name it, we "reviewed" it.

Some days, there were so many gifts that we couldn't open them all. Boxes would sit for days in the hallway, unopened.

We got to go on lots of all-expenses-paid vacations, always with the omnipresent camera. One of our first was to Seattle on a brand deal for a game company. We stayed in an Airbnb on the Puget Sound, which was particularly special because it was where Kevin had attended grad school, and the whole family went, including Ruby's parents.

It was crazy how different our lives had become. We used to make our own granola, spending hours canning fruit and clipping coupons, and buying everything in bulk to save money. Now we had more stuff than we knew what to do with. We'd gone from being a family that was proud of making do with less to one that had too much and more on the way.

I thought about Dad, who'd always been the intellectual powerhouse of our family, dedicating his brilliant mind to understanding earthquakes and making the world a safer place. Yet, it was Mom's newfound obsession with the internet that was finally bringing us true financial success. Point, shoot, upload—and watch the money roll in.

On October 15, 2015, Pregnancy and Infant Loss Remembrance Day, Ruby sat alone on her bed, facing her camera, about to film a video that was a little different from the ones she'd done before. A story she hadn't talked about in years—her miscarriage in 2009.

Her voice cracked as she described the sterile doctor's room, the cold gel on her stomach, and then . . . the deafening silence where there should have been the rhythmic heartbeat of her baby boy. Ruby's pain was palpable as she described the moment she realized her baby was dead and his little body would have to be taken out of her. The confusion she felt, waking up in Kevin's car, feeling utterly empty—both physically and emotionally, without ever being able to see her baby's body before it was disposed of. Nothing for her to take home, no ashes, nothing to hold on to.

Her anger about her lack of agency in the way things were handled still simmered, and by the end, she was weeping, years of buried frustration spilling over. "Anyway, I don't know if this video is going to be helpful to any of you," she said, wiping her tears. "Gosh, this has been really helpful for me."

The video didn't go viral, but it was powerful, and I still have complicated feelings about it. I am glad Ruby felt able to share her story in such a raw and vulnerable way. In the realm of family vlogging, it so happens that rawness and vulnerability are the lifeblood that keeps subscribers engaged and channels thriving. But the line between authenticity and exploitation becomes dangerously blurred when children are involved. My unborn baby brother in heaven would suffer no ill effects from Ruby sharing his story. But what about the rest of us, whose stories were being shared daily?

What are the lasting repercussions of growing up on camera, without any say in the matter? How does that constant exposure shape a child's sense of self, their future relationships, their very understanding of privacy? And what does consent really look like when you're a child, too afraid to say no? Personally, I mourn those precious formative years spent in service to someone else's vision. Ruby might claim her kids were always on board, but the truth is, we never really had a choice in the matter.

And what about Ruby? What might be the emotional repercussions of her snowballing online success? Yes, Ruby's drive was bringing in money for her family and validation for her ego. But none of those superficial rewards could fix what was broken inside her. Instead, they seemed to fuel a vicious cycle, pushing her to seek more validation, more views, more content—often at the expense of her family.

The most problematic element in our family dynamic—Ruby's relentless ambition, fueled by a potent mixture of unresolved pain and narcissism—had become the driving force of our existence. It was as if we had taken the most poisonous plant in our garden and, instead of uprooting it, made it the centerpiece of our lives.

CHAPTER 11

teenage influencer

Toward the end of eighth grade, when I was fourteen, I started my own YouTube channel for one reason: money. I saw what YouTube had done for Ruby. If this could pay for college and save me from working at the grocery store after school, I was all in. Although I'd have to get Ruby's permission first, of course.

Ruby's eyebrow arched. "Your own channel? Better be serious about it."

"I promise I will!"

"You're not old enough for an AdSense account, so I'll have to manage your earnings."

"Oh, okay . . . ," I said, disappointed. I'd forgotten I wouldn't be legally allowed to have my own AdSense account until I was eighteen.

"Don't worry—if your channel is successful, we'll let the earnings build up," she continued. "A little nest egg for the future."

"All you need to do is give me a shout-out on 8 Passengers to get me started, and I'll get a ton of subscribers that way," I said, excited.

Ruby laughed.

"No way, Shari. No shortcuts, no shout-outs. You need to get to one hundred thousand subscribers on your own, just like I did. And *then* I'll give you a shout-out on 8 Passengers."

"Seriously? I have to earn a shout-out from my own mom?"

"Shari, I don't shout out anyone with less than one hundred thousand, you know that. Consider it an incentive for you to treat it like a real business. I'll shout you out once you've built a channel worth promoting."

Challenge accepted, Mom. But make no mistake, I hated every second of filming.

"I'm done!" I'd shout with relief after each video, the camera finally off. It was torture, but it was a job. Then came the editing, writing the captions, figuring out when to post, and uploading. Anyone who says posting online isn't real work clearly hasn't done it themselves.

I posted twice a week. And like my mom, I exploited my own siblings, doing shaving videos with my sisters and talking about periods, because I knew it would get views. The guilt eats at me now, but back then, I was just following the blueprint Ruby had laid out: This is what people like; this is what makes money. The personal stuff.

One day, Ruby brought her laptop into my room, wanting to show me something.

"Look at this," she said, excited. "In case you've ever wondered why YouTube is the most important thing that ever happened to this family."

On her screen, a direct message from an 8 Passengers subscriber. A woman who said she had grown up in a troubled home. Her parents fought constantly, and she often felt lost and alone—until she stumbled upon 8 Passengers.

"'Watching your family, it's like I finally found a place where I belong,'" Ruby read out loud. "'You guys are so happy and loving and above all HONEST, it gives me hope that maybe one day, I can have that, too. I've even started going to church because of you, and I'm thinking about getting baptized in the LDS church. Thank you for showing me the light.'"

Ruby's face glowed as she closed the laptop.

"Isn't that amazing, Shari? God gave us this platform. And now look at the difference we're making in people's lives! Showing them the way!"

When viewers praised her for her "honesty," for showing the unvarnished truth of family life, I saw the pride in her eyes. It made her even more sure that she was doing something noble, something meaningful. But reading the comments, I had a different take.

"My parents are divorced and they fight a lot. When I watch your videos, I feel like I'm part of your family."

"I feel like I've grown up with you guys. You're like my siblings. I know everything about you."

These comments always left me with an uneasy feeling. To me, it felt like a weird attachment, people latching on to families that weren't their own, while inflating Ruby's ego to mythic proportions.

"Wow, thank you for showing the tough side of parenting!"

"I wish my parents had been like you, Ruby. Maybe then I wouldn't have gotten into so much trouble as a teenager."

As much as our fans might have appreciated the story Ruby was selling, they had no idea what they were doing. Enabling her. Fueling her sense of righteousness and power as a mother who could do no wrong, and cheerleading her as she drifted further and further away from reality.

One day, thirteen-year-old me walked into the cafeteria at my junior high, clutching my lunch tray as I navigated the sea of cliques and social circles. I headed toward the corner table where I typically huddled with fellow bookworms. But before I got there, a high-pitched voice cut through the din.

"Hey, Shari, over here!"

I turned, startled, to find one of the cheerleaders waving at me from the coveted populars table. She sat surrounded by her posse, a sea of perfectly coiffed hair and designer labels. She had never spoken to me before, let alone summoned me from the depths of Nerdville and invited me to sit with her. But things had shifted. Now that I was internet famous, I'd become *soooo* interesting in their eyes.

I knew their sudden interest was as fake as their meticulously curated social media feeds. They weren't interested in me, Shari the person, but in Shari the internet celebrity, a potential boost to their own online presence. Still, it felt nice to be noticed and included for once, even if it was just for shallow reasons. So I sat with the popular girls, smiled for the inevitable selfies, laughed at inside jokes I didn't quite understand, and pretended this was all perfectly normal.

Suddenly, Jake, a boy I'd secretly been crushing on for months, approached our table. My heart skipped a beat as he flashed his signature grin.

"How's it going, influencer?" he said, his eyes twinkling with interest.

"Uh, great!" I managed, my smile a mixture of genuine excitement and practiced poise.

"Cool. Hey, are you on Snapchat?"

"Nah." I shrugged, trying to sound nonchalant.

Jake's eyebrows shot up in surprise. "You're like, the biggest thing on YouTube, but you don't Snap?"

"Yeah, I know, it's weird," I said, embarrassed. "My mom won't let me."

"That sucks. My mom's a piece of work, too. Hey, maybe we should hang out and talk about our mothers."

"Ugh, no thanks," I said, before realizing what I was saying, and rapidly correcting. "I mean, yes, we should hang out and do that!"

He flashed another smile before walking away.

I watched him leave, frozen in a mix of elation and disbelief. The other girls at the table were equally stunned. Whether Jake's interest stemmed from my YouTube fame was irrelevant in that moment—all I could think about were his eyes, the way they had looked at me with genuine curiosity and warmth. He was the first boy who had ever shown me any attention.

Of course, there was one little problem, a tiny snag in my grand romantic plans. I wasn't allowed to hang out with boys until I was sixteen. On top of that, Jake wasn't very active in the LDS church, which I knew would be a problem as far as my parents were concerned. Plus, his parents were divorced, and his dad had tattoos. More deal-breakers.

But with Jake's smile still stuck in my head, none of that mattered. For the first time in my life, I was going to rebel.

After school, heart pounding, I swapped numbers with Jake, my hands trembling slightly as I typed my phone number into his cell. It felt dangerous and exciting all at once. From then on, we texted constantly. I was always checking my phone when no one was looking—each message gave me a thrill I'd never felt before.

I downloaded Snapchat in secret, even though Mom would have flipped if she found out. With each funny Snap from Jake, each goofy face and silly meme, I felt like I was getting a peek into a world that had always been just out of reach. A world where I was free to be a regular teenage girl, without worrying about Ruby's moods or the family vlogging business.

It was understood that until I turned eighteen, I would have to get Ruby's approval for anything I posted on social media. This included Instagram and, for a while, YouTube. (Snapchat was always expressly forbidden.) The approval process was quite rigorous. I would text her pictures along with the proposed captions, asking, "Is this okay to post?" Stories were the exception; she usually allowed me to post those without oversight. As I got older, I developed a better sense of what would be deemed acceptable, but Ruby's final approval was still required.

When Ruby vetoed a post, it was usually selfies that could have been oversexualized by others. Looking back, I understand. I think any good mother would have made similar choices. It wasn't about posting anything truly inappropriate—I would never have considered posting underwear pics, for instance. But I remember one time when I wanted to post a picture of myself attempting to do the splits in midair, with a caption joking about my lack of flexibility, Ruby said nope to that one. Whether it was about protecting me or about preserving her wholesome online image, I'm not sure. A little of both, probably. The line between genuine parental concern and brand management was often blurry in our household.

The hallways of our school soon became a hotbed of gossip, all centered around Jake's interest in me. As a result, the same popular girls who had eagerly welcomed me to their cafeteria table turned on me with startling speed. One minute I was their ticket to social media fame, the next I was a threat to their carefully maintained hierarchy. Their whispered comments echoed through the corridors: "Why would Jake be with *her*?" It was funny, how quickly their fake friendship crumbled the moment I became competition rather than an asset.

Things escalated when one of the meaner girls texted me an old photo of Jake kissing another girl, as if this piece of ancient history would somehow shatter my world. I couldn't help but laugh at the desperation of it all. Did they really think I would care about an outdated photo?

These girls, who had seemed so intimidating and powerful just a week ago, now appeared small and immature.

One sunny afternoon, I found myself settled under a sprawling oak tree with Jake, the grass tickling my bare legs, our knees almost touching as we talked and laughed.

"I can't believe it—we're finally hanging out," Jake said, his eyes crinkling at the corners as he smiled. A warm blush crept up my cheeks. As we chatted, I marveled at how easy it felt. Unlike the stilted, surface-level conversations I had with everyone else, with Jake, everything flowed naturally. As if we'd known each other for years.

Suddenly, the air between us shifted. Jake leaned in, his eyes flicking down to my lips.

"Can I kiss you, Shari?" he asked, his voice barely above a whisper.

My heart thundered in my chest. *This is really happening.* I nodded, wide-eyed, tilting my face up to meet his.

"You can close your eyes," Jake said gently.

"O-okay," I stammered, feeling my cheeks burn hotter.

Our lips met, our noses bumping slightly, and a jolt of electricity raced through me. It was like a thousand tiny fireworks exploding beneath my skin, from my lips all the way down to my toes. In that moment, the world around me faded away. There was no YouTube channel, no Ruby, no school drama—just me and Jake, sharing our first kiss under an old oak tree.

As I walked home later, I couldn't wipe the smile off my face. I wanted to etch every detail of this moment into my memory forever. I'd never felt so happy in my life—that feeling evaporated the moment I stepped through our front door.

Ruby and Kevin sat on the living room couch, their faces set in rigid lines, eyes boring into me like lasers.

"Your mother and I need to talk to you," Kevin said, his tone grave.

Panic surged through me. *They must know about Jake!*

My mind raced, searching for an explanation, an excuse, anything . . .

"How dare you download Snapchat without telling us!" hissed Ruby.

Snapchat? That's what they're mad about? Thank goodness . . .

"Oh, I'm sorry, Mom," I mumbled. "It's just . . . everyone at school has it."

Ruby's eyes flashed. "I said no social media unless it's approved by me!"

I hung my head, guilt twisting my stomach. "I didn't mean to . . ."

"Didn't mean to what? Jeopardize everything we've worked for? Put our entire livelihood at risk?" Her words were sharp, cutting.

"No, of course not. I just . . . I just wanted to feel like a normal kid."

Ruby's laugh was harsh, devoid of humor. "Shari, we're not normal. We're public figures. Every move we make, every word we say, directly impacts our income. Can you try to wrap your head around it?"

As she continued her tirade about the brand and the channel "that puts food on the table," I noticed that not once did Ruby say she was worried for my safety. It was about control. About maintaining the perfect image for her precious audience.

"Hand over your phone," Ruby demanded coldly. "Clearly, you're not mature enough to handle the responsibility of a smartphone."

Never before had I felt such profound gratitude for Snapchat's vanishing messages, and for having meticulously purged every text exchanged with Jake, leaving no digital footprint for Ruby to follow.

She replaced my iPhone with an ancient flip phone, in case I needed to make calls. She might as well have sent me to school in a horse and buggy, and I could practically hear the snickers of my classmates already. So, one evening, when my parents were out, I crept into their bedroom, my target clear: the iPhone, imprisoned in Ruby's closet. She kept it locked away, but I had long ago discovered the hiding place of the key.

That night, in the shadows of my bedroom, I scrolled through Jake's Snapchat stories again, stifling giggles at his goofy selfies. Each swipe of the screen was an act of defiance, a stolen moment of normalcy in my increasingly controlled world.

The risk? Off the charts. If Ruby caught me, she would unleash a tempest. But the thrilling cocktail of autonomy and connection with my crush was too potent to resist. For in those moments, I finally tasted freedom. And even if Ruby found out and metaphorically skinned me alive, it still felt worth it.

CHAPTER 12

i don't think my mother loves me

I sat at my desk, journal open before me, pen poised over a blank page. The house was quiet, the cameras were off, and for once, I had a moment truly to myself. As I stared at the empty page, a wave of clarity washed over me, bringing with it a realization that had been lurking just beneath the surface of my thoughts for years. The words seemed to write themselves, stark and undeniable on the page:

I don't think my mother loves me.

A tear escaped, landing on the page with a soft splat, blurring the words. But the truth of the statement remained. I knew these words weren't stemming from just teenage angst. The sentiment felt very real and somehow insurmountable.

Why didn't my mother love me? was the question. *Had I done something to repel her, to drive her away? Did I not smile enough? Was I too sarcastic, too brainy, too self-absorbed? Did I accidentally roll my eyes at her jokes?* I dissected a life's worth of interactions with Ruby, searching for clues, for some logical explanation as to why I felt so very disliked by the woman who gave birth to me.

My mind drifted to the comments I'd read online about myself; words of strangers on YouTube who thought they knew me based on carefully edited snippets of my life.

"Ugh, Shari is such a kiss-ass. She's always ratting out her siblings and trying to be Ruby's favorite. So smug."

Was that why Ruby didn't love me? Because I came across as a suck-up, Goody Two-shoes? Even if it was, I wished that these strangers, who saw only what Ruby wanted them to see, could understand that my obedience was born not out of adoration but fear. *If only they knew the real me*, I thought. The me who dreamed of a life far away from this circus. But no, all they saw was Ruby's obedient little puppet, dancing on her strings.

I thought back to all the times I had smiled and nodded along with Ruby's demands, even when every fiber of my being wanted to say no. The countless moments I had bitten my tongue, swallowing my true feelings and opinions for the sake of keeping the peace and ensuring the money kept rolling in. Our subscribers didn't understand what it was like to live under Ruby's iron fist, they didn't know the consequences of stepping out of line.

I'm not sucking up, I'm surviving, I thought. *There's a difference.*

But was that a reason for Ruby not to love me?

I ping-ponged between trying to understand my mother's coldness toward me and the public comments tearing me down. The result was a new feeling. A sort of emptiness I'd never experienced before. I didn't understand what it was, not until one day, in my eighth-grade year, I took a compulsory unit on mental health in school and I learned about the symptoms of depression. There, I recognized myself. Hopelessness. Self-loathing. And sometimes, a desire to just . . . end it all. I'd never told anyone about those feelings before. But now that I knew they had a name, I felt compelled to say it out loud.

Immediately after the class, I texted Kevin: "Dad, I'm depressed. I don't know if I want to live anymore."

"Thank you for telling me," he wrote back immediately. "We're going to get through this together." He even shared a link to an inspiring talk that he thought might help.

Dad's quick response sent a wave of relief washing over me. For the first time in what felt like forever, I didn't feel so alone. Sure, an inspiring talk wasn't going to fix everything, but knowing that he was there, ready to listen and help—that was everything to me, in that moment.

But as I walked home from school, my relief curdled into dread. Dad would tell Ruby. Of course he would—they always shared everything, united in their parental front. The thought of facing her, of having to lay bare my depression under her scrutinizing gaze, made my stomach churn. I wasn't ready for that conversation. How could I be, when I knew, deep down, that a significant source of my sadness was her?

When I got home, instead of going inside, I sat on a wall at the side of the house. For three long hours, I perched there, my mind a sea of thoughts, waiting for Kevin to get back from work.

As soon as Kevin's car pulled into the driveway, he spotted me. Surprise flickered across his face as he approached. "Shari? Why are you sitting out here?"

I shook my head, the words stuck in my throat, my feelings too tangled to express.

Concern deepened the lines on his face. "How are you feeling, sweetheart?"

"I'm. . . okay," I lied, forcing a weak smile.

Kevin studied me for a moment, clearly not convinced. "Shari, would you like to talk to someone? Maybe. . . try therapy?"

My heart leapt at the suggestion, a lifeline. "Yes," I whispered, nodding emphatically.

With a gentle hand on my shoulder, Kevin guided me inside.

The conversation that followed went exactly as I had feared—Ruby listened, but never truly understood, her eyes glazing over with dismissal.

"Therapy?" she scoffed, waving her hand. "Don't be ridiculous. You just need to sleep better, exercise more, and eat right."

But Kevin surprised me. "No," he said firmly. "We should let her see a therapist. This is serious, Ruby."

Ruby's face flickered with shock, then hardened into stubborn resistance. But Kevin stood his ground, a quiet determination in his eyes that I'd rarely seen before.

I retreated to my room, curling up on my bed, listening to my parents argue about my mental health. My pain was real, I knew that. And for once, it seemed, at least Kevin was seeing me—really seeing me. That small realization felt like hope, somehow.

JOURNAL

Today was Sunday, and Mom has been acting like a little shit all day. She yells because I randomly shut down and shut everyone out. "I'm not the one causing your depression and anxiety!" she yells. Well, hate to break it to you, Mom, but you are. You're the root of it all. But it's up to me to deal with it. And I do that by ignoring you. It's easier that way. No anxiety attacks. No getting worked up and angry. It's just . . . better to shut down. I feel more at peace when I tune you out, when

I retreat into my own world. It's not perfect, but at least it's away from you.

After opening up to Kevin, I also started confiding in my bishop, not about Ruby, specifically—it felt too close to home—but about other things. I'd unpack the same details over and over, a broken record of unrelenting guilt and shame. It was like picking at a scab, never letting it heal, seeking absolution while punishing myself.

"Bishop, I'm sorry to keep bothering you with this," I began, my voice barely above a whisper. "But I can't stop thinking about when I kissed Jake. I feel terrible. Was it too passionate? I keep replaying it over and over in my head. Did I break all my promises to God? Does this mean I'm a bad person?"

I buried my face in my hands, waves of shame and remorse washing over me.

"Shari, we've talked about Jake before, remember? Quite a few times. And I'll tell you what I told you before: God knows your heart. You mustn't be so hard on yourself."

"But," I began, my voice gaining strength, "I thought a good person examines her thoughts and actions every day to root out any sin or impurity. Isn't it our duty to always be vigilant, to never let ourselves become complacent? The moment we do is the moment we open the door for Satan to lead us astray!"

He sighed, removing his glasses to rub the bridge of his nose. I recognized that gesture—it was the same one he made every time I came to him, obsessing over the same perceived crimes, never satisfied with his absolution.

"Shari," he said gently, "I think it might be helpful for you to talk to a therapist about this."

"My mom won't let me."

"Hm. It's okay to take care of your mental health. It's obvious your scrupulosity is causing you a lot of distress."

"Mom says all problems can be solved with prayer, diet, and exercise."

"Please ask her, Shari. Remember, seeking professional help is nothing to be ashamed of. You don't have to go through this alone."

I walked home, certain Ruby would say no. And what was that other thing he said? *Scrupulosity?* What even is that? The word felt foreign on my tongue.

As soon as I got home, I turned on my computer and typed "scrupulosity" into the search bar. There it was, in black and white: the relentless cycle of guilt and self-flagellation that had become my constant companion. The endless loop of worry about every moral misstep, no matter how minor. The hypervigilance that turned every thought into a potential sin, the exhausting mental gymnastics of trying to be perfect, the crushing weight of guilt that seemed to follow me everywhere.

Great, I thought. *Not only am I depressed—now I'm suffering with religious OCD, too? Why am I so broken?*

The websites I delved into painted a challenging picture of recovery. Breaking free from the chains of scrupulosity, they warned, was no easy feat. Unlearning patterns of hypervigilance and self-criticism, etched deep into your neural pathways over years, is a painstaking process. It's like trying to rewire your own brain's circuitry, one fragile connection at a time. I would need to become a vigilant guardian of my own mind. Learn to catch toxic thoughts before they took root and spread like invasive weeds.

Kevin and my bishop were right. I couldn't do this alone. I had to get therapy, and a lot of it, probably. I just hoped that Ruby would agree.

CHAPTER 13

busted

"Shari, let me shape your brows," Ruby cooed one day, brandishing wax strips. She'd learned some cosmetology tricks from her sisters over the years and was always eager to test out her skills on me and my siblings. But this wasn't just about beauty—it was content, and content was currency.

By this point, 8 Passengers had amassed nearly a million followers. That number wasn't just a statistic; it was a force that reshaped our entire existence. Each follower represented a fraction of a cent in ad revenue, a potential customer for sponsored content, a tiny piece of the puzzle that had transformed our family dynamics into a lucrative business model.

The financial implications were impossible to ignore. Ruby and Kevin had traded in our old minivan for a gleaming Chevy behemoth, complete with an "8PSNGRS" license plate and an 8 Passengers sticker emblazoned on the back—a rolling billboard for our commodified family life. Sometimes, cruising down the freeway, we'd catch other drivers waving at us, their faces lighting up with recognition. We were "famous influencers" now, our everyday lives a source of entertainment for millions.

I eyed the wax strips suspiciously. I couldn't help but wonder: was this a moment of possible mother-daughter bonding, or just another scene in our never-ending family sitcom? The line between genuine interaction and performance had blurred so completely that sometimes, I wasn't sure any of us could tell the difference anymore.

"Come on, Shari, it'll be a great video for the channel. I'll give you a hundred bucks. . . ."

"Okay, you can wax my brows," I said, plopping down in the chair she'd set up in the bright glare of the ring light. Ruby had a salesperson's gift of making everything seem like an adventure. And one hundred dollars in the name of beauty sounded just fine by me.

The pain was nothing compared to the horror show I witnessed in the mirror afterward. Ruby had waxed off half my left eyebrow, leaving a sharp ninety-degree angle that made me look like I was perpetually shocked by my own reflection. Who needs symmetry when you can rock the "Spock meets surprised squirrel" look?

I was mortified, but of course, Ruby kept the camera rolling, zooming in on my face like she was documenting a rare species of uni-browed teen in its natural habitat. The money shot, indeed.

"Shari, I'm so sorry!" she exclaimed, her voice quivering with what I'm sure was remorse and definitely not barely contained glee at striking content gold.

Sure enough, the video titled "SHARI, I'M SO SORRY!!" with a thumbnail of me mid-ugly cry racked up hundreds of thousands of views. *Wonderful*, I thought. *I always wanted to be famous for my crazy eyebrows.* I had to wear huge sunglasses for a few weeks, to hide my mother's handiwork. And I don't recall ever seeing that $100, either.

Jake and I barely crossed paths that week. If he noticed my half-missing eyebrow, he was kind enough to stay silent. Every moment with him felt stolen, precious, and slightly lopsided. Ruby would never allow it. We both knew that. Still, I savored our time together. My first romance, now with 50% less eyebrow.

A few weeks later, I came home from school to find Ruby and Kevin waiting for me, looking like a pair of disappointed statues.

"Shari," Ruby began, her voice like frostbite, "we need to talk."

I stood frozen in the doorway, my backpack a lead weight on my shoulders.

"We're pulling you out of school," she announced, dropping the bomb. "At the end of the semester, you'll be transferring to Chad's school."

"*What?*" I whispered, shock coursing through my veins. "But . . . why?"

"It's for the best, Shari," she continued, her gaze unwavering. "We need to do a better job of protecting you."

"Protecting me from what?"

"Jake's mother called me yesterday."

My stomach plummeted.

"She said you've been hiding a laptop and communicating with him," Ruby continued, her voice taking on a razor's edge. "About how you've been . . . spending time together. How long have you been hiding this, Shari?"

"Mom," I protested weakly, feeling the heat rise in my cheeks. "We're just friends. We barely even—"

"Clearly," Ruby cut me off, her words sharp enough to draw blood, "the students at your junior high are a bad influence on you. This move isn't up for discussion, Shari."

I stared at the carpet, fighting back tears and the sense that I was about to dramatically faint like a Victorian lady. "But I like my school," I whispered, hating how small and pathetic my voice sounded.

"You'll like your new school better," Ruby declared. "The classes are much smaller, the teachers are excellent, and everyone there will be of our faith."

Kevin chimed in here, finally remembering he was part of this parental tag team.

"It will be a much safer environment for you, Shari," he said, softly.

A familiar sense of powerlessness washed over me. Once again, my life was being reshaped without my consent, my choices stripped away, this time in the name of "safety."

I asked to be excused and fled to the bathroom, locking the door behind me with trembling hands. My chest constricted, each breath a labored struggle against an invisible weight. The crushing sensation was terrifying—like drowning on dry land. I knew this unwelcome visitor: a panic attack. I'd had them before, but never quite as bad as this.

Unsure what to do, I shed my clothes and turned on the shower. I lay down in the tub, knees drawn to my chest, arms wrapped tightly around myself as if I could physically hold the fragments of myself together. Water cascaded over my body and face, my breaths coming in short gasps as I grappled with the suddenly complex task of inhaling and exhaling.

In that moment, with the water drumming against the porcelain, that chilling thought came:

I want to die.

The idea of not existing brought a perverse sense of relief, even as the rational part of my brain fought against it. The rational part of my brain fought back.

No, God wants you alive, Shari. This must all be part of His plan.

Gosh, though . . . there must be something deeply, fundamentally wrong with me, for God's plan to hurt this much.

Worthless! another voice hissed in my head, a mean girl's whisper in a high school hallway. *You're an ungrateful daughter and a bad person! You deserve all of this. That's why this is happening to you. That's why God is making you suffer!*

I clamped my hands over my ears, attempting to block out the poison darts of my own thoughts.

As the water ran cold and my teeth began to chatter, I uncurled myself slowly, feeling hollowed out, scoured clean of everything except a dull, throbbing ache. Standing on legs as wobbly as a newborn giraffe's, I caught a glimpse of myself in the mirror—pale, sad, exhausted.

As I wrapped myself in a towel, a small, defiant part of me whispered: *God loves you, Shari.*

It was a faint whisper, barely audible. But it was there.

CHAPTER 14

mommy's little drama queen

After the shower panic attack, Kevin had finally been able to convince Ruby that I needed therapy. I'd been going once a week, and while I liked my therapist, Dr. Winters, I was always tiptoeing around the truth, terrified Ruby's name might slip out. What if it got back to her somehow?

"How are you feeling today, Shari?" she asked me as I sank into the oversize armchair, my fingers tracing invisible patterns on the armrest.

"I'm . . . okay, I guess."

Dr. Winters leaned forward slightly. "Just okay?"

Ruby's face flashed in my mind. I swallowed hard. "I've been having trouble sleeping," I admitted. A safe start.

"Can you tell me more about that?"

I stared at my hands. "It's like . . . there's this weight. On my chest. All the time."

"And when did you first notice this weight?"

"I don't know. Awhile ago, I guess."

Dr. Winters nodded, jotting something down. "Shari, remember what we talked about? This is a safe space."

"Yeah, of course."

Nonetheless, I painted around the edges of my pain, never quite touching its core. I spoke of anxiety, of sleepless nights, of feeling lost. But never of Ruby. Never of the cameras. Never of the pressure cooker that was our home. Dr. Winters' office, with its soothing earth tones and gentle light, should have been a haven. Yet for a long time, I found myself instinctively erecting walls around myself, every time I was there.

Little by little, though, I began to unfurl. Words I'd never dared speak aloud started to bubble up.

"Sometimes I see cars driving by and I think about what if I just stepped in front of it . . . ," I confessed.

"Do you feel you can talk to your family about these feelings?" she asked softly.

I laughed, a bitter sound that surprised even me. "No. Not really."

"Why is that?"

I froze. Ruby's face again, looming in my mind. I shook my head. "I just . . . can't."

One session stands out clearly in my memory. I'd finally worked up the courage to tell Dr. Winters something that had been weighing on me for years.

"I really don't like piano," I admitted, my voice barely above a whisper. "Mom's been making me play piano since I was five, and practicing with her is actually a huge source of stress for me."

With my consent, the therapist invited Ruby, who was waiting outside, into our session. "Shari, can you tell your mom what you just told me?" she prompted gently.

I took a deep breath, avoiding Ruby's eyes. "I don't want to take piano lessons anymore," I said, bracing myself for the backlash.

Instead, Ruby just said, "Okay, Shari. You don't have to play piano. And we never have to talk about it again." A strange mixture of relief and unease washed over me. I'd won a huge victory, but Ruby's easy acquiescence felt oddly hollow.

We drove home, without a word, and I went straight to my room, which I shared with my youngest sister. She'd started coming into my room of her own accord and asking to sleep with me, which I thought was so cute. Now it had become a habit, and I didn't mind. Even though it meant I had to be super quiet going to bed, because of our different bedtimes.

We shared my giant king-size bed, me on one side and her on the other, and oftentimes I'd read to her at night, to help her fall asleep. But honestly, I may have needed her more than she needed me. She was my sleeping pill, my lullaby cherub. With her next to me, I always felt safer at night, somehow. As if something about her could keep the demons at bay.

Usually she was in bed long before me, but that night, she was the one who tucked me in as I crawled under the sheets. I was grateful for her presence, this tiny guardian angel who could make even the darkest nights feel a little less lonely.

JOURNAL

I'm shutting down more and more often. I can't help it, even though my silence really triggers Mom. She seems to think that if I'm quiet, that I have a bad attitude. The truth is, I'm quiet because I irrevocably and undeniably hate myself, and I have for a while. She doesn't know I cried on my bed for an hour today. That I'm full of disgust when I look in the mirror. That I'm trying so hard to hold on. I just have to remember—my last day won't be my worst.

I pasted on a happy smile for the camera as Ruby announced my transfer to my new school to her 8 Passengers viewers. Chad, standing beside me, was visibly less than thrilled that his big sister would be joining him at his school. I could practically feel the waves of resentment radiating off him at the prospect of me invading his turf. He had, by then, perfected the art of the passive-aggressive eye roll, and he employed it now with expert precision.

Determined to make the best of this fresh start, even as my heart ached with familiar comfort of my old school, I decided on a coping strategy. I would throw myself into my studies, lose myself in the pages of great books, and find solace in the realm of ideas. It was a defense mechanism, a way to build walls around my heart with knowledge and academic achievement.

"What class you got first?" Chad, now twelve, asked me as we navigated the crowded halls to our classes.

"English," I replied. "We're starting *Lord of the Rings* today."

A flicker of interest sparked in Chad's eyes before he quickly smothered it with a smirk. "Nerd," he scoffed, but there was no real bite to it.

We were so different on the surface—while I was laser-focused on my studies, Chad, the budding athlete, was making his name on the football field, setting numerous records for the 100-meter dash. The possibility of sports scholarships loomed large in his future. Pretty much the opposite of his bookish, introspective older sister, grappling with depression. Yet, a connection had always hummed between us, a shared understanding of our absurd circumstances that went beyond words.

Chad's gaze snagged on a group of athletes roughhousing by the water fountain, their raucous laughter echoing off the cinder block walls. Chad and his friends were all class clowns, the kind of kids who'd run down the hallways in exaggerated "Naruto runs"—an anime-inspired style of running with arms stretched behind them, as if they were being pursued by the ghosts of their GPAs. I always found myself torn between embarrassment and a grudging admiration for Chad's ability to be so carefree.

"Catch you later, sis," he said, directing a casual wave at his friends before vanishing into the throng of bodies.

I watched him go, a half smile tugging at my lips. *Catch you on the flip side, Chad. Don't let the jock straps hit you on the way out.*

I shouldered my way into the English classroom, sinking into my seat just as the bell rang. As our teacher passed out battered copies of *The Fellowship of the Ring*, I felt a thrill of anticipation zipping down my spine. I had seen the movies but never read the books, and there was something about Tolkien's world that had always called to me, even as a child.

Poring over the pages in the classroom, I felt a spark of excitement for the first time in ages. The world Tolkien had created, with its intricate interplay of good and evil, spoke to me on a deep level. Mostly, though, there was something oddly calming about escaping into a world where even the smallest, most unassuming creatures could change the course of history.

In the lesson, we debated which characters could be read as Christ figures; how the hobbits represented the purity of childhood, embodying a love for simple joys of nature, play, food, and companionship; and how it was their inherent goodness that allowed them to carry the ring without being immediately corrupted. I especially loved Sam, that sweet, hobbity cinnamon roll, that loyal little potato, too good, too pure for this world. I wished I could have had a friend like him.

"So, Shari," our teacher said, his keen gaze settling on me. "What do you believe the ring symbolizes, at its core?"

"I think . . . ," I began, my voice quavering before finding its strength. "I think it symbolizes the duality within us all. Our capacity for great good and great evil."

"That's good, Shari. Could you elaborate?"

The classroom fell silent, every eye trained on me, the new girl. The words poured out of me in a rush.

"It's like . . . the ring is inherently neutral, you know? It's what we choose to do with it that matters." I paused, my heart hammering against my rib cage.

"Look at how the ring corrupts Gollum . . . I think it's a warning. Tolkien reminding us never to let our selfishness consume us until we lose sight of what really matters."

Even as I spoke, an image of Ruby flashed through my mind. The way social media had her in its thrall. The lens of her iPhone camera seeing everything, like Sauron, the giant, flaming eyeball of doom.

My teacher nodded, his brow furrowed in thought. "So, Shari, if the ring represents our capacity for evil, for destruction of self and others, what is its opposite?"

"Love," I said, the word carrying more weight than I intended. "Kindness. The kind of bond that Sam and Frodo share, that endures through all hardship."

The kind of love I yearned for but rarely felt at home.

I stared down at my book, cheeks flushed. I felt exposed, as if I'd revealed too much. But when I looked up, the teacher was smiling.

"Yes, Shari, I think Tolkien himself would appreciate that interpretation," he said.

As soon as classes ended that day, I rushed home—my weekly therapy session with Dr. Winters was that evening, and I desperately wanted to eat some dinner beforehand—I always found it difficult to bear my soul on an empty stomach.

I was halfway through a bowl of hastily prepared pasta in the kitchen when Ruby appeared, her footsteps soft on the linoleum. She sat down next to me, a strange smile playing at the corners of her mouth.

"What is it, Mom?" I asked, my fork hovering midair.

"Great news, sweetheart," Ruby chirped, her voice syrupy sweet. "I had a chat with Dr. Winters today, and she thinks you're just fine. She doesn't want to waste our money on unnecessary sessions. So you don't need to eat so fast—no therapy today."

I swallowed hard, trying to process her words.

"Mom," I ventured, my voice barely above a whisper, "she really thinks I'm fine?"

It wasn't that long ago that I had shared my thoughts of suicide with her.

"Yes," Ruby said, her eyes bright with an emotion I couldn't quite place. "You're fine! You're not around Jake, you don't have a smartphone—you're good."

"Is this because I quit piano, Mom? Are you mad about how that happened? Is that why I can't do therapy anymore?"

"Not at all. No more therapy—doctor's orders."

It didn't make sense to me. I needed more time. I was making progress, inching toward something that felt like healing.

"Mom, I'd like to carry on, if I can," I said, pushing my bowl away.

Ruby's smile faltered for a moment.

"Listen to me, Shari. The doctor thinks you're a very well-adjusted girl with—how do I put it—an active imagination?"

"Wait, she thinks I'm making this up?"

"Mommy's little drama queen is looking for attention," Ruby said, reaching out to ruffle my hair. I flinched, but she didn't seem to notice.

I didn't believe her. There was no way my therapist—the one

person I thought I could trust—could have told my mother I was fabricating my struggles. But whether Ruby was lying or my therapist had betrayed me, the result was the same. My little therapy experiment was over. In this family, the only safe emotion was no emotion at all.

CHAPTER 15

one million followers

That same month I started my new school, September 2017, Ruby hit a huge milestone—her subscriber base had reached one million, two and a half years after launching her channel. I remember the day well because I happened to be sick in bed, fighting what felt like either mono or strep, when Ruby's familiar "vlog voice" drifted through my closed door.

"Shari, honey?" she called out, her tone saccharine sweet. "Are you throwing up? Does your gut hurt like you're nauseated?"

"Yes," I groaned, my throat feeling like I'd swallowed broken glass. I knew she was filming this; I could tell by her tone. *Forget chicken soup and a cool compress, Mom*, I thought. *What I really need is a camera rolling while I'm puking my guts out in a bucket.*

I heard Ruby continue to cheerfully address her viewers, her voice filled with excitement.

"Good morning, Passengers! Today's exciting. Crazy day. Number one, we are counting down to a million. Number two, Shari doesn't feel good. I'm going to get her into a doctor to see if she has strep."

Later that day, she filmed herself while running errands, her eyes darting between the road and her phone as our subscriber count climbed steadily toward the big number: 998K . . . 999K. When the counter hit one million, she pulled over, filled with emotion, and triumphantly addressed her viewers.

"It's perfect! Hitting this milestone while doing the little things. That's what makes mothers powerful." In her mind, buying Chad's cheese, mailing my package, driving me to the doctor—these were her superpowers. The everyday acts that built her empire. A million subscribers, earned between errands.

The video cut to me at urgent care. Visibly weak and exhausted, I tried to smile for the camera. Years of conditioning had taught me to always be pleasant, always be amiable for Ruby, no matter how crappy I felt—at that point, I think I was running a temperature of 102. But for once, smiles weren't what Ruby wanted.

"You can't smile while you're in the insta-care, Shari!" Ruby chided, her voice a mixture of playfulness and command. "You're supposed to look like you're on your deathbed."

I complied instantly, feigning death with a touch of theatricality that I knew would please her. Whatever she wanted.

Oh, and I didn't have strep, I had mono, the kissing disease. Not that I'd been doing much kissing, to be honest. None at all, in fact, even though I was in a *kind* of romance? With a kid called Mark, a boy I had met just before switching schools. Our "relationship," if you could call it that, was a study in adolescent awkwardness and the complexities of growing up in the public eye.

Mark and I started liking each other in eighth grade, right after things fizzled out with Jake. Something about kissing Jake . . . it was as if a switch had been flipped. I went from never having made out with someone to suddenly realizing, "Oh my gosh, this is really fun."

This period was marked by what I'd call "moments of noncommittal make-outs." It wasn't about deep emotional connections or starting new relationships. Instead, it was a time of exploration and discovery, both of myself and of this new world of kissing that had previously been off-limits. It was fun, discovering that boys don't taste like frogs after all.

I found myself kissing about four or five boys during this time. A sort of "kissing spree," which, for someone who had grown up in such a restrictive environment, felt revelatory, a small act of rebellion against the rigid rules that had governed my life for so long.

The LDS church teaches that our physical bodies are gifts from God, to be treated with respect and gratitude, and has long held chastity as a core tenet of its faith, with the overarching principle being that sexual relations should only occur between a married man and woman. We weren't ever supposed to lie on top of someone who wasn't our spouse, and we were urged to avoid "passionate kissing" before marriage.

Oops.

After a while, though, I noticed the disconnect between physical and emotional intimacy. These encounters were fun and exciting, but they lacked the deeper emotional connection I had experienced with Jake. And that was what I really longed for. I wanted someone who I really liked, in a deeper way. Someone who wasn't just interested in kissing. You know, a real connection—like when you both reach for the last slice of pizza at the same time.

That's where Mark came into the picture. I liked Mark a lot. And he wasn't interested in kissing me at all, which helped assuage my guilt surrounding my little kissing spree.

Mark and I would go on dates all the time, even though we never went so far as to say we were "dating." And to call him my boyfriend would be a stretch. He never held my hand and was quite uncomfortable with hugging, let alone a kiss. It was more of a "weird friendship" than a romance, and we were like two awkward penguins, waddling side by side, occasionally bumping into each other but never quite figuring out how to huddle for warmth. Of course, that didn't stop Ruby from capitalizing on the situation for views.

"Shari's crush" or "Shari's boyfriend" made for clickbait titles, even if it didn't align with reality or our family's rule about not having boyfriends until at least sixteen.

Either way, our platonic teenage romance was pretty cute, looking back on it. Like this huge build-up, destined for nowhere. A rom-com that forgot the "rom" and doubled down on the "com."

In our family, skiing was always the winter sport of choice. Chad hit the slopes regularly during the winter months, carving through fresh powder with the ease of someone born with skis on their feet. Kevin, having grown up with the sport, was equally at home on the mountainside. But me? I wanted to be different. I chose a snowboard.

Our go-to spot was Snowbasin, my personal favorite among Utah's impressive array of ski resorts. It was about an hour's drive from our home, close enough for day trips but far enough to feel like an escape. We'd pile into the car early in the morning, the excitement building as we wound our way up the mountain roads.

These weren't regular winter vacations with cozy chalets and crackling fireplaces. Our trips were more of the "rise and shine, hit the slopes, and be home for dinner" variety. But there was something special about those day trips, a sense of adventure and freedom that was often missing from our heavily structured lives.

I remember the first time I strapped on my snowboard at the top of a real run. The world looked different from up there—vast, white, and full of possibility. As I wobbled my way down the slope, falling more times than I care to admit, I felt a rush of independence. Yes, I spent more time horizontal than vertical. Chad and Kevin would zoom past me, showering me with snow and unhelpful advice like "Just stand up!" as if I was choosing to be an upside-down turtle. But I didn't care—this was something I had chosen for myself, different from what the rest of my family was doing.

I decided I wanted to make a video inspired by that feeling, for my channel. It was called "Shari Competes in the Olympics," a skit about being in the Olympics and snowboarding in the backyard.

I had so much fun making it. There was a little bit of snow on the ground, but you could still see the grass; less "winter wonderland" and more "sad, melting snowman's last stand." Kevin helped me with it, and the video starts with me asking him, "Hey, can we go snowboarding today?"

Kevin replies, "Oh, I don't think so."

Then I say, "Well, I have an idea." It shows me putting on all my snowboarding gear and going outside, where we see my hand-built re-creation of an Olympic obstacle course, with a half-pipe, made out of some drainage pipe I found.

I jumped on it with my snowboard, crushing the whole thing to pieces. Take that, structural integrity! I also jumped on the trampoline on my snowboard, with hilarious results. Picture a cat on a pogo stick, but with more flailing. By the end, I had more bruises than a dropped bag of plums, but hey, that's showbiz.

I had a blast editing the video, adding a fake banner across the bottom that read, "Shari Franke from Utah. Never competed before." At the very end, I photoshopped a gold medal on my chest. It was cringy and poorly filmed, the kind of video that makes film school professors wake up in a cold sweat, and it didn't perform very well, in terms of views, but I didn't care. I loved just being goofy, being me. This video was my magnum opus, my *Citizen Kane*.

I'd gotten pretty good at vlogging by this point. I'd watched a lot of YouTube tutorials, transforming myself into a regular Spielberg of the suburban wilderness. My weapon of choice? A Canon G7 X camera, the holy grail among vloggers at the time. For shoots, I'd either set it up on a tripod or hold it myself, depending on whether I wanted my video to look professional or like it was filmed during an earthquake.

For more formal Q&A videos where I'd sit on a couch, I had a ring light, but I didn't really know how to use it. The Q&As covered topics like school routines and random questions about my life. My channel was pretty wholesome, all in all. Like a Disney Channel show, but with worse lighting and more awkward pauses. And my subscriber count was ticking up and up, so I guessed people were enjoying the videos. Even the silly ones.

On the morning of my fifteenth birthday, Ruby presented me with a new tripod, the perfect gift for a content creator. Of course she filmed the whole present-unwrapping session. With 8 Passengers now nearing two million subscribers, no milestone, no private moment was left unmined for content.

"Wow, Mom, this is amazing," I replied, genuine gratitude mixing with the familiar sense of performance. "Thank you so much."

"You're welcome." Ruby beamed before turning to address the camera. "Now why would Shari need new equipment?"

"Because I have a channel!" I blurted, the words rushing out. "I started one awhile ago, and I wanted to grow organically, but then we decided not to talk about it."

Ruby's smile remained fixed.

"Yes, she is almost at one hundred thousand subscribers, so give her some love! She did this on her own. I did not shout her out once on Instagram or on my channel."

"Does this mean I can link to 8 Passengers in my bio?" I asked, feeling like Oliver Twist asking for more gruel.

"Yes!" Ruby exclaimed. "Happy birthday, Shari." And just like that, my wish came true.

I knew the shout-out would bring a flood of new subscribers, and linking to 8 Passengers would undoubtedly bring a tidal wave of traffic to my channel. It felt like a milestone of my own, getting that validation from my mom, even though it cemented my public persona as Ruby's mini-me, rather than my own person.

When Ruby posted the video, my numbers got the expected boost—translating to a few thousand dollars per month. In teenager currency, that's like . . . a million Frappuccinos! Alas, I couldn't touch any of it yet—Mom had set up the account in her name, since I was still a minor.

"By the way," she said casually one day, months after I'd started earning, "I'm taking ten percent off the top for management fees."

I nodded, not fully grasping the "Mom Tax" concept. "What do you mean?"

"You really think you would ever have started a YouTube channel, let alone a successful one, without my help? You owe me, Shari! Business is business."

I felt a knot form in my stomach—on one hand, Mom had a point; her influence had undeniably boosted my channel. On the other hand, this felt like she was cashing in on my hard work. But as usual, what could I do about it? Nothing.

JOURNAL

I talked with my teacher Mr. Haymond today. I asked how I could better my relationship with my parents. He knows I can't have deep conversations with them. He said eventually I'll have to tell my mom I want a better relationship. He was kind and understanding, and really listened to what I had to say. Now I'm jealous of Mr. Haymond's kids because I wish I could have a parent like him.

One day, after class, I found myself lingering in Mr. Haymond's classroom. Something about his patient demeanor made me feel safe. Before I knew it, words were spilling from my lips, a torrent of pent-up pain and frustration about life with Ruby, how cold and mean she could be, how the reality differed so greatly from what the world could see. I had never been this honest with anyone about my feelings regarding my mother, not even my old therapist.

As I spoke, I watched Mr. Haymond's expression shift from polite interest to surprise, then to deep concern.

"Shari," Mr. Haymond said softly when I paused for breath, "I had no idea. This must be incredibly difficult for you."

Those simple words, that acknowledgment, felt like a key unlocking something inside me. Mr. Haymond listened patiently as I poured out my heart, nodding encouragingly, his brow furrowed with empathy. He didn't try to offer quick solutions or dismiss my feelings. He just . . . listened.

As I left his classroom that day, I felt lighter than I had in a long time. The world hadn't changed—I would still go home to the same challenges, the same carefully choreographed family life. But something in me had shifted. I had an ally now, a trusted adult who knew the truth about Ruby, and who saw me—the real me, not the version that was too shut down to share her feelings.

Chad, on the other hand, was becoming more isolated than ever, his clownish behavior and defiance being met with a harsh response at school. The rules were quite strict, and he was struggling to stay within the boundaries. It was interesting, the differences between us—while I tended to keep everything bottled up inside, Chad was more like a shaken-up bottle of Mentos and Coke, incapable of restraint. He was like a force of nature, constantly pushing boundaries and testing limits.

One day in class, probably bored out of his mind, Chad decided it'd be hilarious to chuck a piece of candy corn at his buddy across the room. Classic Chad move. Except his aim was about as good as his judgment. The candy corn pulled a curve ball and smacked the teacher instead. Boom. First infraction. After three infractions, a student would face suspension, and then expulsion. In this zero-tolerance minefield, Chad was playing hopscotch with land mines.

It only took a few more missteps—each as boneheaded as the last—before Chad found himself on the wrong side of the school's gates, expulsion papers in hand. My parents' faces when they got the news . . . I'll never forget it. A mixture of fury, disappointment, and bone-deep weariness that made them look like they'd aged a decade overnight.

But the saga wasn't over. In August 2018, Chad almost ruined our biggest family vacation/brand collab—a meticulously-planned road trip to Universal Studios Hollywood, and our biggest brand collaboration to date.

Our itinerary was planned with military precision, each camera-worthy moment scheduled down to the millisecond.

I vividly remember being in our van, when Ruby said she had a plan: "We're going to make a big mess so that we can show how well Wet Ones works." We made it gross—gummy bears smeared on windows, slime everywhere, chocolate all over everyone's faces. All to demonstrate the effectiveness of Wet Ones.

It was all going so well. Until Chad brought the chaos.

The park had opened early just for us, which was a big deal, so we could get footage walking through the empty park. But while

Ruby was filming her brand-deal talking points in front of the iconic globe, Chad was being, in her words, "an absolute punk," making constipated gargoyle faces and photobombing her carefully orchestrated brand content. Ruby's dream of picture-perfect family content was rapidly devolving into a blooper reel, so she banished him to the hotel room while the rest of us enjoyed the theme park.

Chad, ever the rebel, wasn't about to let Ruby's parental decree keep him down. He snuck out of the hotel room, took a taxi, somehow sweet-talked his way back into Universal Studios, and had a great time by himself.

When we got back to the hotel, he was gone. We had no idea where he was for a while. And that, as far as my parents were concerned, was the absolute final straw. In Ruby's and Kevin's eyes, Chad was becoming some kind of juvenile delinquent, a malfunctioning robot, and they just needed to find some way to reprogram him.

They had already considered sending Chad to West Point Military Academy, and had been dragging Chad from one therapist to another, desperate for a diagnosis, some official-sounding label to slap on his misdeeds. Much to their disappointment, most of these professionals said that at fourteen, Chad was too young for them to conclusively pathologize. Not to mention, he usually ran circles around those poor counselors. Chad was often the most manipulative person in the room—turns out, growing up on camera is excellent training for pulling the wool over people's eyes.

Looking back, my parents should probably have just given Chad the space and time he needed to grow up. Teenagers act out; it's practically in the job description. But no, Ruby and Kevin couldn't fathom such a simple solution. Instead, they doubled down, more determined than ever to find a Chad-whisperer, someone aggressive enough to break through his defenses. They were on a mission to find the perfect person to crack his code and rewire him to their liking—which is how the monster came into our lives.

A monster masquerading as a mental health professional, armed with a tight smile and a mind full of psychological warfare tactics.

A monster who would see my mother's inner darkness and cultivate it, nurture it, until it eclipsed all light.

A monster named Jodi Hildebrandt.

PART THREE

the conjurer

CHAPTER 16

snake in the garden

It was during that Orlando trip that Ruby, at her wit's end, sought advice from a family friend on what to do. The friend perked up. "Oh, I know just the person!" she chirped, explaining that she had been attending workshops in Jodi Hildebrandt's life-coaching program, ConneXions.

"Jodi really seems to command a lot of respect," said the friend. "Maybe she'd be a good therapist for Chad, given his spirited nature?"

"Jodi Hildebrandt," Ruby repeated, testing the name on her tongue. It sounded official, important. Like someone who could wrangle a herd of wild teenagers with just a stern glance.

A licensed clinical mental health counselor, Jodi had built a reputation in Utah's LDS community as something of a miracle worker. Her ConneXions program promised to help people overcome everything from porn addiction to "distorted thinking," and she preached a philosophy based on three core principles: impeccable honesty, rigorous personal responsibility, and vulnerable humility.

Intrigued by the idea of turning Chad from Dennis the Menace into an LDS poster child, Ruby immediately set up a Zoom call for Chad and Jodi. This high-stakes video conference took place in our hotel room in Orlando, where Chad had been grounded for the remainder of the trip.

After the initial call, Jodi reported back to Ruby, expressing confidence in her ability to make progress with Chad if my parents committed to weekly one-on-one calls between him and Jodi. Oh, and she had some other ideas for his immediate rehabilitation, including sending him away to Anasazi, a wilderness therapy program in Arizona for "troubled" teens.

Jodi painted Anasazi as a transformative experience, a place where Chad could shed his rebellious ways and emerge as the obedient, spiritually aligned son my parents craved. It sounded like a miracle cure-all, promising to fix every conceivable teenage problem with a bit of fresh air and wilderness survival skills.

Never mind the eye-watering price tag of $13,945 for just forty-nine days of treatment. But my parents, flush with YouTube money and blinded by desperation, didn't even blink at the cost. They were too entranced by Jodi's promises and too eager for a quick fix to question whether this was really in Chad's best interests.

"Whatever you say," said Ruby, desperate for a solution, and thrilled to be collaborating in Project Chad with this supposed guru of self-help.

I looked up Jodi online, and something about her rhetoric made me feel uneasy. Even her photo was off-putting. Her gaze, sharp and efficient. Her smile seemed severe, unyielding. In retrospect, though, it wasn't just her physical appearance that unsettled me. It was the complete absence of any nurturing energy, the warm, comforting aura one might normally expect from someone who has supposedly dedicated their life to helping others heal. Instead, in her messaging and her appearance, she seemed oddly . . . smug.

Later, I'd dig deeper into Jodi's backstory, much of which she herself has shared openly in various media—although it's hard to believe anything she says. She says she was the sixth of seven kids born to a fighter pilot dad and a stay-at-home mom. The family motto was "You're a Hildebrandt. Go hard or go home." According to Jodi, her mom lost a baby boy and was emotionally distant and didn't spend much time with her. Jodi said her dad, while also emotionally closed off, taught her to work hard and not trust people.

Growing up in the desert, Jodi said she found she was more comfortable around animals than humans, milking the family goats and enjoying her time alone. Having grown up with very little affection, she admitted finding the sight of tenderness between parents and children disturbing. Jodi has publicly shared stories of being sexually abused by a fifteen-year-old neighbor when she was two to five, and again by a sixteen-year-old who lived with them when she was seven to nine. She said that at age twenty-one, she finally told a counselor about the abuse.

In 1999, when she was twenty-six, Jodi's ex-husband filed for divorce. Jodi got full custody of her children, who were nine and seven at the time, and in her books, she admitted finding it hard, managing her energetic young kids. She started her journey as a healer in 2003, becoming licensed as a clinical mental health counselor under the Utah Division of Professional Licensing in July 2005. Guided by "heavenly instruction" and "inspired invitations," she devised her specialized coaching program, meant to foster the thing she'd never had growing up—connection. Hence, ConneXions.

What troubled me most was how quickly my mother seemed willing to entrust Chad's fate to this virtual stranger, ready to ship him off to wilderness camp based on Jodi's advice alone. I couldn't shake the feeling that we might be trading one set of problems for another.

The day Chad left for Anasazi was rainy, the sky a heavy gray blanket that matched the weight in my chest. I watched as he stuffed a trash bag with clothes, his shoulders slumped. He caught my eye, and for a second, I saw a flash of the old Chad—that mischievous sparkle, that huge grin. Then he was gone, swallowed by the gloomy morning.

True to form, Ruby and Kevin couldn't resist recording a video to explain their decision. They painted Chad as some kind of juvenile delinquent in desperate need of an attitude overhaul. Kevin, uncharacteristically, took the lead, his voice stern as he laid out the situation. I could almost see Ruby's puppet strings controlling his words.

Then Ruby took center stage. "Chad needs to develop some very basic maturity and skills," she declared. "This is a chance for a reset, a fresh beginning. The idea with wilderness therapy is if you can survive with these peers in the wilderness with nothing more than the clothes on your back and a couple of field supplies, then there's nothing in this world that you can't tackle."

Ruby's excitement bordered on the manic. "It's like the real wilderness out there," she enthused, eyes gleaming. "There are snakes, bears, coyotes, cougars—it's the real deal. We want Chad to have some of those experiences. I think close encounters would be good for him. Because those types of experiences can teach you what's really important. And he'll come home and he'll be like, 'Dude, I survived and there were bears. I can do anything.'"

Beneath her forced levity, the underlying message was clear: This was another punishment, a way to break Chad down and rebuild him into their idea of a perfect, obedient son.

"No one can fix anybody," Ruby continued, oblivious to the irony. "A person must choose if they're going to make changes in their lives. And so I think this experience will reveal Chad and everyone else who's out there to themselves, and they can learn to better themselves . . . or just stay in the mud."

As Ruby spouted this nonsense, I watched Kevin, nodding along at all the right moments. But there was something in his eyes—a flicker of doubt, perhaps? He'd later claim he disagreed at the time, before eventually falling in line. In that moment, though, he was the perfect supportive husband, backing up his wife's delusions.

Those days after Chad left were a blur of confusion and frustration. Ruby, in her infinite wisdom, decided we needed daily challenges to keep us connected while he was off playing Boy Scout Extreme. I remember rolling my eyes at most of them, but one in particular stands out in my memory. We were supposed to look into our own eyes and write about our "light"—whatever that meant—and how to make it grow. I went along with it, if only to avoid an argument. After all, arguing would probably lead to me being sent to the desert, too, and I sunburn easily.

I remember standing in front of the bathroom mirror, trying to do this ridiculous exercise. But instead of seeing any inner light or whatever, all I could focus on were my imperfections. It was like a dermatologist's nightmare come to life. My skin was dry and flaking like I was some sort of human croissant, there was a stubborn zit on my chin trying to form its own sovereign nation, and that one thick hair by my mole that seemed to grow back overnight no matter how many times I plucked it.

I missed my brother so much—how these stupid daily tasks were supposed to somehow make up for his absence, I had no idea. Everything felt off-balance, like we were a clown car with one less clown.

And staring at my oily T-zone in the mirror was hardly going to make it feel any better.

When Chad returned from Anasazi three months later, he talked about his time in the wilderness like it was no big deal, as if he'd just popped out for a quick nature walk rather than being exiled to the desert for a quarter of a year. He said it was fun, in the end, being in nature with a bunch of kids. More freedom than he had at home. No vlogging responsibilities. Building fires. Seeing snakes. Sleeping under the stars.

But my parents weren't done with Chad yet, not by a long shot. Oh no, they'd already decided to hire Jodi, at great expense, to embark on a series of one-on-one therapy sessions for Chad. This, to me, was concerning, perhaps even more so than camp, especially because the more I Googled Jodi Hildebrandt, the more concerned I became. It was like falling down a rabbit hole lined with red flags.

For instance, in 2012, a young man moved to Utah with his new wife and baby to attend Brigham Young University. His bishop recommended he see Jodi for therapy. This turned out to be a terrible mistake. Without any proof, Jodi accused her client of being an abuser, and violated patient confidentiality by reporting him to BYU's Honor Code office as a sexual predator. She also reported him to the church. The fallout was brutal. The man was kicked out of BYU and the church. His marriage fell apart—the very thing he'd gone to Jodi for help with.

Jodi's therapist license was suspended in 2012 as a result. But for her client, the damage was already done. And here she was, still practicing, still wielding influence. It was as if she'd viewed her suspension as a sabbatical, used it to double down on her questionable methods.

Feeling like we were boarding a train headed straight for Crazytown, I pulled Chad aside for a sister-brother talk. We sat together in the basement, and I let it all spill out.

"Jodi's not cool," I said bluntly. "Like, she's bonkers. You should see the stuff online. She's practically a con artist."

Chad shrugged, annoyingly unperturbed, like I'd just told him we were out of milk.

"Chill, Shari. I can handle her. She's just like all the others. All you have to do is agree with what they say."

"No, I think this is a big mistake."

Chad raised an eyebrow. "Shari, she's just some middle-aged lady. If I don't do therapy with her, Mom's going to make my life even worse than it already is."

"Just . . . be careful, okay? They say she tears families apart. Don't let her get in your head."

"I won't. Listen, I survived the desert, I can survive Jodi Hildebrandt."

Chad thanked me for my concern. Then, in typical baby-brother fashion, he went straight to Ruby and told her what I had said.

A few days later, Ruby pulled me aside, fire in her eyes.

"How dare you sabotage your brother's progress!" she hissed. "He's getting help. And honestly, Shari, you could probably use some help, too."

I stared at her, shaking my head. "I don't need help from Jodi."

"Yes, you do. You don't like Jodi. Anyone who doesn't like Jodi is hiding something. It means you're threatened by the truth she speaks."

Ruby nodded sagely, as if she'd just imparted the wisdom of the ages.

I couldn't believe what I was hearing.

"But, Mom, she had her license suspended. Her own kids don't speak to her!"

"Her kids couldn't handle the truth. She's been called by God to help people." Ruby's eyes gleamed with the fervor of a true believer. She was sold on Jodi hook, line, and sinker.

CHAPTER 17

the cult of conneXions

My first car was a hand-me-down from Kevin, a 2016 Ford Focus in pristine white. Every morning, as I slid into the driver's seat to head to school, I felt a small thrill of freedom. With the radio humming softly and the world rushing by outside the windows, I could breathe, think, and just be myself without any prying eyes or expectations. It represented the first real taste of adulthood, of making my own decisions and charting my own course. Sure, that course was mainly between home and school, with the occasional rebellious detour to the drive-thru, but still. Freedom!

Like many aspects of my life, this newfound freedom came with a caveat. The car's title remained in Kevin's name, a detail that nagged at the back of my mind. In those quiet moments behind the wheel, I couldn't help but wonder: *Can Ruby swoop in one day and take this small piece of independence away from me?* The lack of legal proof that the car was truly mine was always a source of anxiety, a reminder that my autonomy was still very tenuous and hinged on Ruby's unpredictable moods, which were about as stable as a Jenga tower in an earthquake. There had certainly been some strange shifts in her behavior now that she was soooo obsessed with ConneXions.

One day, Ruby and Kevin went to a ConneXions conference, and when Kevin came back, he seemed stressed. He wasn't sure he liked the community and would later say he felt like he was surrounded by a bunch of "man-hating women." Still, a lot of people who he respected were part of ConneXions at this point, so he ignored his doubts. Besides, Ruby seemed so enraptured by Jodi and her philosophy, he dared not burst her balloon. It was easier to go along with it than to risk becoming the next target of Jodi's "Truth-seeking" missiles.

But that was the beginning of the end for them. Ruby became more and more involved with ConneXions, diving into Jodi's concepts of Truth and Distortion—two innocuous-sounding words that would soon become the bane of my existence. The program was as expensive as it was extensive. The six-week team leadership training, which included six ninety-minute sessions with a "certified ConneXions trainer" and access to Jodi's ever-growing library of more than one hundred podcasts, came with a hefty price tag of $4,995 per person.

For those truly committed to Jodi's philosophy—or perhaps those she deemed in need of more intensive "help"—there was the eighteen-week company leadership training, costing $14,985. It seemed Jodi believed in the old adage: If you're going to fleece someone, might as well go for the whole sheep.

The fruits of her labor were evident in her $5 million luxury home in Ivins, a picturesque town four hours south. Complete with a pool and a safe room, it stood as a gleaming testament to how lucrative the business of "fixing" people could be—and just how persuasive Jodi was at reeling in disciples and indoctrinating them.

Jodi's playbook focused on isolation and control. To fully embrace her teachings, ConneXions students were urged to distance themselves from anyone not living by Jodi's truth. It was like watching a real-life *Invasion of the Body Snatchers*, observing my parents' sanity circle the drain as they morphed into Jodi's devoted disciples.

At first, I hesitated to use the word "cult." It seemed extreme. But as I delved into some casual online research—nothing says "normal teenager" quite like Googling "Is my family in a cult?"—ConneXions ticked all the boxes. Sure, we weren't being physically relocated to some remote compound à la Jonestown. But we didn't need to be. Our dedicated enclave within Utah was the perfect setup for someone like Jodi—a ready-made, isolated community ripe for manipulation.

Jodi's followers were compelled to confess their "distortions" in group sessions and through constant phone calls with each other. Her little army, informing on each other, recruiting anybody who'd listen. The key to connection, paradoxically, was disconnection—isolating yourself from anyone who didn't speak Jodi's language, making yourself totally dependent on your new "ConneXions family," who would police your every thought until you existed in a hive mind of groupthink.

At the heart of it all was Jodi, running the show with an iron fist. To those outside her inner circle, she was a respected pillar of the community, a beacon of hope for those seeking healing. Through sheer force of personality, she had positioned herself as the ultimate "life coach," seemingly preying on LDS people who had started out simply wanting some coping tools, new ways to heal and look at the world. Instead, they found themselves trapped in a rigid script and tyrannical system designed to strip them of their autonomy while Jodi monetized their so-called healing.

Ruby's descent into Jodi's world hit warp speed when she took the six-week life-coach training course. Suddenly, she wasn't just drinking the Kool-Aid; she was brewing it. On Saturdays, I'd watch her hang on Jodi's every Zoom-broadcasted word like she was the second coming. The stars in my mom's eyes were blinding.

Before long, Ruby had become a certified ConneXions life coach, leading support calls and women's groups. Client confidentiality became a joke as she reported weekly to Jodi. Big Sister was here.

One night at dinner, Mom casually mentioned that a woman in her support group, had been "cheating." The offense? Noticing the mailman was attractive. In ConneXions' warped reality, this constituted infidelity. Jodi's teachings were extreme: a married man talking to a female coworker could be unfaithful, and glimpsing attractive people online might be classified as porn addiction. Only absolute purity of thought was acceptable.

In Jodi's rigid world, innocence was rare. Those deemed "distorted"—usually husbands—were told to abandon their families to work on themselves. Alone. Jodi seemed to specialize in guiding wives to distance themselves from their husbands. Or kicking them out entirely. ConneXions language framed it as "inviting him to leave," code for "I'm going to make you isolate yourself from everyone you know, except Jodi." Shockingly, the husbands often went along with it, fully convinced that it was in the best interest of their families. It was like watching lemmings jump off a cliff.

This self-imposed isolation was part of Jodi's twisted "rings of responsibility" concept. If you were distorted, you'd be stripped of every responsibility except self-improvement. No job, no community, no family. Just you and Jodi's teachings in a vacuum, solitary confinement, but you have to pay for the privilege, all in the name of "healing."

These separations typically lasted at least six months—the minimum time Jodi deemed necessary to demonstrate genuine change. Her logic was that anyone could fake remorse or make short-term adjustments, but sustaining change for half a year proved sincere transformation. Adults were essentially put on probation in their relationships, expected to prove their worth to Jodi to earn back the privilege of family closeness. The six-month rule also applied to kids, and any significant transgression could result in a half-year sentence of restricted privileges, increased scrutiny, and constant pressure to demonstrate "change."

It's interesting to compare Ruby's glacial approach to parenting with Jodi's rigid philosophy. The two weren't just similar—they were symbiotic. Jodi's ConneXions doctrine wasn't so much a revelation to Ruby as it was a mirror, reflecting and magnifying the harsh worldview she'd always held.

After all, Ruby had always doled out love like a miser with coins, making her affection contingent on a prolonged demonstration of "good" behavior. In her world, love wasn't a given—it was a prize to be earned through perfect conduct, a carrot dangled just out of reach to keep us constantly striving, constantly proving ourselves worthy.

ConneXions wasn't introducing Ruby to a new way of thinking; it was giving her the vocabulary and pseudo-scientific backing to justify what she'd been doing all along. Jodi's system had simply slapped a fancy label on this emotional starvation diet and called it therapy. In the end, ConneXions didn't change Ruby's tactics; it just gave her a manual to refine them.

Ruby didn't announce Jodi's arrival or her newfound interest in ConneXions with any fanfare on 8 Passengers. Instead, the shift was subtle, a slow integration of new ideas and terminology into her existing content. It was as if she were testing the waters, gauging her audience's reaction to this new philosophy.

I remember noticing the change in her language first. Suddenly, "Truth" became a buzzword in her videos and blog posts. She'd casually mention how she'd "found this self-help program" that was revolutionizing her approach to parenting and life in general. It was presented as just another tool in her parenting arsenal, another piece of advice she was sharing with her followers.

Ruby began promoting ConneXions events to her audience, though she didn't immediately reveal the depth of her involvement. She'd mention upcoming conferences or encourage her followers to sign up for free Saturday classes. It was framed as an exciting opportunity for self-improvement, a chance for her audience to access the same wisdom that was supposedly transforming our family life. She positioned it as an evolution, a natural next step in her journey as a mother and influencer. Her followers, already primed to trust her advice, began to show interest in these new ideas, even though they couldn't see how ConneXions was already starting to destroy our family.

For instance, when Jodi decided that Chad wasn't "improving" fast enough, she advised my parents to immediately pull him out of track and football, crushing all his teenage dreams. For Chad, track and football were his lifeline, his ticket to a brighter future. He had won first place in the district 100-meter dash, also in the 200-meter dash. Coaches whispered about his potential, and the dream of a football or track scholarship seemed within reach. It was more than just a way to pay for college; it was Chad's chance to prove himself, to carve out an identity beyond the constraints of our family's dysfunction.

But with one nod from Ruby and Kevin, Jodi's interference shattered all those dreams. How could Chad possibly commit to track and football when he couldn't even be "fully responsible" for himself? Nope, Chad would be barred from sports, until he was "fixed." And that meant taking away the one thing that gave him purpose and joy.

I stood in the doorway of Chad's room, watching him methodically pack away his football gear.

"Chad," I said softly, "do you really have to do this?"

He looked up at me, his eyes hollow. "You know I do, Shari. Mom and Dad made it clear. Jodi says—"

"Who cares what Jodi says!" I blurted out.

Chad's lips quirked in a sad smile. "Yeah, well, try telling that to Mom and Dad."

As if on cue, Ruby's voice floated up from downstairs. "Chad! Jodi's on the phone. She wants to talk to you!"

I watched my brother's shoulders slump even further. He stood up, casting one last longing look at his gear before heading downstairs, like a condemned man walking to the gallows.

This isn't right, I thought, my heart aching. In the world of competitive sports, especially at the high school level, timing is everything. You can't just pause your athletic career and expect to pick it up again years later without consequences. They effectively ruined his chances at the scholarships he had worked so hard for, all in the name of . . . what? Even now, I struggle to understand their reasoning.

I followed Chad down, hovering at the edge of the living room as he took the phone from Ruby. Her face was beaming, as if she were handing him a gift instead of a death sentence for his dreams.

"Hello, Jodi," Chad said, his voice flat.

I couldn't hear Jodi's words, but I could see their effect on my brother. With each passing moment, the light in his eyes dimmed a little more.

"Yep, I get it," he mumbled. "I need to focus on being responsible for myself before I can be responsible to a team."

I wanted to scream. *Don't you see what you're doing to him? Don't you understand what you're taking away?*

In that moment, I saw flashes of a future crumbling away—Chad scoring the winning touchdown, scouts clamoring to offer him scholarships, a path out and away from all of this madness . . . all that, now gone.

As Chad handed the phone back to Ruby, Kevin clapped him on the shoulder. "This is for the best, son. Jodi knows what she's talking about."

CHAPTER 18

isolation tactics

As I watched my family, and so many others, succumb to Jodi's twisted dogma, I couldn't help but wonder—what on earth was the source of that woman's power? Why did this woman in her ugly khaki shorts and long-sleeved shirts have such a hold on people? Was it the promise of absolute truth? Her supreme self-confidence that offered some illusion of certainty in a world that seems to be unraveling at the seams? Or was it the way she enabled people's hatred of others and themselves?

I noticed how Ruby was beginning to turn on her parents and siblings, confronting difficult memories of her past in ways she'd never dared before. Always the poster child for "moving forward," she'd spent her life plastering over her childhood wounds with a veneer of perfection and daily phone calls to her mother. Her relationship with her mom bordered on codependency—a fact I'd always found unsettling, given my own emotional distance from Ruby.

But Jodi's emphasis on "ceaseless inventory and inner work" cracked that carefully constructed facade.

Suddenly, Ruby's wounded inner child emerged, raw and angry, recalling incidents that she'd long buried, sending shock waves through the entire Griffiths clan. None of them had shown an interest in joining ConneXions, despite Ruby's glowing reviews. Increasingly, though, Ruby felt that unless they embraced ConneXions, healing would never be possible.

This severing didn't manifest overnight. It took around two or three years before Ruby would cut ties entirely with her family. And as I watched Ruby delete contact after contact from her phone, I couldn't help but wonder: Was this healing?

It was as if Jodi had flipped a switch in Ruby's brain, turning familial love into contempt overnight. In the back of my mind, a terrifying thought took root: If Ruby could cut off the entire Griffiths family so easily, what would stop her from doing the same to us? Would I wake up one day and find myself deleted from the family iMessage thread?

I wanted to support my mother, despite the complex emotions I harbored toward her. Perhaps it was because I could empathize with the experience of holding resentment against one's parents and grappling with unresolved childhood trauma. I instinctively understood that unaddressed pain often perpetuates cycles of hurt, passing from one generation to the next.

I'd never thought about it before, that even those who present a flawless facade to the world, like my mother, might be struggling with deep-seated issues that remain hidden from view. How their polished exterior can serve as a mask, concealing the inner turmoil and unhealed wounds that continue to fester beneath the surface.

Recognizing this for the first time, I did feel a sense of compassion for my mother, kinship even, acknowledging that her seemingly perfect demeanor, and the darkness behind it, might have had a lot to do with her own unresolved past.

One evening Ruby pulled me aside after dinner for a little talk.

"Shari, we're taking you out of track so you can focus on what's really important—your personal development," my mother said.

I was stunned. Track—the only sport I actually enjoyed—was being taken away from me? What would be next, banning me from breathing?

"But why?" I asked, desperately hoping this was just a really bad joke.

"You're not emotionally vulnerable with me," Ruby said. "There's a wall between us. Imagine how it'll affect your husband in the future. You think any man wants to put up with that? A cold, shut-down wife?"

"I don't understand!"

"Shari, you don't have empathy. You're not compassionate. As your parent, it's my job to help you fix your flaws, before it's too late. That's why your father and I have decided to give you the gift of one-on-one sessions with Jodi."

My stomach dropped. Over my dead body was I letting that woman anywhere near my brain! I'd rather lobotomize myself with a spoon!

"Chad is making so much progress with her," Ruby continued. "Now it's your turn."

I dug my nails into my palms, fighting the urge to scream. Instead, I just stayed silent, turned to stone. Maybe if I didn't move, they'd think I was a statue and leave me alone.

Ruby's eyes flashed, sensing my anger.

"The choice is yours, Shari. You either do one-on-one counseling with Jodi, or we take away your car, your phone, and pull you out of school entirely. You decide."

My jaw dropped. They couldn't be serious. But one look at my mom's face and I knew she absolutely was. She would quite happily derail my entire life in my senior year of high school in order to force me into therapy with her totally sus life coach.

Who were these pod people masquerading as my parents?

I fled to my room, rage boiling beneath my skin. I opened up my laptop, my trembling fingers typing "how to emancipate yourself from your parents" into the search bar. But as the results loaded, reality crashed down.

Where would I go?

What would I do?

Who would I be?

The questions echoed in my mind, each one a painful reminder of my puppet status. At seventeen, I was a prisoner of circumstance—no friends outside our community, no support system, no escape route.

I wished I could have walked out that door and never come back.

But the cold truth was, I had nowhere to walk to.

CHAPTER 19

winning the self-loathing olympics

The following week, I got on my first one-on-one phone call with Jodi Hildebrandt. I took the call while sitting in the corner of my closet—I wanted to make sure no one could hear what was said.

"So, Shari," Jodi began, her tone matter-of-fact. "Let's dive right in. Our goal with these calls is to isolate, and ultimately address, the distorted thinking that is causing you to behave in a cold and entitled manner that is creating issues in the family. Can you tell me more about that, from your perspective?"

"I don't know," I said, already irritated. "I really try to be a good person."

"But *are* you a good person?"

"Yes, I think so. How do we even know, for sure?"

Jodi let the question hang in the air for a moment.

"Everyone has areas where they can grow," she said finally. "Questioning yourself rigorously is a healthy start. It shows self-awareness."

"I agree with that," I said truthfully. "Actually, I question myself all the time. It's kind of a problem."

"But are you asking yourself the right questions, Shari? I don't think so, otherwise, why would we be here?"

I listened as Jodi explained how people engage in what she called "logical fallacies," meaning the lies we tell ourselves. She said I might be lying to myself about being a good person, for instance, because it suited my distorted narrative. Then she explained how it's crucial, in order for us to get closer to the truth about ourselves, to identify every single way we are in distortion. In order to do that, we were going to embark on a new way of thinking. One involving radical self-honesty and rigorous personal inventory.

"Fine," I said. "I'm open to taking inventory. I think our time's up, isn't it?"

"Yes. Before we hang up, I'd like to address something, Shari. I heard you had some disparaging things to say about me."

Oh crap. Blood rushed to my cheeks.

"Oh. I'm sorry about that."

"Don't be sorry, be real."

"Fine, yes. I had some concerns."

"I said be honest, Shari. You were spreading gossip, lies, and rumors. Would you consider that to be compassionate behavior? Or do you prefer to blindly believe everything you see on the internet?"

"I mean, if it's the truth . . ." I started, feeling like I was walking into a verbal minefield.

"Oh, you're going to learn a lot about Truth, Shari. You'll love it. Chad does, and he's much better now, isn't he?" Jodi said brightly, shifting gears.

"He seems more respectful," I said quietly.

"And your mother doesn't shout as much as she used to, does she?"

It was true. Ruby didn't raise her voice as much as she used to, since she'd been in ConneXions.

"The question is, are you willing to do the same work, to be a happier and more fulfilled person for your family and, one day, your spouse?"

"Sure I am," I said, feeling like I'd just signed a deal with the devil. Or at least, the devil's life coach.

CHAPTER 20

dirty laundry

Weekly calls with Jodi became a part of my routine, each session lasting about fifty minutes, a standard therapy hour, for which she charged my parents $175. Typically, our sessions were freeform conversations, focused on analyzing my thoughts and experiences from the week before.

She never ever talked about herself. Even though she'd been very open about her history in her books, she always remained guarded in her personal interactions with me, never hinting at any past trauma. She didn't invite inquiries into her personal life, and I never felt comfortable asking her about herself directly. The relationship she was cultivating didn't leave room for such personal exchanges; it was all about quietly asserting domination while encouraging me to open up about my flaws and self-loathing, which I was happy to do.

On our second call, Jodi listened intently as I read from my list of distorted thinking episodes for that week. I was quite proud of my work, actually. Very thorough.

Monday
- *Jumped to conclusions—3x today*
- *Thought in black and white about that hard test seven times*
- *Competed with Sara and assumed I was better at math than she*

Tuesday
- *Catastrophized about upcoming presentation—4x*
- *Overgeneralized my abilities based on one bad grade—2x*
- *Personalized professor's general criticism of class performance—3x*

Wednesday
- *Engaged in "should" statements about my study habits—5x*
- *Magnified importance of minor social faux pas at lunch—2x*
- *Discounted positives in feedback on my essay draft—3x*

And so on.

Jodi sighed when I finished, her voice heavy with disappointment.

"Clearly, you have serious issues with adulation," she said.

"I don't understand," I whispered, frustrated.

"Adulation is when you think you're better than everybody else," Jodi said. "Denigration is the opposite. Most people lean toward one or the other. It's clear to me you heavily lean towards adulating."

"But I thought if anything . . . I tend to self-denigrate?"

"But at your core, it's the opposite, Shari."

Jodi informed me that for next week's homework, I'd have to

write down every instance of self-adulation I indulged in, on top of all my other distorted thoughts. To my horror, there were quite a few.

Yes, list number two was a real page-turner, bullet point after bullet point of damning evidence that I was, as Jodi suspected, an insufferable smarty-pants. A teacher's pet. A grammar snob.

Monday
- *Felt smug when I answered a question in class that no one else could*
- *Silently congratulated myself for using "whom" correctly in a sentence*
- *Thought I was better than others for reading a book "above my grade level"*

Tuesday
- *Felt superior for finishing the math test first*
- *Privately judged classmates for their music tastes*
- *Believed I was more mature than my peers for enjoying documentaries*

Wednesday
- *Felt proud of my extensive vocabulary during a presentation*
- *Thought I was special for understanding a complex scientific concept quickly*
- *Silently criticized others' grammar mistakes in group chat*

And so on.

I'd always been obsessed with micro-analyzing myself, so in a twisted way, being forced to notice even more possible ways in which I was a terrible person was right up my alley. Before long, I was documenting and second-guessing every single word that came out of my mouth.

Working with Jodi was like a dream come true for my inner mean girl. We'd been training for the Self-Loathing Olympics for a while, but now it was finally showtime. And the best part? It was all framed as a healthy way of building self-awareness. A noble pursuit of personal growth and enlightenment. And so, each week, I continued to write, to document every flaw, each failing, each moment of possible hubris, my pen a weapon turned inward.

"Okay, this is much better, Shari," Jodi said five weeks in, her eyes scanning the pages of my meticulously documented mess-ups. "Now I'm going to teach you a very important technique. A way to transmute the adulation and turn it into something useful."

"Okay," I said, my voice filled with an eagerness that was surprising, even to my own ears.

"Next time you identify your adulation, Shari, I invite you to explore its opposite," Jodi continued. "Think of it as a balancing exercise."

"So, I should self-denigrate instead?"

"Very good, Shari. So, let's say you assume you're going to ace a test, because, of course, you think you're so very clever. Change the language in your mind. Flip it. Think to yourself, *Oh my gosh, I'm going to fail this test because I'm a very stupid little girl.*"

"Excuse me?"

"Yes, I want you to imagine what it feels like to fail that test. Really inhabit the feeling."

"Uh . . ." I hesitated, my stomach churning. Failing a test? Was she kidding? I had never done that in my life. It was outside everything I knew.

"Shari, be humble. You are far less clever than you think you are. Now tell me how that feels. Be honest."

I took a shaky breath and tried to imagine what it would feel like not understanding my favorite books. Confusion and frustration washed over me.

"Uh, this sucks," I whispered.

"Good. What else? How do you feel?"

I thought about trying to navigate the world, and Ruby's mercurial moods, without the anchor of my mind, my imagination. My ability to compartmentalize and cleverly pretend like everything was okay—it had gotten me out of trouble so many times. If I didn't have that guile, that wily understanding, I'd be like Chad, facing punishment and reprimands every five minutes.

"I feel scared," I said, my cheeks burning. "Exposed."

"There it is!" exclaimed Jodi. "You feel *vulnerable*. Vulnerability is what Shari Franke experiences when she realizes that she is not right about everything. And that, my dear, is what we call living in Truth."

As much as my gut tried to rebel against her methods, my mind couldn't refute her logic. By telling myself I was less than I thought I was, I found myself literally drowning in emotional vulnerability. And wasn't that the whole point of this therapy circus in the first place? To strip me down to my rawest, most vulnerable core, so that my mom would finally approve of me?

Jodi's convoluted math seemed to add up: self-deprecation plus vulnerability equals "truth." And who was I to question her infallible calculations?

"I'm going to tell Ruby we had a real breakthrough today," said Jodi afterward. "I'm very proud of you, Shari."

"Thank you," I said. "And I'm so sorry for the things I said about you, Jodi. I guess we shouldn't believe everything we see online."

She chuckled.

"No, we shouldn't," she said, her voice dripping with the satisfaction of a predator who knows she has finally caught her prey.

CHAPTER 21

jodi says

Like Ruby, Kevin, and Chad, I drank the ConneXions Kool-Aid. More like chugged it by the gallon.

Within a few months of starting my one-on-one therapy sessions with Jodi, I was a card-carrying, insufferable ConneXions convert, obsessed with analyzing every thought that crossed my own mind, as well as every thought that crossed anyone else's mind, too. As you can imagine, I was a real joy to be around, and every interaction became an opportunity for me to showcase my newfound "enlightenment."

Oh, you think you did well on that test? That's just your adulation talking. Let's explore the opposite, shall we? How does it feel to imagine failing miserably?

I could practically hear my friends' eyes rolling back into their heads as I launched into yet another lecture on the dangers of distorted thinking. But I couldn't help myself, couldn't resist the urge to "correct" their flawed perceptions, to show them the error of their ways. Not now that I understood Truth.

I managed to drive away most of my friends at school. Surprise surprise, no one wanted to be around a preachy seventeen-year-old firebrand, a mini-Jodi obsessed with calling out their every cognitive distortion. But hey, their loss, right? They just couldn't handle my superior grasp of the human psyche.

Watching them drift away, along with their laughter and easy camaraderie, I sometimes wondered if the price of my "enlightenment" was worth it. Then I realized that losing all my friends was just part of the process. It was a test, to see how strong and dedicated I was to Truth. Just like the Widow had been dedicated to her faith.

We must be willing to sacrifice for our beliefs, I told myself, every time I alienated another friend. *Anyway, unlike me, they're all going to hell.*

And so, I soldiered on, my head held high, my mind brimming with Jodi's teachings. I was a warrior, ready to take on the world, one distorted thought at a time. I didn't need anyone's validation. I had Jodi's approval, which meant I had Ruby's, and that was all that mattered.

One day, a good friend and I were sitting on the worn wooden benches outside school, the sun beating down on us, when she turned to me, her voice lowering to a conspiratorial whisper.

"Shari, I kissed three boys over the weekend, and I was telling Sarah about it, and she basically called me a whore," she said guiltily. "What do you think?"

I couldn't believe my friend since ninth grade was expecting me to sympathize. As a fellow member of the LDS church, sworn to a vow of chastity before marriage, she was treading on thin ice. *She is so damned*, I thought.

"And what was your motive for kissing all of those people?" I asked icily.

She looked at me like I had sprouted horns.

"*Motive?* Um, they were cute? Why does there need to be some deep reason?" Her voice was rising with each word, attracting curious glances from nearby students.

I gave her my best ConneXions look, a perfect blend of condescension and pity, and placed a sympathetic hand on her shoulder, as if I were a wise sage bestowing my profound insights upon a lowly peasant.

"As your friend, I must ask, what does a kiss actually mean to you? What part of your ego was it serving, when you chose to share yourself in that way?"

She shrugged me off, her eyes narrowing. "Shari, why are you interrogating me?"

"I'm just curious."

"You're judging! You're being so mean! I thought you were my friend! Don't you remember when you were the one going around kissing boys?"

"True growth comes from confronting our deepest flaws. Are you willing to do the work?"

"Oh, get *lost*, Shari! Who even *are* you anymore?"

Tears spilling down her cheeks, she got up and stormed off. A flicker of remorse stirred within me, a tiny voice whispering that maybe, just maybe, I had crossed a line. But that voice was quickly drowned out by the deafening roar of my own self-righteousness, my unwavering conviction that I, Wise Shari, was merely trying to guide this sweet poor lamb out of Distortion and toward Truth.

I guess she just isn't ready, I thought. *She'll thank me later.*

She didn't. In fact, she never spoke to me again.

Even teachers weren't safe from my sanctimony. In English

class, I decided to take it upon myself to shred the book we were reading, *The Chosen*, by Chaim Potok, a poignant and well-written story about a friendship between two Jewish boys growing up in Brooklyn at the end of World War II. Personally, I felt ready for a more challenging text, something that would truly test my superior intellect.

"This feels a little babyish; I think we should be reading harder things," I announced to the teacher at the beginning of class. *Behold, mortals, for Shari has spoken.*

My teacher raised an eyebrow.

"I think you'll find it has a lot to offer, Shari. It was nominated for some big awards. It's a very well-respected text, not a children's book by any means."

His gentle rebuke pricked my conscience, and I wondered if maybe I was being a bit of a pretentious jerk. But what did he know? I was the one learning to dismantle Distortion. Awards? Respect? Those were just societal constructs designed to keep us from Truth!

"What is it, Shari?" said the teacher, as if reading my disdainful thoughts. "Go on, tell us what you think."

"I think you're engaging in emotional reasoning, letting your positive feelings about *The Chosen* cloud your judgment about its suitability for the class," I said. "Just because you personally find it poignant and well-written does not mean it is the ideal choice from an objective educational standpoint. You're worshipping the 'should' without rationally evaluating whether it truly meets students' needs, which means your thought process is distorted by unexamined assumptions and an overly adulatory view of the book's merits for this particular purpose."

Boom. Mic drop. Shari: 1; Teacher: 0.

He asked me if I was finished, which, of course, I wasn't. *Finished? I'm just getting started.*

My classmates could not believe my preachiness, their faces a mixture of confusion and annoyance. I could feel their silent pleas for me to just shut the hell up and let them learn in peace. My teacher, fortunately, seemed to think it was all quite funny.

"Ever considered going into law, Shari?" He chuckled, before telling us to turn to page 52.

"Actually, yes, I have," I muttered, flipping to the page, annoyed, my cheeks burning with a mixture of embarrassment and self-satisfaction. How strange, being someone who'd always felt so shy but was now compelled to yell from the rooftops that she was the only one who truly understood the world.

When I told Ruby about the incidents at school, she was thrilled.

"Wow, that was so truthful and loving of you to reflect that to your promiscuous friend!" she said, pride in her eyes.

"So you don't think it was bad that I asked her what her motives were?"

"No, that was a good question of you to ask, Shari. And how did she respond?"

"Well, she got kind of upset."

"Can you see how that's a reflection of her distortion? She wasn't comfortable with your questions, even though you were just reflecting Truth. My sweet Shari, you're so brave and clever!"

I wasn't brave or clever. I was just riding high on my wave of self-righteous ConneXions zeal. That's what being in a cult like ConneXions feels like. Like you're special, and no one else understands the special knowledge that you have. It's addictive. My eyes were sharp and my tongue sharper as I sought out every imperfect, distortion-filled soul that crossed my path. In my eyes, I was a crusader for Truth, a warrior for enlightenment, determined to expose the flaws and weaknesses of those around me. In other words, I was a mean, judgmental scold—but I couldn't see that. And I didn't care if I lost every friend I had, if it meant hearing praise fall from my mother's lips.

I'm so proud of the woman you're becoming, she'd say, her words filling me up like a balloon.

I drank in this new, and hard-won approval like a flower turning toward the sun. My whole life, all I'd ever wanted was to be seen and truly appreciated by my mother. With Jodi's teachings as my guide, it seemed as though now I was learning how to access all that love and acceptance I'd been craving for so long.

Finally, Ruby liked me—some days, it almost felt like we were friends.

CHAPTER 22

burn it and be damned

In 2019, thanks to the channel's continuing success—two and a half million subscribers and climbing!—Ruby and Kevin bought a new house in Springville, just a block away from the first 8 Passengers house, and a far cry from our modest beginnings.

This new house was a sprawling three-story structure with an epic, tree-filled backyard made for entertaining (hello, hot tub!). With seven bedrooms and six bathrooms—well, five full and one half—it was more than spacious enough for our family and our adorable new Cavapoo puppy, Dwight, who we'd gotten after Nolly passed away.

All the girls had bedrooms upstairs, sharing the top floor. Ruby and Kevin's master suite occupied the main floor, a buffer zone between the gender-divided levels. The boys, Chad and my youngest brother, had claimed the basement as their domain, complete with their own bathroom, a pool table and a Foosball table, and even a full kitchen (although Ruby quickly commandeered it for extra freeze-drying storage).

Ruby's two large freeze dryers ran ceaselessly, humming away twenty-four hours a day, preserving everything from leftovers to bulk-bought sale items. Nothing was safe from their grasp—leftover steak, vegetables on sale at the store, entire meals would be processed and stored away for some future crisis that lived only in Ruby's imagination. She even experimented with freeze-drying greens, grinding them into a powder that could be reconstituted later.

For all its grandeur, the house felt oddly sterile. Spacious yet confining, modern yet soulless. A house built for show, not for living. Ruby's obsession with camera-friendly minimalism meant our walls remained bare, save for the occasional picture. The lighting in our house was clinical—rows of bright white studio lights instead of warm, homey fixtures. It made everything look clean and pristine, but it lacked warmth. Like everything else in our lives, it was designed for the camera, not for comfort. We weren't even allowed to decorate our rooms or put up posters—Ruby feared tape would rip the paint or nails would damage the walls. The whole place felt more like a showroom than a home.

Perched on the upper floor, my bedroom overlooked the backyard, a slice of nature framed by two windows. From my vantage point, the view was a tapestry of green. Dense box elder trees lined the creek at the bottom of the garden, their leaves rustling in the breeze, creating a natural curtain that partially obscured the fields beyond. On clear days, I could just make out the neighbors' horses grazing in the distance.

For months after we moved in, I slept on a mattress on the floor, topped with a comforter that I struggle to remember clearly now. I think it was striped blue and white, but the details have faded with time. It's funny how such a central part of my daily life could become so hazy in my memory. And to be honest, I didn't love having my own bedroom—I missed sharing with my youngest sister, whose bubbly energy had always helped take me out of my dark thoughts.

At night, I'd often leave my windows open, letting the gentle murmur of the creek wash over me. The soothing sounds of rustling leaves and trickling water gradually eased my restless mind into sleep. Come morning, I'd wake with itchy eyes and a stuffy nose, courtesy of the box elders in the yard. But I welcomed these minor discomforts. In this house—a monument to artificial perfection—nature provided my only taste of authenticity and warmth. Those open windows became my lifeline, a portal to a world that still felt real and alive, unlike the sterile emptiness that surrounded me indoors.

On March 3, 2020, my seventeenth birthday, Ruby finally allowed me to paint my bedroom wall. I chose a geometric blue-green triangle pattern, a small rebellion against the stark whiteness that dominated our home. It felt like a breath of fresh air, a tiny slice of personal expression in our tightly controlled world. But the respite was short-lived—just ten days later, the world ground to a halt as Covid-19 swept across the nation. If life felt suffocating before, it was about to become truly unbearable.

As the pandemic took hold, Ruby continued posting to 8 Passengers, but her demeanor had shifted. The channel she'd painstakingly built from the ground up now seemed to hold less allure for her than Jodi's ConneXions venture.

"This is going to be big," Ruby would say about ConneXions, with the same fervor she once reserved for our YouTube channel. "Jodi is changing lives. She's changing me."

It was true—she had changed. The yelling had stopped. She seemed calmer, more in control. She no longer flew off the handle at minor infractions or disagreements. But something else had taken its place. Something worse. Ruby's punishments became more psychological in nature, more focused on our emotions and minds than our bodies.

Punishments themselves took on a more elaborate, almost theatrical quality. Instead of swift, straightforward consequences—a flick in the lips, a slap on the cheek—Ruby began devising complex object lessons meant to teach us about empathy, responsibility, or whatever virtue she felt we were lacking. These often involved grand gestures or prolonged periods of deprivation, all designed to make us truly "feel" the weight of our transgressions.

May 2020. In a video titled "What We Haven't Told You," Chad dropped a bomb that would soon detonate our family's carefully curated image. He mentioned, casually, that he'd been sleeping on a beanbag on the basement floor. For seven. Whole. Months. On Jodi's advice, Ruby removed Chad's bedroom privileges as punishment for continued defiance. His options? A pullout guest bed, an inflatable mattress, or . . . wherever. That "wherever" became a beanbag in the basement.

Seven months—210 nights. On a beanbag.

Ruby saw nothing unusual about this. Chad acted like he didn't care. It was a master class in emotional suppression, a skill we'd all been forced to perfect. When he let slip during filming what his current sleeping arrangements were, he did it so coolly, I doubt Ruby really even noticed.

But Ruby's new editor did, and he made Chad's revelation the focus of the video, misguidedly thinking it would be interesting content. Ruby didn't hesitate to post it. Why would she? Jodi had been pumping her full of misplaced confidence, convincing her that her "unique" parenting philosophies were not just acceptable, but admirable.

As the upload bar reached 100 percent, Ruby sat back, satisfied.

In her mind, she wasn't just a mother anymore. She was a truth-teller, a revolutionary parent. Ruby, high on Jodi's toxic positivity, was about to (proudly) display her son's dehumanization for millions to see. Even Dwight, our dog, had more comfortable sleeping arrangements.

The internet went ballistic.

Ruby's face paled as she scrolled through the comments. YouTubers and TikTokers were accusing her of child abuse.

"But . . . but this is all wrong! They don't understand!"

"Ruby," Kevin suggested, "maybe we should take the video down. So we don't lose subscribers."

"No!" Ruby snapped. "Jodi says we need to stand firm in our Truth. We can't let the haters win!"

That one video burned down the 8 Passenger's YouTube channel overnight and cost our family 90 percent of our income. Hundreds of thousands unsubscribed, and brands, once eager to associate with our wholesome family image, couldn't distance themselves fast enough. Overnight, we went from wholesome family influencers to social media pariahs.

Ruby seemed oddly defiant regarding the crash and burn of her own channel. "People have been asking for years how I've raised such well-behaved children," she declared, chin held high. "Now they know. If they can't handle the truth, that's on them."

Financial concerns, once the cornerstone of our family's decision-making, now seemed secondary. It was as if Jodi's approval had become the only currency that mattered. In my mind, Ruby wasn't just brainwashed; she had become a devoted daughter to a mother figure who seemed to demand nothing less than total obedience.

As for me, I was secretly thrilled about our new status as YouTube's most unwanted. Did this mean we'd finally get our lives back?

Could I actually eat a meal without it being broadcast to millions? But on the other hand, watching our livelihood circle the drain wasn't exactly cause for celebration.

As for Chad, well, he seemed almost amused by the whole thing. Revenge is sweet.

Ruby kept the channel up, a ghost of its former self, posting only occasionally. Mainly, though, people were hate-watching 8 Passengers (which still lined our pockets) digging deep into the archives, trawling through five years of our lives with a fine-toothed comb, looking for more evidence of Ruby's cruelty.

Some videos became infamous: Ruby threatening to behead my youngest sister's stuffed animals; an "eye for an eye" punishment after my youngest sister damaged something. I remember that day, the horror in my little sister's eyes, the mocking determination in Ruby's voice.

Ruby's rationale seemed to be "You murdered someone else's possession, so how would it feel if we murder yours?" Her approach, intended to teach consequences, totally disregarded the emotional capacities of a young kid because for a child of five, a stuffed animal is more than just a toy, it's a source of comfort, a loyal friend, a crucial coping mechanism for navigating the big, scary world around them. Threatening to guillotine a beloved buddy wasn't just a punishment; it was emotional terrorism. Now, years later, thousands of strangers were revisiting that moment.

Ruby posted a vlog where she bragged how she wouldn't bring a packed lunch into school for my youngest sister, who had forgotten hers that day. Ruby explained how the teacher had called her to say she was uncomfortable with my youngest sister being hungry and would like Ruby to drive her lunch over.

"I told the teacher, my daughter is responsible for making her own lunches in the morning," Ruby said, in the video. "The natural outcome of forgetting your lunch is that you are going to be hungry."

Ruby went on to say that she hoped no one shared their lunch with her child that day; she should go hungry in order to learn her lesson. Ruby tried to defend herself afterward, saying the school was a forty-five-minute drive from our house, there were only two hours left of school that day. But that did nothing to calm down the masses; all they'd heard was Ruby's cold contempt for her hungry child.

Angry viewers didn't just leave mean comments—they went after what remained of our family's livelihood. People bombarded BYU with calls and emails, demanding they fire my dad from his professor job. Someone even started a Change.org petition accusing my parents of abuse. Just like that, Ruby and Kevin were canceled. The truth was out there, replayed in countless reaction videos and commentary channels.

Ruby and Kevin sent cease and desist letters to content creators who dared call her abusive. They were desperate to silence the criticism, to stuff the genie back in the bottle. Things got real when Child Protective Services showed up at our house. They didn't find any evidence of child abuse. But the damage was done. There was no going back to our picture-perfect online image. Ever again.

Watching all this unfold, I felt conflicted. Part of me was glad others finally saw what I'd known for years. But I also worried if the public shaming would only make Ruby double down on her strict methods. Would the very attention meant to help us end up making things worse?

As the backlash intensified, Ruby's rage burned brighter, fueled by a mix of self-righteousness and victimhood. In her mind, she wasn't a controversial figure being held accountable; she was a martyr, crucified for her unwavering dedication to tough love.

I am Mother. I know best.

The very public outcry meant to shake my mother awake was driving her deeper into delusion, and instead of acknowledging her mistakes, Ruby burrowed deeper into the safe space of Jodi's poison dart philosophy.

ConneXions became her bunker, a fortress against the onslaught of public condemnation, as Jodi played her part with calculated precision. Never questioning, always supporting, offering comfort to Ruby's wounded ego. She validated Ruby's every action, every decision, and encouraged Ruby to move on to greener pastures. To hell with 8 Passengers. Why not focus on the ConneXions Classroom. The place where she could truly carry out God's will and share the truth about divine motherhood, with Jodi at her side.

CHAPTER 23

obedient little drone

Summer rolled around. Ruby, leaning into Jodi-approved strictness, declared that our favorite TV shows were banned—no more *SpongeBob* or *Simpsons*. In addition, it would be an "electronics-free" summer. Away went our iPod Touches—our gateway to music, apps, and games—locked in a safe in Ruby's closet.

I didn't mind so much—I was always more of a reader, but I remember the mixture of disbelief and resignation on everyone's faces as Ruby gathered up our electronics—these were our connections to the outside world, a small taste of normalcy in our household.

That summer stretched before us, seemingly endless without our usual digital distractions. I started crocheting, and taught my sisters to. But Chad was absolutely livid. How dare Ruby lock away his precious Xbox? With the determination of a master thief and the stealth of a cat burglar, he'd find ways to break into it, liberating the Xbox for clandestine gaming sessions in the dead of night, frantically trying to level up before the house stirred to life.

Chad was still in therapy with Jodi—but he'd figured out how to play along, how to agree with everything she said while still living by his own rules. I, on the other hand, was earnestly living by ConneXions rules, almost addicted to my weekly self-flagellation sessions with Jodi.

"This week, I had black-and-white thinking seven times," I reported to Jodi proudly. "And I caught myself telling myself stories five times."

"You're not getting it yet, Shari!" Jodi snapped. "This is about more than just tallying thoughts like an obedient little drone."

"I'm sorry," I mumbled, my voice barely above a whisper, cheeks burning with shame.

"Stop apologizing! See, this is exactly what I'm talking about, Shari!" she barked, her voice rising.

I was completely lost. *What does she want from me? Why can't I ever get it right?*

"Look, it's much easier to point out everyone else's distortions than to confront your own, isn't it? If you truly want to grow, you must be willing to look at the ugly parts of your psyche."

For clarity, I asked her exactly what kind of ugliness I wasn't seeing.

"You see how focused you are on getting approval from me?" she said. "You're still in self-adulation, Shari, you still need to hear that you're the best, the cleverest. Your areas of weakness are compassion and empathy. But all you seem to do, even now, is look for ways to boost your own ego."

Frustration welled up inside me. I had been trying so hard, putting in so much painful introspection, doing my best to correct everyone's distorted thinking—I'd probably lost more friends in the past month than most people do in a lifetime—but I still wasn't getting it right. I was still just a self-absorbed adulator. A garbage person living in complete distortion.

That night, I sat at my desk, the soft glow of the lamp illuminating the pages of my journal as I poured my heart out, my pen scratching furiously against the paper.

JOURNAL

Jodi thinks I am relying too much on external validation. She said I was an obedient little drone focused on getting approval from her and Ruby. Then she said I'm just not understanding compassion and empathy. It was awful. I don't want to be a cold and unfeeling person, which is how she described me.

The next week, my heart pounded in my chest as I confessed to Jodi how much her words had affected me. "Jodi," I said, my voice shaking slightly, "I just wanted to tell you how much it hurt me when you said I was an obedient little drone. But you were right, and I'm very grateful for your honesty. Hearing Truth is the only way we can bring about change."

"I never said those things, Shari," she replied calmly.

"Excuse me?"

"That's not how I talk. You must have misinterpreted my meaning and then remembered it as fact."

"Oh, okay," I said. Tendrils of doubt wrapped themselves around my mind, but Jodi seemed so sure, so confident in what she was saying. I guess I must have hallucinated the whole exchange.

After the session, I took a look at my journal, flipping to the entry I had written right after last week's call. Just to check. And there it was, in black and white.

obedient little drone
unempathetic
not getting it

I stared at the words, a sinking feeling in the pit of my stomach. Thoughts like tiny spiders began crawling up my spine. How many other times had she twisted my own memories against me?

After that, I became hypervigilant, less focused on finding evidence of my own distorted thinking than on monitoring hers. I zeroed in on the ways she didn't play by her own rules. It became a game, spotting her inconsistencies, slyly pointing them out to her, innocently calling her out on her own lies.

During a session, Jodi mentioned how a family friend had visited her and brought their young kids. Afterward, Jodi noticed the remote control for her curtains was missing.

"I just know those kids took that remote, to spite me," she said.

"How did you know they took the remote?" I asked coolly.

"I just knew."

"Isn't that an assumption? One of those stories we tell ourselves without facts?"

I felt a rush of adrenaline, using Jodi's own language to correct her.

"Assumptions are different when you have evidence behind them, Shari," she said. "The evidence being that those kids have a pattern of being vindictive troublemakers."

The remote showed up under Jodi's couch a week later.

The final straw for me was when Jodi started talking about how babies are distorted. Those tiny, innocent bundles of joy, with their soft, downy hair and their wide, trusting eyes. According to Jodi, they're manipulators who feel entitled for their mothers to come and tend to their every whim.

"The problem with society today is that we coddle children," she told me. "We give them everything they want, and then we wonder why they grow up to be selfish and lazy."

"But they're just babies, Jodi. They can't help it if they cry or need things."

Jodi's eyes glinted with something dark and unsettling. "Shari. You think a baby doesn't know how to manipulate? How to get what it wants?"

I swallowed hard, my mouth suddenly dry. "I think a baby cries because it needs food, or comfort, or . . ."

Jodi waved her hand dismissively. "A baby cries because it's entitled and it knows someone will come running because it believes that the world revolves around them and their needs. Unless you train it not to be entitled, you're just reinforcing that behavior in them. It's our job, as women and mothers, to break that cycle of manipulation, to teach children from an early age that they need to earn their blessings. Only then can we hope to create a society free from distortion."

Bile rose in my throat. *Who is this monster?*

In my mind's eye, I saw a baby, denied the comfort and love she so desperately needed. A baby left to "cry it out" by her mom, her wails trapped in the emptiness of a dark room. That baby was me.

A fire lit in my chest, and as it grew, it burned away the fog. The invisible shackles binding me to Jodi disintegrated and turned to ash. No more would I let her poison my mind.

It was as if I had been holding my breath, and now, I could finally exhale. I told myself then, unequivocally and forevermore, that never again would I trust one single word that came out of that woman's mouth.

As I finally started to break free from Jodi's hold on me, I began to ask questions. How had I, and so many others, been so vulnerable to being manipulated by someone like Jodi? Had the emphasis on obedience that I'd grown up with created a "follow the leader" mentality that made it all too easy to fall under the sway of someone like her, who claimed to have special knowledge and the ability to guide us toward righteousness? The fact that she had been able to so easily convince my family and me of her supposed spiritual authority was worrying.

Cults are thought to prey on the vulnerable, the lost, the broken—but here's the thing, they also can ensnare anyone who is simply a human searching for meaning. Or people who are in a state of transition in their lives—young adults coming of age, for instance.

Intelligence is no defense—my own father, a professor, was shockingly quick to abandon his own judgment in favor of hers. Our dedication to thinking critically and analyzing complex ideas was the very thing that Jodi used against us. She twisted our inquiring minds into knots, using our own logic and reason to lead us down a path of self-doubt and self-deception. But it was all a lie, a carefully crafted illusion designed to keep us trapped and compliant.

For Ruby, the allure of Jodi was more about climbing the ranks and amassing power within the ConneXions system so that one day she could glory in it herself. She had always yearned to lead, and the ConneXions system, with its rigid hierarchy and defined steps toward enlightenment, offered her a tantalizing path to power. Ruby envisioned a future where she, like Jodi, would stand at the pinnacle, basking in the adoration of followers, wielding the authority she so deeply craved.

But of course that was never going to happen. Jodi, the master manipulator, had no intention of ever sharing her throne. The system she had crafted was designed with a single purpose: to keep herself firmly at the top, surrounded by devoted acolytes who would never quite reach her level. Jodi's grip on power was absolute, her control over her followers unshakable. She had cultivated in Ruby and others a desperate need for approval, an insatiable hunger for enlightenment that only Jodi could satisfy. It was a brilliantly crafted trap, and Ruby had walked right into it, dragging our family along with her.

CHAPTER 24

the demon in my room

Jodi's paranoia about her position at the apex of ConneXions was palpable. In a move that revealed both her greed and her fear, Jodi demanded that all her certified life coaches sign a new contract: No one could use her "teachings" or "materials" as independent life coaches unless they paid her a cut of their earnings.

It was a watershed moment. The majority of Jodi's followers, finally confronted with the reality of Jodi's boundless greed, balked at these demands, seeing the contract for what it was—a desperate attempt to maintain control and monetize every aspect of their hard-earned skills. One by one, people started walking away from ConneXions, choosing their freedom over Jodi's increasingly unhinged requirements.

Not all of them, though.

My mother, in her blind devotion to Jodi and her teachings, signed the contract without hesitation, hell-bent on cementing her position as Jodi's most loyal disciple.

Of course, the narrative spun within the ConneXions bubble was vastly different from reality. We were told that Jodi had "fired" all those disobedient life coaches because they were too "distorted" to truly understand and implement her teachings. It was a classic example of Jodi's gaslighting techniques, rewriting history to paint herself as the victim and the sole arbiter of Truth.

As I pieced together the real story—that these coaches had quit once they saw Jodi's true colors—I felt a mix of admiration for their courage and deep, gnawing frustration with my parents. Why couldn't they see what was so obvious to others? I found myself wishing desperately that they had followed suit, that they had walked away.

But they didn't. They remained steadfastly loyal to Jodi, and by extension, to the warped reality she had constructed. Their commitment to this destructive path stirred something within me—a need to assert my own identity, to push back against the suffocating control that had seeped into every aspect of our lives.

My rebellion started small, in ways that might seem inconsequential to an outsider but felt monumental to me at the time. One of these small acts of defiance was my friendship with Derek. It started innocently enough, I suppose. A friendship that turned into something . . . else.

Derek was high up in the church, a family man and landowner in his late forties. In May 2021, right after I graduated high school, he asked for my help with social media strategy for his company, offering me a side gig to help him put together videos for YouTube. Having just turned eighteen, it meant a lot to me that a respected adult like him had singled me out and recognized my skills and talents.

After my first meeting with Derek, he couldn't stop singing my praises.

"I have to say, Shari, you really impress me," he said once. "The way you think, the way you see the world . . . it's refreshing. You're mature, way beyond your years."

"Oh, I'm just normal," I said, embarrassed.

Derek chuckled, shaking his head. "No, Shari. You're anything but."

He asked me to tell him about myself and my family. He seemed intently curious, genuinely interested in getting to know me better.

"My family . . . we don't get along the best," I said with a shrug, and he seemed surprised.

"Tell me more," he said.

Remembering how Mr. Haymond had been such a positive source of paternal support for me, I decided to open up. Just a little.

"My mom's super involved with a group called ConneXions, have you heard of them?"

"Oh, I know Jodi Hildebrandt, she used to be my neighbor," he said. "And I can tell you, she was not very well liked."

"She wasn't?"

"No, not at all. I can't stand the woman, personally."

Hearing that from Derek, I knew right then that he was someone I could trust, someone I could confide in about what was going on at home.

A friend.

Derek and I fell into a routine, meeting at his office once a week to work on his social media projects. I felt very safe with this regular-middle-aged guy with a happy family and a nice wife he'd been with for years and years. Although sometimes he did say things that felt just slightly off color, remarks bordering on flirtatious. Like, complimenting my appearance a bit too enthusiastically or letting his gaze linger a moment too long. Each time he made one of those comments, I felt a twinge of unease. But I tried to brush it off, reminding myself of his upstanding reputation. When I finally worked up the courage to tell him to stop telling me how pretty I was, he apologized profusely, almost overdoing it. He assured me it would never happen again.

He started doing little things, kind gestures that made me feel seen, cared for. A DoorDash delivery when I was having a tough day, a little shopping trip if I needed something. Even if I didn't. One day he told me, his voice low and intense, "I'm the only one who really cares about you, Shari. You know that, right?" Each time he sent me gifts, I felt a little guilty, pressured somehow. This man who was showing me so much kindness, but for some reason, I wasn't always sure I liked it.

One day, I accidentally called him "Dad," and that was the first time I saw Derek angry.

"I think we're more than that, aren't we?" he said, his face a storm cloud.

"I didn't mean to offend you. Please don't be mad."

When I eventually told Ruby that I was working with him, she had a fit and forbade me from seeing him any further. "I have a really bad feeling about this guy," she said. "Jodi and I don't think it's appropriate for you to be working with him one-on-one like that. Tell him you'll have to stop."

"Okay, sure, I'll stop talking to Derek," I lied.

I was sick of people telling me what I should do. I was eighteen and old enough to make my own decisions. Besides, I knew why they didn't like him—it was because Derek had been Jodi's neighbor and probably knew too much. *That's* why Jodi didn't want him in my life. Well, guess what, Jodi wasn't the boss of me anymore, and very soon, Ruby wouldn't be, either, because I was going to college in the fall, which meant I was an adult now and no longer answerable to anyone, except God.

So, I carried on working with Derek, behind everyone's backs. And despite the secrecy, it felt nourishing, and empowering, having his constant support, someone to lean on. Lord knows, I was about to need it more than ever.

PART FOUR

◇◇◇◇◇◇◇◇◇◇◇◇◇◇◇

mankind

beset

by

devils

CHAPTER 25

ninth passenger

About two weeks before my freshman semester started, my phone rang while I was hunting for last-minute college supplies. Ruby's name flashed on the screen. Her voice crackled with a frantic energy.

"Jodi's not well," she blurted out, skipping any pleasantries. "She's being bombarded by the adversary. Her soul is under siege from Satan himself, Shari! He's trying to silence her truth. So . . . she's moving in with us. We're going to help her get better."

I nearly dropped my phone. "Wait. *What?*"

My mother's unhinged guru was locked in a battle with evil, and her solution was to crash at our place?

"Yes, she'll be taking over your room," Ruby continued, as if this were the most natural thing in the world. "It's the biggest of all the kids' rooms, and you're leaving for college soon anyway. I need you to come home right now and clear out. Like, now, Shari. She's arriving this afternoon."

According to Ruby's breathless explanation, Jodi was being plagued by nightmares, visions, and crippling bouts of anxiety; clear symptoms of dark forces seeking to destroy the righteous. Jodi, handpicked by demons for destruction, urgently needed protection.

And Ruby had decided that protection would be us.

"By the way, we can't talk to Paige or that family anymore," Ruby said, her voice bitter.

Paige, our family friend, had been one of Jodi's biggest supporters, and one of her longest-serving life coaches. Until she quit, that is.

"What? I like Paige," I protested weakly. "She's nice."

"Well, Jodi was staying with Paige, and now she's in league with Satan," Mom snapped, as if she were discussing someone who'd committed a social faux pas rather than joined forces with the ruler of Hell. "So that's that. Now hurry up and clear out your bedroom; Jodi's arriving this afternoon. Thank goodness she's staying with us now. We'll take good care of her."

I drove home, my mind reeling. Was I the only sane person left in this circus? My room was being commandeered by a woman battling demons, my mother had appointed our family as spiritual bodyguards, and I was supposed to just roll with it, pack up my life and evacuate my room to make way for our mad prophet?

I went home, climbed the stairs to my bedroom, and began stuffing belongings into bags. I couldn't believe the epic battle for Jodi's redemption would have to take place here, in my teenage sanctuary, amidst my stuffed animals. Glancing over my shoulder every few minutes, I half expected to see Jodi standing there, her eyes black and soulless, her mouth twisted into a demonic grin. My childhood nightmares made flesh.

Get a grip, Shari, I thought to myself, even as my heart threatened to pound straight out of my chest. *Jodi is just a person—a deeply problematic person, yes, but a person, nonetheless. If she is suffering, then we probably should help her.*

I descended the stairs slowly, lugging my bags behind me. As I reached the bottom, I heard the front door open. And there she was—Jodi standing in the foyer in her khaki shorts, her eyes blazing with a feverish intensity, her hair wild, like an Old Testament hermit who'd been wandering in the desert wastes.

"Hello, Shari!" she crowed, her voice strangely raspy and raw. "Thank you for offering up your bedroom like a Good Samaritan. I appreciate it."

"Hello, Jodi," I said brightly, forcing an amiable smile. "The room's all yours. Uh, get well soon!"

I watched Jodi sweep past me, headed toward my bedroom like a conquering general, and felt a chill in my bones. This wasn't just a temporary inconvenience—this was the beginning of an occupation.

CHAPTER 26

in spirit and in truth

JOURNAL

The house's spirit feels weird with Jodi here. Something's going on between her and my parents that we don't know about, and the whole thing is super secretive. I'm trying to spend as much time out of the house as I can.

Those few weeks after Jodi moved in were a total mind warp—a bizarre, chaotic blur, in which each new day seemed to outweird the last. Jodi had taken up residence in my bedroom, and once installed, she never left, lingering like a bad smell, while I was relegated to the couch downstairs, a refugee in my own home.

Thank goodness for Derek—the only person I could confide in at the time. He urged me to stay calm as best I could, reminding me that in just a few weeks I'd be a free bird, an independent woman, at college all by myself, away from Ruby and Jodi.

Even knowing that I was moving out soon, it wasn't easy being in that house. Jodi was in a dark place mentally. Night after night, she'd fall into these mysterious trances—not quite seizures, not quite sleep, but something eerily in between. Ruby and Kevin, suddenly embracing a level of mysticism I'd never seen before, would conduct what they called "spiritual interventions" for her; hushed, intense sessions meant to heal her.

Ruby soon decided it was best for her to bunk with Jodi, so her friend didn't have to suffer through her demonic night terrors alone. I never remembered her being that sympathetic toward me when I was having similar issues, as a kid. But this was different, I guess.

Apparently, Jodi was experiencing incredibly detailed visions. In some, she saw Ruby walking on water alongside Jesus. In others, she envisioned herself riding a massive lion named Charles through the gates of heaven—Charles has since gained something of a cult following on Reddit among those tracking my family's story.

All of these fantastical visions were meticulously recorded in a hefty leather binder that Jodi referred to as the "Pen Papers." In her delusion, she believed these scribblings would one day be elevated to the status of holy scripture, personally validated by God Himself.

I felt helpless watching all of this unfold. Dad, who seemed like a shell of his former self, wasn't doing anything to stop it, either. I wanted to intervene, to shake him out of this compliance, but I didn't know how. I yearned for my dad to find his backbone, to step up and be the protector he was supposed to be. To shield us, somehow, and convince Ruby that Jodi needed the kind of care that we simply weren't equipped to give.

In the end, he never even tried.

Meanwhile, Jodi and Ruby hunkered down in their upstairs sanctuary, rarely leaving except for occasional ice cream pilgrimages to Dairy Queen. Their dietary habits were a cardiologist's nightmare—a steady stream of sugar, saturated fat, and fried foods, liberally garnished with Jodi's sole contribution to our household: gallons of ranch dressing.

Pam, Jodi's oldest and dearest friend, high up in ConneXions, was always popping by with a case of soda and a high-pitched hello that set my teeth on edge. The three of them—Ruby, Jodi, and Pam—would hole up in my old bedroom for hours on end. They went boating in Lake Havasu in Arizona for a week and would make little "shopping trips" down to Mexico, coming back with grocery bags full of pills. When I asked about it, Ruby claimed it was all part of their grand plan to stockpile antibiotics for the end of days. It was as if they'd formed their own exclusive Apocalypse Collective, and the rest of us were decidedly not on the list.

They, like many doomsday preppers in the LDS church, were obsessed with a book called *Visions of Glory*, published in 2012. The book, not endorsed by the mainstream LDS church, was a wild ride of near-death experiences, apocalyptic visions, and doomsday prophecies. It became the basis for many LDS prepper fantasies, feeding into their fears and justifying their extreme preparations.

The book's contents ranged from New Age–style spiritual encounters to graphic descriptions of impending disasters—foreign invasions, viral plagues, massive earthquakes devastating the entire United States, including our own Wasatch Front. It was all very trippy, and apparently, very convincing to Ruby, Jodi, and Pam.

Strange as it may sound, I don't think I've ever seen Ruby happier than when Jodi was living with us, battling entities and riding Charles the Lion. She seemed to have a glow about her. She had always complained about her lack of close female friendships, about the loneliness of motherhood. But now? Now she had her girlies. Jodi and Pam had become her ride-or-dies, her squad, her soul sisters. They were the Three Musketeers of the apocalypse, ready to follow each other literally to the ends of the earth—or at least to the nearest Mexican pharmacy for another antibiotics run.

As Ruby, Jodi, and Pam grew closer, bonding behind closed doors and sharing whispered conversations, Kevin found himself increasingly on the outside looking in. He was told that upstairs was off-limits. He could leave the house when he wanted, but he couldn't return without Ruby's permission. Even access to the kitchen for meals required her approval. And Ruby dictated if and when they were allowed to communicate. New house rules, inspired by Jodi.

Ruby even tried to transfer control of the 8 Passengers YouTube brand to Jodi. When our longtime manager Larry raised concerns about her plans, Ruby dismissed his warnings, claiming that this wasn't about money but about "doing God's work." Then they parted ways. Ruby was isolating herself from anyone who might question her increasingly erratic decisions.

Relegated to the couch downstairs, I found myself grappling with a cocktail of emotions: frustration, confusion, and a growing sense of displacement. This wasn't just an invasion of privacy; it was a fundamental shift in our family dynamic. I'd grown accustomed to Ruby's boundary-pushing over the years, but this, inviting Jodi Hildebrandt to reshape our entire household, felt like a point of no return.

"Shari, don't be blind," Ruby would admonish, any time I'd timidly inquire if Jodi was feeling well enough to go home yet. "Jodi is a powerful being, which is why she's under spiritual attack. The least you can do is share your space with her while we fight. Can't you see beyond your entitlement for a moment, and think bigger picture?"

Ruby imposed a gag order on the entire household, insisting that Jodi's presence be kept under wraps, as if we were harboring a fugitive. Here we were, Ruby and Jodi preaching truth in their ConneXions videos, while concealing the juiciest plot twist of all.

Pulling off this charade required some serious smoke and mirrors. Jodi was still running her ConneXions Zoom meetings from our house, with Ruby playing sidekick as a senior emotional fitness coach. They'd set up their laptops in separate rooms, backgrounds blurred to maintain the illusion of distance. A slick master class in digital deception.

When I decided to film a video for my own channel—which was chugging along despite the 8 Passengers backlash—I had to use my sisters' shared room, since my own bedroom was now a shrine to Truth and Dairy Queen. I didn't mention a word about Jodi, but before I could upload, Ruby swooped in like a hawk.

"I need to watch that video before you post it," she said, eyes narrowed.

"It's okay, I just talked about getting ready for college and my packing list."

"I don't care, I need to review all content shot in this house. We can't risk Jodi's voice slipping through in the background."

I'm sure that Jodi was behind this information blackout. As cracked as her marbles might have been, she still possessed strategic forethought. Moving in with a client/student because she was suffering from mental issues/demonic attack was not the look she was going for, publicly, so she had to ensure she was still projecting power and strength, even as her world crumbled around her. For Jodi, optics were everything. Another thing she and Ruby had in common.

"This home situation isn't healthy for you, is it?" Derek said one afternoon, when I'd gone to do some work for him at his office, mainly because I wanted to get out of the house.

I shook my head, feeling the tears prick at the corners of my eyes. "No," I whispered. "It's not."

During those two weeks, Derek could tell I was very stressed—

he was intuitive like that, and always seemed to take a close interest in me and how I was feeling. I confided in him, and he always listened, patiently, allowing me to share the pain and confusion of my family life without judgment.

Derek studied me intently. "Must be lonely, going through all this on your own . . ." His voice was soft, his eyes full of concern.

I shrugged, picking at a loose thread on my sleeve. "I'm used to it."

"I wish you had more support, Shari. Everyone needs someone they can count on."

I looked up, surprised by the emotion in his voice.

"I've never really had that, to be honest."

"Well, now you do."

Derek smiled, his hand brushing mine as he reached for his coffee mug.

I spent most of the day at Derek's office, and it was sunset by the time I arrived home. The house was eerily quiet. For once, nobody was home. Taking my chance, I made my way upstairs to my room, figuring I'd take advantage of the situation and grab a couple of books.

I pushed open the door to my bedroom and looked around, confused. The room was bathed in the soft glow of candles. The air was heavy with the scent of lavender and vanilla wafting from the massage oils on the dresser. I quickly grabbed what I needed and got the hell out of there, feeling like I had just walked into someone else's honeymoon suite. The only thing missing was rose petals on the bed.

That night, I couldn't sleep. Maybe it was the fact that the couch was hurting my back, or maybe it was the sense that I'd seen something I wasn't supposed to. I tossed and turned, thoughts swirling. It must have been around 5:00 a.m. when I heard a creak of footsteps upstairs. I cracked one eye open, just in time to see Ruby tiptoeing out of my room, her hair messy, her cheeks flushed and her robe hastily tied, heading back to the bedroom she shared with my dad. A strange smile on her face. She looked... mischievous.

What the hell was going on?

Why was Ruby sneaking around in the middle of the night like a teenager trying not to get caught by her parents? Were they really doing candlelit massages in my bedroom? How could this be happening, with all of us in the house?

In that moment, I felt a bone-deep pity for my father, a once proud and rational man who seemed completely oblivious to what was happening right before his eyes.

It was equal parts fascinating and horrific. Two women who preached "Truth" while living lies. Who condemned queerness very publicly in their ConneXions videos, while embodying it privately. In my room. On my bed, most likely.

The next day, I left the house as early as I could and just drove around, going to random places. I couldn't bear to be home, not with all these thoughts in my head. At the mall, I bumped into a couple of neighborhood acquaintances who I knew to be gay, and without giving too much away, casually asked them their thoughts on Jodi Hildebrandt, the life coach, and if they had heard of her.

"OMG that woman is *so* closeted," said one of them, arching an eyebrow.

My other friend nodded, adding that oftentimes the most homophobic people were the ones who are hiding something about themselves.

I know my community isn't exactly leading the Pride parade when it comes to queer acceptance. A lot of the older folks are still clutching their pearls at the mere mention of it. But times are changing, and the younger generation (myself included) see things a little differently.

Personally, I like to remember that Jesus taught us to love everyone.

There was a story that kept coming to mind, during this time. The story of Jesus speaking with the Samaritan woman at the well. She was an outcast, a sinner, who had been shunned by society. But Jesus looked at her, His eyes full of compassion, of understanding. He spoke to her, not with condemnation but with love.

"You should worship in spirit and in truth," Jesus told her, and those words had always stuck with me. Since Jodi moved in, I'd been hearing them louder than ever, playing on a loop in my mind.

In spirit and in truth.
In spirit and in truth.
In spirit and in truth.

"Truth" was a word Jodi and Ruby wielded like a weapon. But this story reminded me that truth should always be connected to spirit, the essence of the divine. People thank God all the time, but do they live by God's teachings? Their words might honor God, but do their actions align with the Bible?

In spirit and in truth.

True truth isn't just quoting scripture while behaving exactly the way you want to when you think no one is looking. That's the opposite of truth.

I asked myself, How would I have felt if Ruby and Jodi had actually embraced honesty, practiced the authenticity they preached, and told me and the rest of our family about what was really happening between them? And the answer was, yes, it would have hurt. But I would have supported them. It would have been preferable to living like . . . *this*. In this house of lies that I couldn't bear to step foot in anymore.

CHAPTER 27

dirty. shameful. ruined.

Two weeks after Jodi moved in, college started, which meant I was finally able to escape. Oh, the joy I felt, fleeing that festering wound of a household.

Brigham Young University—the LDS college where I would be majoring in political science—was close by, only ten minutes' drive up the 89 North freeway. But still, it felt a million miles away. No more fake smiles and performative laughter to placate my mother and the demon in my bed. Now, it was just me. Shari and her books. Freedom. What a chef's kiss of a feeling!

Ruby and Kevin drove me to my college dorm and helped me move in—all caught on camera, and later uploaded to 8 Passengers, which Ruby was still clinging on to for dear life. Standing there, watching Ruby, all fake smiles and tearful embraces, feign maternal love for me for the camera, filled me with a rage so intense it nearly knocked me off my feet. How could she stand there, pretending to be the perfect mother waving her beloved eldest goodbye, when I knew all she cared about was that monster in my bedroom at home?

As my parents drove away, I stood there, waving, rooted to the spot. I had craved this moment of freedom, yet now that it arrived, I felt . . . strange.

I trudged back to my dorm room, each step echoing in the unfamiliar hallway. The space felt cavernous, my meager belongings dwarfed by the emptiness of my roommate's untouched side. Silence pressed in from all sides. For the first time in my life, I was truly alone. No siblings' laughter to punctuate the quiet. No familiar routines to fall back on.

Suddenly, a text lit up my phone.

"How's your first day of freedom, Shari?"

It was Derek, right on cue.

"Want to stop by the office later, once you've settled in? I got you some back-to-school gifts. Remember that North Face jacket you said you wanted?"

"Wow! Thank you! See you later."

I don't remember the drive to his building. I just remember the way my heart was pounding, and how my skin felt too tight, like it might split open at any moment. I wasn't sure why I felt so nervous. In hindsight, perhaps it was my intuition, trying to tell me something, to turn around, go back to my college dorm and never talk to this middle-aged man again.

But I didn't do that, and by the time I arrived, I was gasping for breath, my vision narrowing to a pinpoint.

"Shari? What's wrong?" I heard him say as I stood at his door.

"I can't . . ." I choked out, my chest heaving. "I can't breathe. I think I'm having a panic attack."

Derek guided me to the couch, his hands gentle on my shoulders. I tried to focus on his voice, on the steady rhythm of his words, but the panic was rising like a tidal wave, threatening to pull me under.

"Shari, listen to me," he said, his voice cutting through the static in my head. "I think skin-to-skin contact will help you calm down. Can I take your shirt off?"

I froze, my mind reeling. *No,* I thought, *no, no, no.* But my mouth wouldn't work, the words stuck in my throat. I shook my head, tried to push him away, but he was stronger than me, his grip iron-tight around my wrists.

"Trust me," he murmured, his breath hot against my ear. "Just let me help you, Shari."

And then his hands were on me, rough and insistent, yanking my shirt up, exposing my bra, my skin. I squirmed, I fought, but it was useless. He was bigger than me, stronger than me, and the more I struggled, the more powerless I felt.

"See?" he said. "It's not so bad. Now just relax for me. Be a good girl."

His hands roamed over my back, my stomach, snaked up to cup my breasts through the thin fabric of my bra. I felt myself go numb, felt my mind detach from my body, floating up and away until I was looking down at the scene from above. A girl on a couch. A man looming over her, his hands possessive, greedy. This was the first time someone had touched me like this. It couldn't be me. It couldn't be happening. Not to me.

"That feels better, doesn't it?" he asked, and I heard myself say yes, heard my voice, small and distant, agreeing with him.

I don't know how I made it back to my dorm that night. All I know is that when I finally collapsed onto my bed, I couldn't move. Couldn't think. Couldn't feel.

I laid there for hours, staring at the ceiling as the world went on around me. I heard the laughter, the chatter of my fellow freshmen through the walls. But I was separate, cut off.

I've sinned, I thought. *I've ruined everything.* It felt like a punishment, a divine reckoning for all the ways I had failed, all the ways I had fallen short.

In my mind, my frozenness, my inability to move was a sign from God, a punishment for my transgressions. *This is the Spirit telling me I need to repent*, I thought.

When I finally managed to drag myself out of bed, to fumble for my phone with numb fingers, I saw the missed calls, the texts from Derek.

"Where are you?" he demanded. "Why aren't you answering? Is everything okay?"

I stared at the screen, my heart pounding, my mind reeling.

He's worried, I thought guiltily. *I should get back to him so he doesn't get more upset.*

With trembling fingers, I typed out a response. "I'm okay. How are you?"

The reply was instant.

"Are you talking to any boys?"

I frowned, confused. "No," I typed back.

"Good," came the response.

"Thank you," I typed, not knowing what else to say.

I fell back on my bed again, closed my eyes, and tried to summon up the image of the Samaritan woman at the well, the outcast, the sinner who had been offered living water, a chance at redemption. But I couldn't find her. All I could see was my own face, in the harsh light of judgment. *Dirty. Shameful. Ruined.*

Is this who I am now? I wondered, a dull ache in my chest. *Is this all I'll ever be?*

CHAPTER 28

grateful

College life introduced me to the peculiar experience of having a non-sibling roommate. To say we were an odd couple would be an understatement. I was the quintessential early bird, greeting the dawn with enthusiasm, while she was a night owl of Olympic proportions. Our schedules were so misaligned that I'd often be crawling into bed just as she was applying her makeup for a night out.

And I certainly never felt able to confide in her about what I was going through with Derek, and how possessive he had become since . . . what had happened on the first day of school.

I had blanked it out, pretended it never happened.

I was enjoying a rare moment of normalcy at the campus creamery with a male classmate when my phone buzzed. Derek's name flashed on the screen, and I felt a familiar knot form in my stomach. His text was innocent enough, asking where I was, but when I replied truthfully, he didn't take it well.

"Ah, you're with a boy? You don't care about me anymore. That's not very nice."

I stared at the words, a mix of confusion and guilt washing over me. Was I doing something wrong by simply hanging out with someone else?

Logically, I knew I should keep my distance from Derek, especially after what had happened. But there was a traitorous part of me that clung to the attention he gave me, filling a void I hadn't realized was there. My own father had become a ghost in our family, more present in his absence than in reality. In comparison, Derek's intense focus on me felt . . . validating, even if it came with strings attached.

Maybe, I thought, trying to rationalize, it was okay to keep Derek as a friend. After all, he liked me, noticed me. In a world where I often felt invisible, wasn't that worth something?

About halfway through my first semester, I went home, partially because I needed to grab a book but also because I was missing my siblings.

I walked through the front door, tentatively calling out: "Hello?"

I could hear Ruby and Jodi in my bedroom, talking and laughing.

Kevin emerged from the backyard.

"Hello, sweetie," he said. "You're home. It's good to see you."

I wished I could talk to him, tell him what had been going on with Derek. Instead, I shifted uncomfortably under his sad, listless gaze.

"Well, I'm just popping in to say hi to everyone," I said.

"That's nice."

"Oh, and I need to grab something from my room."

"That won't be possible," he said, more firmly than was necessary.

"Why not?"

"Jodi and Ruby are in there. They're busy."

Busy with what? I thought. *Braiding each other's hair? Wrestling demon warlords? Debating the merits of Dairy Queen's Peanut Butter Bash versus Chocolate Chip Cookie Dough Blizzards? Which is it, Dad?*

"If you want to go in there, you have to text your mother first and get permission," he said. "Then she can tell you a convenient time to get your book."

"Dad, really? Why on earth would I have to schedule a visit to my own bedroom?"

"Because that's just the way things are now, Shari," he said sadly.

It was hard for me to believe this was the same person who used to delight me with geological fun facts, impromptu jazz piano sessions and a childlike enthusiasm for rocks. How quickly minds can become eroded, weather-beaten into blank, featureless expanses. I hated to see him in this state.

It was a relief when, after texting Ruby and being allocated five minutes to retrieve my book, I could hug my siblings and then swiftly retreat back to school, away from my sad-sack of a father, and that house, where nothing made sense anymore.

Thanksgiving was a few weeks away. Would we go to our grandparents, like we usually did? Or would this year be different, thanks to our new guest?

In the early years, our Thanksgivings had followed a predictable pattern, alternating annually between Kevin's parents and Ruby's. These were big, boisterous affairs, each side of the family bringing its own unique flavor to the celebration.

At Kevin's parents' house, the sheer number of people was always overwhelming. With all of Kevin's siblings, their spouses, children, and even their children, we'd easily have more than fifty people crammed into the house. It was chaos, but the kind of chaos that comes with warmth and laughter. The downside? Like I mentioned, my grandparents weren't much for cooking, so we often ended up with a spread of store-bought dishes that left much to be desired.

Still, the joy of family connection always outweighed the culinary disappointments.

Ruby's family gatherings were smaller but no less lively. With about ten adults and twentysomething kids, it was a more manageable chaos. The cooking here was the star of the show—homemade dishes that filled the house with mouthwatering aromas and left us all in a pleasant food coma by the end of the night.

As I entered high school, our Thanksgiving traditions began to shift. The rift between Ruby and her parents meant that side of the family was no longer an option. Kevin's parents, advancing in age, found it increasingly difficult to host such large gatherings. Our celebrations became smaller, more intimate.

The year before, we'd had one of my favorite Thanksgivings ever—just the eight of us, at our house. Kevin, who had recently gotten into smoking meats, produced a turkey that was nothing short of miraculous. Ruby's homemade rolls filled the house with a comforting, yeasty aroma. I took charge of the mashed potatoes, determined to make them creamy and lump-free.

Chad's contribution was . . . unique. He decided to make a giant pot of queso, which seemed like a great idea until it solidified into a cheesy brick within minutes of being served. We teased him mercilessly, but there was genuine affection in our laughter. It became one of those cherished family moments I'd hold on to.

I wished we could have just had a repeat of the previous year. But with Jodi around . . . I knew it was unlikely. I pictured her at the head of our dining table, our resident psychic vampire, gorging herself on turkey and my family's lifeblood, my mother crowing by her side, my father silently pushing mashed potatoes around his plate as my siblings and I cast awkward glances at one another.

"Hi, Shari, just letting you know we're all going to Jodi's house for Thanksgiving this year," Ruby relayed, in a phone call.

"Nope!" I blurted.

I could have handled Thanksgiving at our home with Jodi, but I would have rather gouged out my own eyeballs with a spoon than step foot in Jodi's house. Hard pass. Invitation declined. Return to sender. Every cell in my body was telling me to stay away.

An awkward silence as Ruby's indignation revved up like a chainsaw.

"Did you just say *nope?*"

"Uh, I can't make it, unfortunately, Mom. Thank you for the invitation."

I could almost see the gears turning in Ruby's head, as she processed the fact that her eldest daughter was defying her. *Error 404, obedient daughter not found.*

"Sorry, Mom, it's just, it's a four-hour drive to Jodi's and I have a ton of homework I need to do this weekend."

A pause, while Ruby decided how mad she wanted to be.

"Your siblings will be disappointed," she said, and I noticed how she didn't include herself in that sentiment. But I didn't care—honestly I would have rather spent Thanksgiving slurping instant ramen alone.

In the end, I wound up going to Kevin's parents' house, close by in Ogden, and watching *The Andy Griffith Show* on TV while eating store-bought snacks and Stouffer's macaroni and cheese.

I picked at the remnants of my meal, my eyes darted to the basement door.

"Grandpa," I said, setting down my bowl, "can I look at the old family photos? The ones you keep in the basement?"

Grandpa's eyes lit up. "Of course, Shari! I'd be happy to grab 'em."

As he stood up, Grandma called out, "Don't be down there too long. I'm putting the pie in the microwave."

Grandpa brought upstairs a folder and set it on a small table, gesturing for me to sit. As he opened it, I was met with the stern gaze of a man with piercing eyes.

"Who's that?" I asked, slightly unnerved by the intense stare of the guy in the photo.

"That's your great-grandfather," Grandpa said proudly. "An orphan, came over from Germany aged 18, right before the Nazis took over. Landed in New York with his sister, headed straight to Salt Lake City to find him a wife and settle down. He was the first in our family to be baptized into the church."

I leaned in, studying the photo. "Why isn't he smiling?"

Grandpa chuckled. "People didn't smile in photos back then. Too long of an exposure time."

He glanced up at me, his eyes softening. "Shari, why didn't you want to do Thanksgiving with your family this year?"

I bit my lip, considering my words carefully. "Because I wanted to be here with you guys."

Grandpa's brow furrowed. "Shari, is everything okay at home? Really okay?"

"Yes, Grandpa. Everything's fine. Really," I lied. "I just . . . I don't get to see you and Grandma as often as I'd like. That's all."

Grandpa studied my face for a long moment, and I held my breath, afraid he'd see through my facade. Finally, he nodded, seemingly satisfied with my answer.

"Well, we're always happy to have you here, sweetheart," he said, patting my hand. "Any time you want to visit, our door is open."

I swallowed hard, fighting back the sudden urge to cry. "Thanks, Grandpa. That means a lot."

Part of me wished I'd had the courage to tell him the truth. But for now, at least, I could pretend that everything was normal, that I was just a granddaughter enjoying time with her grandparents on a cozy Thanksgiving afternoon.

And for that, I was truly grateful.

CHAPTER 29

jingle hell

I may have escaped Thanksgiving with Ruby and Jodi, but I wasn't out of the woods just yet—Christmas was just around the corner, which would mean another two whole weeks sleeping on the couch, my mom and Jodi acting like giggling schoolgirls in matching Christmas sweaters, filming their preachy, hateful ConneXions videos in my bedroom in front of the little mural I'd painted, in between daily Dairy Queen runs.

The day the semester ended, I showed up at the house; Chad greeted me at the door with a sympathetic look and a whisper.

"Hey, sis. Welcome to hell."

The atmosphere in the house was, somehow, even stranger than I remembered.

My dejected father was now sleeping alone in the marital bedroom, with Ruby and Jodi permanently installed upstairs in my room.

Ruby, on the other hand, was full of Christmas cheer, hugging me and saying she was thrilled to have me home, insisting that she and Jodi take me and my two eldest sisters out to dinner for a welcome-home girls' night out.

"Jodi really wants to feel closer to you," Ruby said, smiling in a way that made me feel uncomfortable.

"Sure," I said. "What time are we going out to dinner?"

"Let's leave here at seven. Sound good?"

Seven o'clock rolled around, and no sign of Ruby or Jodi—I could hear them laughing it up in my room. Meanwhile, I was starving. Figuring dinner plans were off, I made spaghetti for myself and my siblings and flopped down on the couch, throwing on *Order of the Phoenix*.

Around eight o'clock, Ruby and Jodi came downstairs, all dressed up.

"All right, girls, we're ready to go!" Ruby chirped.

"Already ate," I said from the couch, my eyes glued to the wizards battling on the screen.

"Excuse me! You committed that you were going to go out with us!" Ruby was incandescent with rage.

I looked up at her.

"Well, Mom, isn't one of the principles of Truth being on time?" I said coolly.

Mic drop.

"Shari, if you'd ever paid attention in your sessions with Jodi, you'd know that another important principle is that you need to be *flexible* in your relationships!"

"Which is why I went ahead and made my own dinner tonight. Very flexible."

I could see the shock in my mother's eyes that I would dare answer her back in this manner, in front of Jodi, no less.

"Your poor future husband, Shari. I feel sorry for him. Good luck finding a man who wants a selfish wife like you."

There she was again, wielding my apparent unmarriageability like a weapon. Any aesthetic misstep, any hint of individuality, any flicker of rebellion was so often met with the same crushing refrain: *How would any man want to marry a girl like* you?

I glanced over at my dad, who was shuffling past, mumbling something about spark plugs—as if Ruby, with her own disintegrating marriage, was the arbiter of marital bliss. I knew her taunts of "unmarriageable" were nothing but poisoned arrows, designed to murder my self-worth and keep me small and compliant. And I no longer cared.

Ruby, sensing that her usual insults weren't having the desired effect, changed tack.

"May I remind you, you're only an invited guest here, Shari. This isn't your home. It's mine. And frankly, I don't want you in it if you're going to talk to me like this."

"*Then uninvite me!*" I said, voice sharp. "I'm serious, Mom. Just say the word, and I'll walk right out that door. Save you the trouble of enduring Christmas with your inflexible daughter."

I stood up, more than ready to grab my things and leave, but Ruby, true to form, wouldn't let me have the last word.

"*I can't take this abuse!*" she wailed, voice pitched to shatter windows. She bolted for the door, Jodi rushing after her.

I stood there, caught between laughter and tears. The absurdity of it all—my mother playing the victim card while holding all the cards. As she always had.

Ruby and Jodi went to dinner on their own, without any of us. My sisters and I ended up finishing the movie, and, honestly, I was absolutely thrilled to have them to myself without Ruby and Jodi's negative energy in the house.

After the kids went to bed, I decided to wait up for my mother and Jodi to come home. Might as well face the music sooner rather than later. Maybe try to clear the air—we had to spend the holiday together, after all.

Close to midnight, Ruby and Jodi walked into the house, both of them sobbing uncontrollably.

"What's wrong?" I gasped, genuinely alarmed. "Did something happen?"

Jodi looked at me with tearful, bloodshot eyes, whimpering.

"Your fight with your mother . . . it reminded me of my daughter. She *left* me! There's no greater pain than being abandoned, Shari! You can't do that to Ruby! She loves you more than anything in the whole world!"

Her words found their mark.

I imagined what it would feel like, truly walking away from Ruby, despite all the heartache she had caused me. Would the hurt she caused me every day be less than the agony of never being able to see her again? And how would Ruby feel, if I shut her out forever?

Suddenly, I realized I was crying, too.

"I'm so sorry, Mom . . . ," I whispered, tears rolling down my cheeks. "I never meant to hurt you. I'll never talk to you like that again."

They engulfed me in a suffocating embrace. "We're *so* glad you're home, Shari!" Ruby whispered, and I noticed how wrong it felt, being held by the both of them.

CHAPTER 30

children are not entitled to a magical childhood

A few days before Christmas, the adults gathered us children in the living room. Ruby and Jodi, addressing the four oldest of us, relegated my two youngest siblings to a corner.

"We're making you aware of something," Ruby began, her tone unnervingly calm. "Your youngest siblings won't be receiving any presents this year."

"We're teaching them not to be selfish and entitled," Jodi added, her face a mask of self-righteousness. My father, ever the silent supporter, nodded along.

I glanced at my youngest siblings. Their faces were pictures of dejection and confusion. Christmas should be magical for children—a time to feel cherished and celebrated. This punishment felt cruel and vindictive.

"Furthermore," Jodi continued, her voice hardening, "they must ask permission before speaking to any of you. If they interrupt, you must reprimand them. This is nonnegotiable. We all need to present a united front to correct their behavior."

"If they're not getting presents, none of us should," I interjected, my voice trembling with anger. "It's not right for us to open gifts while they watch empty-handed."

Jodi's eyes narrowed. "Shari, your discomfort shows you're struggling with the consequences of their actions," she said, her tone dripping with condescension.

"Yes, I am," I admitted firmly.

"Do you want your siblings to remain entitled? Do you understand the suffering that mindset will cause them later in life?"

As always, Jodi had a knack for making me feel like I was always the one in the wrong.

A few days later, on Christmas morning, 8+1 Passengers gathered around the Christmas tree to open their gifts. The presents beneath the tree looked a little thin on the ground this year. And we all knew why.

"Now, everyone, open up your presents, and in doing so, give the young ones the gift of this precious, beautiful lesson that will serve them for years to come," crowed Ruby.

As the eldest sister, every fiber of my being screamed to protect my siblings. But standing there, dwarfed by Jodi and Ruby's united front of adult authority, I felt microscopic. Impotent. Useless.

We opened our Christmas presents while my two youngest siblings watched, wide-eyed and silent. When the flurry of torn paper settled, Jodi's saccharine voice cut through the air: "Clean this up," she ordered them.

As they wordlessly gathered the debris, Jodi launched into a sermon, her face glowing with self-satisfaction. "Children are *not* entitled to a magical childhood," she cooed, each word dripping with poisonous sweetness. "You can't just *expect* love and presents. Many have nothing at all."

White-hot rage boiled within me, searching desperately for an outlet. How had I let it come to this? I was supposed to be their guardian angel, their rock. Instead, I was a silent bystander—no better than my mute, nodding father.

The voice of the Widow of Nauvoo echoed in my mind: "Burn it all down, Shari." I knew I wanted to, somehow. I'd always felt an invisible "Protector" badge pinned to my soul, a responsibility I'd tried desperately to fulfill. But how could I be their safe haven when I was drowning in the same storm?

Shortly after New Year's, I fled back to college, my survivor's guilt a lead weight in my chest. As I unpacked in my dorm room, the truth hit me: I'd abandoned my siblings to face the emotional apocalypse alone. I'd been thrown a life preserver, while the ones who needed me the most remained in treacherous waters.

I swam in that guilt for a week or so, until a text from Kevin heralded new hope on the horizon: "Jodi's feeling better. She's moving back to Ivins."

I hesitated before typing, "How's mom taking it?"

"She's sad Jodi's leaving, wishes she could stay. But Jodi says she's ready to go home."

I could picture Ruby's reaction—the facade of supportive friend crumbling to reveal the desperate, clinging need beneath. Jodi had been her toxic lifeline, her twisted mirror of validation. Now, with four hours of desert between them, what would fill that void?

A chill ran through me as I realized the likely answer: us. Her offspring. She'd take her feelings out on us, as she always had. Based on the way she'd behaved over Christmas, drunk on Jodi's empowerment, I imagined things might even get worse. I worried about the youngest ones, who were least able to fight back.

Still, a spark of hope flickered. Maybe, just maybe, this separation would force some much-needed change. With Kevin there to watch the little ones, perhaps Ruby would spend more time in Ivins with Jodi, giving us all some crucial breathing room.

In which case, Jodi's departure might just be the best thing that could have happened. I would certainly return home more often, to be there for my siblings, if it didn't mean suffocating under Ruby's presence. And being home would maybe mean I could get away from Derek.

Things had escalated, physically. He said he was training me for marriage. Showing me the things I would need to do in order to please my future husband.

"Never all the way," he'd insist, as if this boundary made his actions noble. But he insisted on practicing everything else he said I would have to do as a wife, if I wanted to keep my husband happy.

"Your husband is going to be so disappointed on your wedding night if you are uncomfortable being touched like this," he'd say. "See how you flinch when I do that? You don't want to do that in front of your husband, do you?"

"No, you're right," I'd say, convincing myself that this was some kind of exposure therapy, meant to help me get over my issues and be a better wife.

I pretended it wasn't happening. I kept my feelings hidden, deep inside. But slowly, and surely, I noticed the colors of my world fading to shades of gray. Depression crept up on me once again, and suddenly I didn't seem to care about anything anymore—other than getting my homework done, and making sure Derek wasn't upset with me.

"How's your day?"

"What are you doing?"

"Who are you with?"

"Hello?"

"Miss you."

Every day, his messages came in a relentless stream, every fifteen minutes like clockwork.

"I want to make sure you're safe, Shari," he'd said. "Maybe you could share your location with me, just in case something goes wrong. I know you're all alone."

I wasn't all alone. I had friends, and Kevin was on campus most days. But I was so hungry for any scrap of fatherly attention, any hint that someone truly gave a damn about me, that I'd agreed to share my iPhone location with him, without a second thought. Before long, Derek turned into Big Brother, tracking my every move, grilling me about every little detour or pit stop. Parties? Forget it. Boys? Not a chance. A single moment of peace? Absolutely out of the question.

His messages took on a new tone, filled with longing and desire. Reading those words made me want to hurl. They also forced me to face the reality of what his interest in me was about. But even then, I made excuses, remained in denial. I couldn't make myself cut the cord. On one hand, his attention made me deeply uncomfortable. On the other, it was the only form of support I had in my tumultuous world. The contradiction tore at me, leaving me paralyzed and unable to act.

"He's the only protection I have," I repeated like a mantra, even as a part of me screamed that this "protection" came with a terrible price. "Without him . . . I really will be all alone." The truth hovered at the edges of my consciousness, too terrifying to fully acknowledge. Cutting ties with Derek meant facing a world where I truly had no allies. And so I remained in limbo, caught between revulsion and desperate need, unable to break free.

As Derek's grip on me got tighter, I felt myself shutting down more and more. I became skittish, secretive. I stopped going to the dining hall, scared to death of running into someone who might start asking questions I couldn't answer. I cut off my roommates, quit my clubs, let any hint of a social life wither up and die. Dark circles bloomed under my eyes, and I turned into a ghost girl, washed-out and hollow-eyed, jumping at every buzz from my phone.

Sometimes, I'd hover my fingers over my phone screen, knowing what I needed to say . . .

"Derek, I'm sorry, but I can't do this anymore. I'm not your doll. I'm not your pet, your plaything, your anything. I'm my own person."

And then I'd delete it all, every word. It was easier to stay silent and play along than say something that would upset him.

CHAPTER 31

poisoned well

One day, as Derek and I sat in his office, the curtains drawn, I tried, meekly to confront him and address our situation. It took all the courage I had. "I don't know if this is right, Derek," I said, slowly, my heart racing. "I shouldn't be here, right? Not like this. What if someone finds out? It would be terrible for everyone."

He leaned back in his leather chair, cool as a cucumber. "Shari, you worry far too much. In God's eyes, we're not doing anything wrong. And that's all that matters."

I fidgeted with the hem of my skirt, my stomach twisting in knots. "But how can you be so sure?"

"Shari, I'm an elder in the Melchizedek Priesthood. I'm responsible for the spiritual and temporal well-being of the men in my quorum. Do you really think I would do anything to jeopardize my calling?"

It was true, he was a man of God, a worthy member. Suddenly, I felt very ill.

"Oh, honey, you're so pale," he said, reaching out to pat my hand. "Stop with these bad thoughts. It's your anxiety disorder making you overthink things."

He kept pushing, kept taking things further and further over the line. I didn't have those kinds of feelings for him, I wasn't attracted to him and didn't want him like that. But I was too addicted to the scraps of validation he gave me, the morsels of support he'd toss my way when it came to my family. He was the only one who knew how messed up it all was, the only one telling me I wasn't crazy, wasn't making it all up in my head.

I needed that lifeline, that hint of warmth in a world that felt hard and unforgiving.

But it was confusing. Crazy-making. My rational mind knew that what I was doing was wrong, while my traumatized mind convinced me to stay quiet and compliant.

I don't know why I thought Ruby could possibly help, but one day, in a moment of desperation, I mustered up the courage to text her. I think on a deep and primal level I just needed my mother, and it came out as a plea for her attention. I wanted her to understand that I still needed her. So I just blurted out my feelings.

"Mom, I feel like you don't care about me," I wrote. "You never answer the phone when I call, but I know you're always talking to Jodi. I just feel ignored. I feel like you don't love me."

I hit send and immediately felt like I had just signed my own death warrant. *What have I done?* I thought, my stomach twisting into knots as I anticipated Ruby's response. She never responded kindly to demands for affection. Affection had to be earned, and it was always on her terms.

She took her time getting back to me. It was torture. For twenty-four hours, I lay in bed, my body paralyzed, every ping of my phone sending jolts of fear through my veins.

The next day, Ruby decided to grace me with a response.

"I sense a lot of aggression in your text. A lot of resentment. I'm going to invite you to invite me to talk about this with you, in person."

So I did. I invited her to talk about it in person, and she accepted my invitation, telling me to meet her and Kevin for dinner at a local restaurant.

I sat there, pushing my french fries around my plate, Ruby taking the reins of the conversation, as usual.

"You were very selfish in writing this text to me," she said, shaking her head.

I sighed and shrank further into myself, not saying anything.

Ruby fixed me with a penetrating stare.

"What was your motive in sending me that text, Shari?"

I shifted in my seat, anger suddenly flaring in my chest. "Honestly? I was hoping you might actually hear me for once."

"And what is it you think I'm not hearing?"

"This dinner was supposed to be about me feeling like I don't matter. Like my feelings don't matter."

Ruby glared at me.

"Shari, I need you to really examine your motives. Because it feels to me like you're hiding something."

And I was. But I couldn't tell her about Derek, could I? I just needed to hear, somehow, that she cared about me. But that wasn't in the cards.

By the time dessert arrived, I was broken. Sobbing into my chocolate cake. Apologizing for being selfish enough to put them through this ordeal.

"Thank you for allowing me to mirror Truth to you, Shari," Ruby said, patting my hand as the server dropped off the check. "And since you're an adult now, we'd like to invite you to pay for dinner."

I nodded meekly and pulled out my wallet, watching as $80 disappeared from my bank account, faster than my will to live.

For days after that disastrous dinner, I lay in bed, catatonic. Every thought that popped into my head was tinged with paranoia and self-doubt.

Is this me?
Is this Jodi?
Is this God?
Is this just my anxiety talking?

I found myself truly questioning my own sanity, wondering what was real and what wasn't.

I couldn't even bring myself to go to class. My body was reacting with physical symptoms that I couldn't ignore.

What would happen if I actually stood up to my mother? I wondered, my stomach churning with fear at the thought. But I knew the answer. Ruby had the power to turn my siblings against me, to cut me off from the only people in the world who also understood the insanity of our upbringing. And she would pull that trigger without a second thought.

What would my life look like without my family? I wondered, my heart aching at the thought. Immediately, I knew that I would rather endure this soul-crushing depression for the rest of my life than risk losing them completely.

And through it all, there was Derek, whispering in my ear. "I see how messed-up your parents are," he would say. "I see how wrong this is. Let me help you."

He had my number the first time we met—he knew I'd been trained to fall in line, to never make waves. And because I had let him get close, because I had spilled my guts to him about the mind games and power trips that passed for love in my family, he knew just which buttons to push.

My body, my space, my very being . . . none of it was really mine. So, when Derek started pawing at me, started treating me like his personal property . . . I went away inside my head. Fell back on that big fake smile that had gotten me through so much already.

What irony—while all his was happening, I was studying "abuse of power" in my college classes. Learning about the dynamics of coercion, about the ways in which abusers groom and manipulate their victims. But even as I intellectualized these concepts, even as I wrote papers and participated in discussions about the insidious nature of abuse, I was unable to apply that knowledge to my own life. My brain wouldn't let me go there.

But deep down, I think I knew what Derek was. He was just another one of them. Just like Ruby and Jodi—he was yet another one of the poisonous adults in my life, sucking the very marrow from my bones.

CHAPTER 32

seeds of healing

It was one of those picture-perfect early-summer days—the kind that feels like a slap in the face when your life is falling apart.

"Shari, I think you need therapy," said my bishop, watching me stare listlessly into space.

"Oh, sure," I said. "I've done it before; I liked it. But Ruby won't let me. I'm on the family health insurance. She won't allow it."

"Well, the church can take care of that," he said. "We'll cover whatever you need, no questions asked."

True to his word, the church stepped up and covered the costs of my therapy and medication without ever involving my family. It was a weight off my shoulders.

I settled into the plush armchair in my new therapist's office, the leather cool against my skin. My new therapist's name was Dana, and I liked her, so far.

"So, Shari," Dana began, her voice gentle. "What are your hopes for therapy? Do you have any specific concerns?"

I picked at a loose thread on the couch cushion, avoiding her gaze.

"Well. Things at home . . . they're not great."

I willed myself to open up more, remembering how guarded I had been last time, with Dr. Winters.

Dana leaned forward, nodding. "What do you mean, Shari? What's been going on?"

I took a deep breath, trying to steady my racing heart. "It's my mom. She's very intense. Controlling. I don't think she likes me very much."

Dana nodded, her pen poised over her notepad. "Can you give me an example of a time your mother has made you feel that way?"

I huffed out a laugh, shaking my head.

"Where do I even start?" The words came tumbling out, a flood I couldn't stop.

I told her about piano, about being pulled out of school, about being forced to be on camera all the time, even when I felt sick and tired. I told her about Jodi moving in and my father shutting down. I told her how our house just didn't feel like a home anymore.

Dana's eyes softened, and she set down her pen. "Wow, that sounds very tough, Shari. It's a lot for anyone to handle."

I felt tears prick at the corners of my eyes, and I blinked them away. "I just . . . I don't know how much more I can take."

"Shari, I want you to know that what your mother is doing, the way she's treating you and your siblings . . . it's not okay. It's emotional abuse."

Abuse?

I imagined Ruby laughing at us if she were here. *Don't be so dramatic, Shari.* But this was Dana saying it. A real doctor. And I knew she was right. I'd known for a long time.

"Thank you," I whispered. "She always made me feel like I was just being too sensitive, too selfish. My last therapist thought I was making everything up."

Dana raised an eyebrow.

"Did your mother tell you that?"

I nodded.

"You're not weak, Shari. And the fact that you're here, that you're seeking help and support . . . that's a testament to your strength."

It felt like I was waking up from a long, hazy dream. The fog was lifting, and in its place was a blinding, brilliant truth: It wasn't me. It had never been me. The dysfunction, the chaos . . . it was all Ruby. It always had been.

In the safety of Dana's office, surrounded by soft lighting and the comforting scent of chamomile tea, I found myself teetering on the edge of honesty. A part of me longed to unburden myself, to lay bare the complexities of my relationship with Derek. But I couldn't yet.

When Dana gently probed about my personal life, asking if I was involved with anyone, I felt the familiar tightening in my chest. My palms grew clammy, and I shifted uneasily in the plush armchair that suddenly felt too confining.

"Well . . . ," I began, my voice barely above a whisper. "There is this one friend. He's older than me, but it's not like that. He's more of a father figure, really." The words felt hollow as they left my lips, a half-truth that didn't begin to capture the complexity of my feelings for Derek.

Dana cocked her head, her keen eyes searching my face. I could almost see the gears turning in her mind, picking up on the subtle cues I was inadvertently giving away. "A father figure?" she echoed, her eyebrows arching slightly. "Can you tell me more about that?"

I forced a smile, willing my features to remain neutral. "There's not much to tell," I said, my voice steadier than I felt. "He's just someone I can talk to, someone who understands what I'm going through with my family." As I spoke, I realized how true those words were, even if they didn't tell the whole story.

I could sense Dana's skepticism, the unspoken questions hanging in the air between us. But to her credit, she didn't push. Instead, she steered our conversation back to familiar territory—strategies for coping with my mother's behavior and the ongoing family drama.

As the session wound down and I prepared to leave the sanctuary of Dana's office, I felt a mixture of relief and guilt. Relief that I had managed to keep my secret, and guilt that I wasn't being entirely honest with the one person who was trying to help me.

But I wasn't ready to examine it too closely, to hold it up to the harsh light of therapy, to understand why this was happening to me.

Maybe one day I would. I just wasn't sure when.

CHAPTER 33

puppets and puppeteers

In June 2022, between my freshman and sophomore years, the Frankes gathered for our annual photo shoot; the last time the eight of us would ever be in the same place again, as a family.

When we arrived at the small clearing overlooking the valley, the scene was breathtaking. Wildflowers dotted the hillside in a riot of color. The light was golden and buttery, the kind of light photographers dream about. It should have been perfect.

Ruby's eyes were darting around the clearing, her gaze sharp and assessing. When they landed on Dwight, our three-year-old Cavapoo, her lip curled in distaste. He was sitting at Kevin's feet, his tongue lolling happily, his tail thumping against the ground in a steady rhythm, oblivious to the crackle of unspoken anger in the air.

"I don't want him in my pictures," Ruby said. "He's not part of the family; he's a dog."

I felt a hot rush of anger. Dwight *was* a part of our family, a constant source of love and comfort in a household sorely lacking in both. How could she say he didn't belong?

But the kids pushed back. We all wanted Dwight there. Maybe it was the heat, or the pressure of the photographer's curious gaze, or maybe some small part of her recognized the need to preserve at least the illusion of unity—but Ruby relented. Dwight would make the cut.

We arranged ourselves for the camera as we always had. Dwight nestled in the center of our strained, uncomfortable poses. As the camera clicked and whirred, I felt detached, like I was watching the scene unfold from outside my own body.

Ruby's smile was fixed and brittle, her eyes hard. Kevin's expression was distant and closed off. And the rest of us wore expressions painted on like masks. The smiles were too wide, the eyes too bright. When the photographer tried to coax Kevin and Ruby into a kiss, Ruby flat-out refused and turned away from him as though he were a stranger.

The result was the most awkward family photos in the history of family photos. No amount of photoshop could ever fix that. Even Dwight looked a little off, like he could sense the tension radiating from us in waves. He knew a sinking ship when he saw one.

In the car ride home, I caught Chad's eye in the rearview mirror. I think we both sensed the ground was about to shift beneath our feet, the carefully constructed edifice of our family life about to come crashing down around us.

Shortly after the shoot, Kevin and Ruby prepared for our annual summer trip to the Wasatch Mountains, an hour's drive away. This getaway was supposed to be a family bonding experience, but this year, they'd decided to leave Chad and the two youngest kids behind, deeming them too "selfish" to come along. Because nothing says "family bonding" like excluding half the family.

They had invited me, but I declined due to classes. Kevin then texted our family group chat—including me, Ruby, and Chad—

asking if I could watch the little ones while they were gone. I agreed without hesitation but asked if he could cover my gas money since I'd be driving back and forth from campus daily on a tight budget. Kevin agreed.

While they were up in the mountains, Kevin invited Chad and me to visit for a day. I thought it was a nice gesture.

"Yes, we'd love to join," I texted back. "By the way, are you guys still willing to help with gas?"

Kevin's response was swift and cold: "No, Shari. You have plenty of money for gas and we have offered to purchase your lunch. If somebody invites you to join them at an event, it's brazen and impolite to ask them to pay for your gas."

The abrupt shift in his tone left me stunned. One moment, I was a responsible adult entrusted with childcare; the next, I was an ungrateful child being scolded for my "brazen" behavior.

I was so confused.

"Okay," I wrote. "It's just, when you asked me a few months ago to stay with the kids, you agreed to pay for my gas."

"Shari, I hope you can see the difference between these two requests. They are very different. Please do not make money your God. Obsessing over and pursuing money will destroy every beautiful relationship in your life. That's true for everybody."

Huh?

Kevin had never, ever talked to me like this before. But it sounded *exactly* like something Ruby would say. It had her fingerprints all over it, her signature blend of holier-than-thou rhetoric and ConneXions-style criticism. But coming from my dad, it felt like a knife to the heart.

Maybe this is just a momentary lapse, I thought, even as the doubts swirled in my mind. Because the alternative—the idea that my father was truly lost to me, that the person I loved had been completely erased and rewritten in Ruby's image—was too devastating to contemplate.

I tried to diffuse the situation.

"Very good advice. I've been trying to keep a budget so that is just something I'm aware of. But I'm happy to spend the gas money in order to spend time with my siblings and build family relationships."

Then Ruby chimed in.

"Shari, I'm deeply concerned for you. Can you see that what dad offered you was not advice? He was giving you feedback on your presentation. We offer it because we love you. Rather than sidestep the feedback it would be better for you to thoughtfully consider it and get curious if you don't see it."

"OK," I responded, not knowing what else to say.

My fingers hovered over my phone. I wanted to write something that could break through and reach the dad I once knew. But after several agonizing minutes, I had nothing.

Who are you, Kevin, and what have you done with my father?

Kevin had about as much autonomy as a wet noodle in a hurricane. His every thought and action was dictated by the whims of his unhinged masters, Ruby and Jodi. The groundwork had been laid long ago, the seeds of doubt and obedience sown deep. As it had with me. The only difference was, I'd gotten out. Years of subservience to Ruby had left Kevin's psyche weakened, and now he was easy prey, low-hanging fruit.

With meticulous precision, Jodi had finished the job, dismantling the last remnants of Kevin's independence, stripping away layer after layer until nothing remained but a pliant puppet awaiting her command.

With all her pieces in place, Jodi was poised to make her final move. To eliminate Kevin completely.

CHAPTER 34

facsimile father

As a high-ranking member of ConneXions, Kevin was duty-bound to make his weekly confessions to Jodi, each call a ruthless dissection of his psyche, picking apart the carcass of what remained of his self-worth. Just like my sessions with Jodi had been.

One innocent incident from my childhood had become a major weapon in Jodi's arsenal. I was five years old, and Ruby had made chicken alfredo for dinner. I had developed an intense hatred for chicken alfredo and spent the entire meal hiding under the kitchen table, refusing to take a single bite.

At the end of the dinner, Kevin snuck me a bowl of ice cream. He slid it right under the table, like we were secret agents on a covert mission. It was such a small thing, but it meant the world to me. My dad, my hero, making sure I didn't go to bed with an empty stomach.

That memory had always made me smile. Until he told Jodi about it.

Now that bowl of ice cream was one of many exhibits in the case against Kevin's character.

"Do you see how you were being entitled in that moment?" she told Kevin. "Giving her ice cream, undermining Ruby's authority as a mother?"

Alongside this, there was the damning evidence of his "lustfulness" in noticing an attractive woman at the gym (not even talking to her, mind you, just noticing), and the unforgivable crime of speaking to a female coworker. That long-ago act of kindness was now proof of his "extreme distortion."

Jodi saw sex everywhere, in every interaction, every glance, every fleeting thought. In her mind, the world was a cesspool of lust and distortion, a roiling sea of desire, a twenty-first century Sodom and Gomorrah with only her twisted version of "Truth" offering any salvation.

A part of me pitied her—a repressed, self-loathing, deeply damaged woman trapped in an environment in which she felt compelled to conceal her true nature. Surrounded by women she couldn't have—women who were married to men she resented—in her mind, there was only one path to justice: crush the sperm donors and liberate the females.

In the twisted matriarchy Jodi had orchestrated, Kevin's innermost thoughts were a weapon to be wielded against him. With ruthless precision, Jodi would extract each secret shame, each hidden doubt, and turn it back upon him in service of her one true goal—to claim Ruby as her own, knowing full well that Kevin's shattered spirit no longer had the strength to fight back.

The accusations took an even darker turn when Jodi twisted the happiness he felt in hugging his daughters into something sinister and perverse. She filled his mind with doubts and self-loathing, making him second-guess every interaction, every display of affection.

"Can you see how messed-up it was, when you gave your girls those hugs? You enjoyed it, didn't you?" Jodi would ask.

I can only imagine the horror and disgust that filled Kevin's mind. The shame, the fear, the sickening idea that he might not be a safe person for his own children to be around.

It was all nonsense, of course. But these kinds of sexual accusations were Jodi's go-to tactics, her nuclear option in the game of psychological warfare. She had used it time and time again to tear families apart, planting seeds of doubt and spinning false narratives of incestuous thoughts, infidelity, or porn addiction.

And once the accusations were made, the supposed perpetrator was as good as done for; it was only a matter of time before they'd be "invited to leave."

The Haymonds had been a constant in my life since high school, when Mr. Haymond, my teacher, had become the first adult I felt safe confiding in about Ruby's behavior. As that summer of 2022 unfolded, Mr. Haymond and his wife realized just how dysfunctional things had become at home. One day, Mrs. Haymond pressed a shiny new key into my palm. "Shari, sweetie," she said, her eyes filled with warmth and concern, "you're always welcome here, anytime. Our home is your home."

That's why, one muggy midsummer evening in July 2022, I found myself driving to their house. I had chosen to stay at college during the summer break, reluctant to return home, but on this particular night, I couldn't face the solitude of my dorm room, either. Almost without conscious thought, I knew where I wanted to be.

The Haymonds didn't know my parents too well. They had briefly taken one of Jodi's classes when I was a freshman in college but quickly dismissed ConneXions as "dumb" and dropped out after only a few weeks. Ironically, this fleeting exposure proved invaluable, giving them just enough insight to understand the world I was trapped in, without being pulled into its orbit.

Their daughter, who was close to my age, had become like a sister to me. We'd spend hours watching old movies, bingeing on *Little House on the Prairie* and black-and-white Deanna Durbin musicals from the 1940s.

Their house, always filled with laughter and warmth, had become my safe haven, a place where I could breathe freely and just be myself.

I walked up to the Haymonds' front door, let myself in, only to realize that nobody was home, just their dogs. *Right, they'd mentioned something about going to see a play*, I reminded myself.

I plopped down on the Haymonds' cozy living room couch, intending to zone out in front of the TV for a while. Just as I reached for the remote, my phone buzzed, Kevin's name flashing across the screen. I answered the call.

"Hey, Dad."

"Are you alone?" he asked, his voice serious.

"Yeah, why?" I replied, unease creeping up my spine.

"Your mom and I need to talk to you," he said. I heard the faint echo that told me I was on speakerphone, though Ruby remained silent.

My mind raced, immediately jumping to worst-case scenarios. *Have they found out about Derek?*

"Shari, I . . . I don't know how to say this."

I gripped the phone tighter, my palms sweating. "Just say it, Dad. Please."

"Your mom has invited me to leave the family home so I can work on myself," he said, his voice cracking. "Once I'm better, I'll come back, and we can be a happy family again. I'll be gone for at least a year."

The words hit me like a sucker punch. *A year?*

Tears streamed down my face as I choked out, "You're moving out of the house, leaving the kids?"

Kevin sighed heavily. "Yes, I'm leaving, and taking Chad with me. Chad is also selfish, and I guess selfish people belong together.

"I don't want you to end up like me, Shari," he continued. "Maybe this can be a learning experience for you."

Learning experience? Is he serious right now? I thought, my mind reeling.

Kevin then dropped another bombshell: He wouldn't be communicating with the other kids. Only me.

None of this made any sense.

"How are you feeling about all this, Shari?" he asked, his voice flat.

"Confused," I said. "Really, really confused."

"I understand. But this isn't the end of our family—it's the beginning."

The *beginning.* The word echoed in my mind, hollow and meaningless.

When the Haymonds finally returned home, they found me curled up in a fetal position on the couch, my body wracked with sobs that seemed to come from a place deep within me. They didn't ask questions, just helped me to the guest room and told me I was safe.

The next morning, I woke to the buzz of my phone—this time, a lengthy text from Kevin.

"Shari, things have changed, and Chad and I are going to ask that you don't contact either of us until we're ready and we reach out to you. Please don't contact me. Don't be selfish about this, and don't hold resentment for this. Use this time to get close to your mom and your siblings."

I read the message once, twice, three times, each word cutting deeper than the last. The urge to hurl my phone against the wall was almost overwhelming. *Don't be selfish? Don't hold resentment?*

He was cutting me off with this poor excuse for a goodbye. How could he expect me to just accept this without question, without any explanation?

The Haymonds' guest room became my cocoon. Hours stretched into days as I lay there, my mind a labyrinth of unanswered questions and half-formed theories. But there was no logic to be found, no hidden meaning to uncover. All I knew was that this was Jodi's doing.

JOURNAL

I went to counseling today and talked it through. I'm so angry with my dad for not sticking up for himself and for abandoning his family. And I am furious at Mom and Jodi for ruining our family. I feel like a part of me has died and I will never get it back. I don't know how I'll ever recover or forgive them. I don't know how to help my siblings. I don't even know how to help myself.

A week passed in a haze of grief and confusion before Ruby finally reached out. Her message popped up on my phone: "How are you doing with all of this?"

I was surprised she'd contacted me at all, given the state of our relationship. Part of me was relieved she hadn't reached out earlier; I'd needed time to process. Still, her belated concern felt hollow.

"I'm having a really hard time. I'm really sad."

Her response was as comforting as a bucket of ice water. "Yes, this has been really hard. I hope that all of us will use this as an opportunity to become humbler, especially you."

Humbler? Was she serious?

I couldn't bring myself to dignify that with a response. I tossed my phone aside, burying my face in my pillow and sobbing until my throat was raw.

A few days later, Ruby suggested we meet for lunch to "discuss the situation."

What's there to discuss? I thought bitterly. *You've kicked Dad out because you're obsessed with Jodi. Now the rest of us are left to pick up the pieces.*

Mustering every ounce of courage I possessed, I declined her invitation.

"How come you don't want to meet with me?" she wrote.

"This has been a hard time for me. Text is what I'm available to do right now."

"My concern is texting leaves a lot open to misinterpretation."

I left it there, unable to engage further.

As days turned into weeks, I found myself reflecting on Kevin's role in all of this. He was far from perfect. Over the years, he'd made his share of mistakes, enabling Ruby's toxic behavior and standing idly by as she steamrolled over everyone. He was her faithful servant, catering to her every whim, no matter how unreasonable. But Kevin was never a selfish man. In fact, his greatest weakness was his selflessness—he gave and gave until there was nothing left. Now, he had gone willingly into exile, cutting off all contact with us, his children, to please his wife and to protect us from the vile monster Jodi led him to believe he was.

He'd said it would be temporary, a year to focus on personal growth before returning to his family. But I knew Ruby would never welcome him back, no matter how much time passed. This was a one-way ticket. This was permanent.

To this day, it's a miracle to me that he survived the misery of his exile and didn't end it all. A chilling thought has crossed my mind since then: Maybe that's what Jodi and Ruby wanted. Maybe they were hoping he'd just . . . disappear. Forever.

CHAPTER 35

care package

As summer faded into fall, I found myself facing a new chapter of my life: sophomore year of college. The relative safety of dorm life was behind me now, replaced by the daunting prospect of off-campus living. I moved into a cramped apartment with two girls, fellow students whom I'd met on campus, the three of us squeezed into two bedrooms like sardines in a tin.

The stress of the move, compounded by the ongoing family drama, left me feeling raw and vulnerable. But nothing could have prepared me for the shock that awaited me in our new bathroom. What I had initially mistaken for sloppy spackling on the walls turned out to be black mold, creeping across the surfaces like some alien invasion, sending my anxiety into overdrive.

Panic rising in my chest, I did the unthinkable: I called Ruby. As the phone rang, I realized how desperate I must be to turn to her for help.

"Mom," I blurted out, my voice cracking, "I can't live here. I'm going to die from black mold!" The words tumbled out in a rush, part plea for help, part childish exaggeration born of fear and stress.

I don't know what I expected. Comfort, perhaps. Maybe even an offer to come and help me sort out this mess. What I got instead was pure Ruby: no sympathy, just a clinical list of cleaning tips delivered in her matter-of-fact tone.

"Now that you're eighteen," she concluded, her voice devoid of any maternal warmth, "it's time for you to take care of yourself."

And I tried, as best I could, to do just that, alongside my two roomies, each of us battling our own demons in our cramped, moldy apartment.

One was a twenty-six-year-old, down in the dumps that she was still stuck on a campus she'd long ago outgrown. The other was a walking, talking pillar of faith, living her LDS principles with such an upbeat, unyielding intensity, that even I—no stranger to conservative values—was impressed by the way she'd lunge for the remote and hit fast-forward during PG kissing scenes in movies.

We were a stressed-out little sisterhood, all very different from one another, but I found great comfort in not being alone, an odd sort of solace in these young women's company.

I shared fragments of my story with them—they knew that I wasn't speaking with Ruby, for instance. But the full extent of my family drama remained locked away, too heavy to share.

They didn't know about the unanswered texts I sent to my father, each one a desperate plea for some sign that he still cared, that I wasn't dead to him.

Derek? That was a secret I held close. I could already imagine their eyes widening, lips pursing in poorly concealed disapproval if they knew. Telling them—or anyone, for that matter—would invite judgment I wasn't prepared to face.

I couldn't even find the words to explain to my roommates what was happening with Chad, who, I'd discovered through some covert detective work involving sympathetic neighbors, wasn't living with Kevin as I'd been told. Instead, he was out on his own, playing house with a bunch of roommates in an apartment complex in Provo, practically around the corner from where I was living.

When I found out, my brain nearly short-circuited. An urgent need to find him, to talk to him, consumed me. If he was living alone, did that mean he was estranged from Ruby and Kevin, too? And most importantly, was he okay?

I racked my brain, trying to think of anyone who might have the inside scoop on Chad's actual address. I remembered that one of our neighbors was a big-shot landlord in Provo, and something told me he might have helped Chad get his apartment.

I fired off a message to him. "Do you happen to know where Chad's living?" I wrote. "If so, can you please, PLEASE tell me? It's urgent!"

His reply was frustratingly tight-lipped. "I can confirm that he's living in one of my properties," he wrote, his tone maddeningly neutral. "But I'm afraid I can't give you the specific apartment number. Confidentiality agreements, you understand."

Then, out of the blue, I got a text message from an unknown number.

"Building 6, Apartment 38."

To this day, I have no idea who sent me that message.

I ransacked my kitchen, stuffing a bag with Chad's comfort foods—Doritos, Oreos, and those bizarre cheese crackers he'd devour by the fistful. Nestled among the snacks, I tucked a letter pouring out my heart: my love for him, my fears about our family's implosion, and my unwavering promise to stand by him as both big sister and friend. With this lifeline packed, I jumped in my car and raced to his apartment.

I timed my visit for when I thought he'd be out, hoping to leave the care package and letter without ambushing him. The plan was to give him space to process everything on his own terms.

But when I knocked on the door of apartment thirty-eight, one of Chad's roommates opened the door, revealing my brother in the kitchen behind him. My heart leapt at the sight of his familiar face—the same smile that had brightened so many of my days, the eyes that had twinkled with mischief during countless shared jokes. Our eyes locked, his wide with surprise, as he slowly approached the threshold.

"Shari?" he said, his voice low. "What are you doing here? How did you find me?"

I swallowed hard, suddenly feeling like an intruder.

"Can we talk? Please?" I said, my voice shaking slightly.

For a moment, I thought he was going to slam the door in my face, tell me to get lost. Instead, he stepped into the hallway, and gazed at me warily.

"I miss you, Chad," I said, tears brimming.

"What's in the bag?" he asked, voice flat.

"Snacks!" I chirped, false cheer straining my voice. "You know, for the bottomless pit you call a stomach. Here."

He shook his head, declining the bag.

"All good, Shari. So why are you here?"

I could feel the tension radiating from him, suspicion and anger simmering just beneath the surface of his carefully controlled exterior. *What lies had they used to turn him against me?* I wondered, my heart clenching painfully in my chest.

I took a deep breath, trying to gather my thoughts. Then the words I'd been holding back for so long came pouring out.

"I'm here because our family is falling apart! Because our mother is *abusive*, Chad!"

Chad's eyes widened, a flicker of something—recognition? denial?—passing across his face. "Shari, come on . . ."

I pressed on, desperate to make him understand. "Dad leaving, the way they're isolating him, isolating us . . . You have to know, deep down, that something is very wrong here."

Chad crossed his arms over his chest, his jaw clenched tight. The gesture was so familiar, so reminiscent of our mother, that it made my heart ache.

"There's nothing wrong, except that some of us need to work on our responsibilities."

I reached out, my hand hovering inches from his arm. "Chad, please. Just hear me out."

He jerked away from my touch as if burned, his eyes flashing with a mixture of anger and something that looked suspiciously like fear.

"I'm trying to protect you!" I whispered. "Can't you see, Mom and Jodi are dangerous?"

Chad laughed. "*Protection*? I'm doing fine, Shari. I'm working two jobs; I'm paying my bills." His eyes raked over me, critical and cold. "You should worry about yourself."

"Why are you so loyal to her, after everything she's done to you?"

"She's our mother, Shari."

I opened my mouth to respond, but Chad held up a hand, cutting me off.

"You should leave," he said, his voice low and final.

And with that, he turned and disappeared back into the apartment, slamming the door behind him.

I stood there, staring at the closed door, clutching the care package I'd brought, trying to gather my thoughts. I felt so drained, and the hope I'd felt just hours ago had vanished. Despite my joy at seeing Chad, the coldness in his eyes was devastating. It was painfully clear that my entire family had turned against me. I wanted to scream, to pound on the door until my fists bled, to make him listen. My chest tightened, each breath a struggle against the growing knot of panic. I had to get out of there. I had to lay down.

As I was getting back to my apartment, my phone buzzed—a long text message from Ruby. Chad must have told her I'd tracked him down. She twisted my actions, painting my attempts to protect Chad as a malicious attack. The fact that I'd called her "abusive" seemed to have struck a nerve.

Shari.

You have been deceiving me for quite some time. This makes sense now why you didn't want to talk to me . . . you couldn't handle the duplicity! It's clear to me that you are not interested in being part of our family and you have chosen to disconnect by sneaking around attempting to harm other members of our family.

I feel great grief and loss at your choices. I will honor your agency of disconnect. Disconnection means you are not interested in being around me and the family. You don't get to disconnect emotionally and tell stories about your mother . . . and then get the perks of familial and financial connection that I provide.

It has come to my attention that you called me "abusive." Wow, Shari, that word is heavily loaded with intimation. It is hurtful you would use that word knowing the pain that this lie has caused.

This is my way of being very loving and inviting you to see the reality you are in. You don't get to use me or any members of my family. When you are willing to humble yourself and acknowledge your aggression and deception I am open to talking to you.

I will keep you in my prayers. You appear to be a very lost

soul. You don't even know where the enemy is. Your arrogance has kept you from heeding my warnings.
Love,
Ruby

I hurled my phone onto the bed, its screen still glowing with Ruby's words. My hands trembled as I yanked open drawers, grabbing fistfuls of clothes and shoving them into an overnight bag. I couldn't be here anymore, knowing Chad was so close, and yet so far away. And Ruby . . . her words echoed in my head, dripping with a cruelty that seemed to have deepened, if that were even possible.

As I slung the bag over my shoulder, I caught a glimpse of myself in the mirror. The woman staring back looked lost, hollowed out. I barely recognized her. With a shaky breath, I tore my eyes away. "Hey, I'm staying with some friends for a bit!" I called out to my roommates.

The door slammed behind me before they could ask me why.

CHAPTER 36

fawn

After leaving the apartment, I drove straight to the Haymonds' house, my sanctuary in the storm. When I asked if I could stay for a while, they welcomed me without hesitation or interrogation. I caught a glimpse of concern in their eyes—they could sense that things with my family had taken a turn for the worse. But they knew better than to pry, offering instead the quiet comfort of their presence and the safety of their home. As I set my bag down in the guest room, the knot in my chest loosened just a little, allowing me to take my first real breath since leaving my apartment.

But Derek, for some reason, didn't seem to like that I was there.

"I hope you're not overstaying your welcome," Derek's text glowed on my screen. "You don't want to be a burden. They're nice people, but everyone has their limits."

His words lingered in my mind, poisonous and persistent.

Suddenly, every kind gesture from the Haymonds felt tainted. Were their smiles strained? Were their welcomes fully sincere? Did they think I was a parasite, feeding off their generosity?

I found myself analyzing every interaction, searching for signs of resentment or fatigue. The warmth of their home felt precarious, like a fragile bubble that could burst at any moment.

I cornered Mrs. Haymond in the kitchen, my eyes wide and pleading.

"Are you sure it's okay for me to be here?" I asked. "I can leave if you want. Or I can pay rent."

"Shari, you're very, very welcome here. It's not a problem," she said, fussing around the sink.

"Are you absolutely, positively sure?" I asked.

"Honey!" she called out to Mr. Haymond, who was puttering around in the garage.

"Can you come in here for a minute? I need you to tell Shari something."

Mr. Haymond ambled into the kitchen, his face creased with concern.

"Listen, I need you to tell Shari that she's not a burden, that she's welcome here for as long as she needs. I think she needs to hear it from both of us."

Mr. Haymond's face softened, and he turned to me. "Shari," he said. "You are a part of this family now, whether you like it or not. You're stuck with us, you hear me? And we wouldn't have it any other way."

I could feel the tears welling up in my eyes, the lump rising in my throat. *Is this what it feels like?* I thought, my heart swelling with a fierce, aching love. *Is this what it's like to have people in your life who actually care about you?*

Despite the Haymonds' kindness, I couldn't shake off Derek's words. He kept texting me, each message a carefully crafted barb designed to sow doubt. "I'm sure they're just being polite," he'd write, or "You know people start to resent houseguests after a while."

Deep down, I knew his comments probably stemmed from jealousy—he couldn't stand the idea that I had found comfort and support outside of him. Yet, even recognizing his motives, I couldn't bring myself to confront him or ask him to stop. Instead, I'd simply respond with noncommittal agreement, swallowing my frustration. It seemed easier, safer, to let him have his say than to disagree and risk provoking his anger.

"Shari, have you ever heard of the fawn response?" Dana, my therapist asked.

"Fawn response?" I asked, shaking my head. "What is that?"

"Well, we often talk about fight, flight, and freeze as trauma responses. But there's a fourth—fawn. It's when a person tries to please or appease their abuser to avoid conflict or further harm."

Dana leaned forward, her eyes kind but intent. "Fawning can look like always agreeing with others, even when you disagree inside. It's constantly trying to keep the peace, putting others' needs before your own, even when it hurts you. People who fawn often become hyperattuned to others' moods, trying to anticipate and meet their needs before they're even expressed."

I felt my breath catch in my throat as she continued.

"In abusive situations, fawning can manifest as smiling and nodding while you're screaming inside. It's doing whatever it takes to keep an abuser happy, because you've learned that's the safest way to survive. Does any of this sound familiar, Shari?"

"Oh my gosh," I whispered, my voice barely audible. "That's . . . that's me. That's what I've been doing my whole life."

Dana nodded encouragingly, allowing me space to process this revelation. "It's a common response to prolonged abuse or trauma. Recognizing it is the first step toward changing the pattern."

I sat there, stunned, as years of memories suddenly clicked into place with this new understanding.

"That must be why I never fight back with Derek!" I exclaimed, the words tumbling out before I could stop them. "I just fawn, and make sure he's happy. Because that feels safer."

"Shari . . . who's Derek?"

I raised my hand to my mouth, my eyes filling with tears as I realized my slip.

No, I wasn't ready to talk about this yet.

"Is he the friend you mentioned, a few sessions back? The older gentleman?"

I shook my head, unable to meet her gaze.

Dana handed me a tissue. "It's okay. Go at your own pace. I'm sure this is all very overwhelming. And you don't have to talk about it unless you want to. But understanding this fawning pattern may help."

I nodded, dabbing at my eyes.

As the session came to a close, I felt a strange mix of vulnerability and relief. Derek's name had finally been spoken in this room, even if I wasn't ready to say more. But now I understood why I couldn't say no to him, why I never rebuked him or showed anger—it wasn't weakness, it was a pattern etched into my very being by years under Ruby's thumb. Some way, somehow, I'd have to figure out how to break it.

CHAPTER 37

showdown

> They gave me also gall for my meat, and in my thirst they gave me vinegar to drink.
> —PSALM 69:21, KING JAMES BIBLE

Ruby's vindictiveness was legendary, and I knew she wouldn't hesitate to pull the trigger if she felt like she had a point to prove. The signs were all there. She'd already stopped signing her texts with "Mom," opting instead for the cold, impersonal "Ruby." I knew what this meant. I knew what was coming. Ruby always had to have the last word. She had to win. I better get ready for what was coming. She was going to cut me out, just like she had Kevin, and the rest of her family.

Then I remembered—she had access to my bank account.

All my money, every last penny I had scrimped and saved, was sitting in an account that Ruby could empty at any given moment. *I have to get my money out*, I decided. That night in early September, I set about transferring every cent into a new account, one that bore my name and my name alone. As I hit the final "confirm" button,

I flinched. Ruby was a master of retaliation. As soon as she realized what I'd done, she would punish me.

An email pinged into my inbox the next morning, a message from our family's insurance agent.

"Shari," it read, "your mother has asked me to remove you from the family's car insurance policy. Effective immediately, you will need to secure your own coverage. Please do not drive until you have done so."

Indignation burned hot in my veins. *Who just cuts off their own daughter's ability to drive without so much as a heads-up?* Then I realized that I had a bigger problem on my hands. *The title to my car. It's still at the house. And if I want to get my own insurance, I need that damn piece of paper in my name.* The thought of having to face Ruby, of having to beg and plead for what was rightfully mine, made my skin crawl. But I had no choice. Time to grovel.

I typed out a message, my words carefully chosen and painfully polite. I brought our congregation president, Jim Nelson, into the text conversation, as a form of emotional backup. I knew Ruby would be less likely to ignore the text if someone powerful was included.

"Mom, I'm going to get my own car insurance and I would like the title of the car as proof of ownership. Is there a way I can get this from you?"

I hit send and waited, my heart pounding in my chest. And then, after what felt like an eternity, her response came through.

> *Shari, this is just another example of your lying and manipulating—bringing President Jim Nelson into this text thread. You are just asking for the title for your car, which I have no problem getting to you. You could have just asked me. You've been very active in deceiving and creating chaos, pain, destruction and turmoil. My own daughter has turned*

on Truth and me. And the outcomes are devastating to your siblings.

Shari, I am your mother. I am only guilty of teaching you Truth. Truth is the only thing that matters in this life and you have fought against it since you were little. It breaks my heart you are at war with God. The Lord has blessed you with a quick mind and it is devastating to watch you use that mind to fight against Truth.

I will give the title to Pam. Feel free to collect it from her.

I texted Pam, my words carefully neutral and polite. How did one even begin a conversation like this, a negotiation with a gatekeeper?

"Hi Pam, Ruby mentioned that she would be leaving some documents with you for me to pick up. Is there a convenient time for me to come by and collect them? Thanks, Shari."

Her response came quickly, setting a date and time the following week when I should come by.

That was easy, I thought, feeling a little better. *I can just swing by, grab my documents, and be done with this whole mess . . .*

But a couple of things happened before I was able to get my car title back.

The situation at home had escalated. With Kevin gone, and Ruby increasingly absent, I felt a growing sense of dread about my younger siblings' welfare. The final straw came when a neighbor informed me that the children had been left alone for five days while Ruby was off doing God knows what with Jodi.

I was stunned. Five days. No adult supervision. No one to make sure they were fed, safe, looked after. The thought of my younger siblings fending for themselves for nearly a week made my blood boil. In that moment, I knew I had to do something, consequences be damned.

I made a call to the Division of Child and Family Services (DCFS), requesting a welfare check on the children. The police went to the house, knocked on the door, and looked inside the windows. They reported back that the kids were there and apparently everyone was fine. I was relieved they were okay but frustrated at the lack of action. While there might not be specific laws against leaving minors alone, surely five days crossed some kind of line?

My relief was short-lived. Somehow, Ruby had discovered that I was the one who called DCFS, and now she was on the warpath. I don't know how she figured it out, but she wanted my head on a stick.

Now, I found myself in the awkward position of having to face Pam to collect my car title, all while knowing about Ruby's fury. As if things weren't awkward enough already.

I paced back and forth across the Haymonds' living room, probably wearing a hole in their carpet as my brain went into overdrive, conjuring up all sorts of nightmare scenarios. *What if Pam straight-up refuses to give me the title? What if she tries to use it as a bargaining chip, to force me back under Ruby's thumb?*

Panicking, I fired off a text to Pam, hoping and praying that Ruby had been too embarrassed to tell her what had happened.

"Hey Pam, I'm really anxious to get those documents. Would it be possible for you to just leave them in your mailbox for me to pick up? I'm kind of in a rush today. Thanks again, Shari."

Her response was swift and unequivocal.

"Absolutely not, Shari. These are valuable legal documents, and I won't risk them being stolen or lost. You'll need to come to the house and collect them in person. See you at the appointed time and day. Pam."

As if the situation wasn't stressful enough, a few days before I was supposed to go and pick up the documents, Reddit exploded—word had gotten out that Kevin and Chad were no longer living at home, and the internet, with its insatiable appetite for our family drama, had latched on to this information. Rumors were spreading, theories were being formed on Reddit and other forums about what was going on, questioning my role in everything.

In the face of this growing speculation, I felt compelled to make my position clear, and posted an Instagram story:

> "I know that there are many rumors circulating online about my family. While it is true I am not in contact with my immediate family, and don't support the extreme beliefs of ConneXions, please remember that this is my real family. Despite good intentions, speculating, rumors and gossip doesn't help us. I'd like to ask for privacy for me and my family as we work through this very difficult situation. Please know that many are working on this situation, and I hope one day we can be whole again. Please respect my privacy as I work on my own healing as well."

I knew that by posting this statement, I was effectively burning whatever flimsy bridge might have remained between me and Ruby. But something inside me had shifted. The need to stand up for what I believed in, to distance myself from Ruby and Jodi, and all they represented, had become stronger than my fear of the consequences.

As I posted it, I felt a mix of terror and exhilaration. It was as if I'd jumped off a cliff, not knowing if there was water or rocks below. But for the first time in a long time, I felt like I was being true to myself. Whatever came next, I would face it.

My heart was racing as I approached Mrs. Haymond in the kitchen. The words felt heavy in my mouth, but I forced them out.

"Mrs. Haymond," I said, my voice small and shaky. "I have to go pick up some documents from Pam today. Would you... would you maybe come with me? I don't think I can do it alone, and I'm not supposed to drive without insurance."

Mrs. Haymond's face softened, her eyes filling with a compassion I'd grown to rely on. "Of course I'll come with you, Shari. We'll do this together."

The drive to Pam's house was a blur. As we walked up the front steps, each footfall felt like it was bringing me closer to some inevitable confrontation. My hand trembled as I knocked on the door.

When it swung open, my worst fears were confirmed. There stood Pam, her face pinched with disapproval. But it was the figure behind her that made my blood run cold. Ruby, my mother, stood tall and regal, my documents clutched in her hand like a hostage.

It was an ambush.

"Hello, Shari," Ruby said, her voice dripping with false sweetness.

I swallowed hard, my mouth suddenly dry as sandpaper. "Can I please have my papers?" I asked, holding out my hand, willing it not to shake.

Ruby's eyes narrowed. "Not so fast. I'm not giving you the title until you listen to what I have to say. Come inside. Let's have a little chat."

In that moment, I felt a surge of strength I didn't know I possessed. "No," I said, my voice trembling but clear. "I'm not coming inside. If you want to talk, we can do it out here."

And so, there we stood, the four of us on Pam's front porch, locked in a bizarre standoff. Ruby, clutching my documents like a weapon. Pam, hovering like a shadow. Mrs. Haymond, calm and unflappable behind me, a silent pillar of support. And me, shaking like a leaf, but refusing to back down.

Ruby's face contorted with anger and hurt. "I can't believe you called the police on me," she began, her voice rising. "After everything I've done for you, after all the sacrifices I've made. How could you betray me like that, Shari? How could you be so selfish?"

I could feel Mrs. Haymond's steady presence behind me, reminding me that I wasn't alone, that I had support beyond the toxic web of my family.

"Selfish?" I repeated, finding strength in my voice. "I was worried about the kids. They were alone for five days, Mom. Five days!"

"They're fine," Ruby snapped. "They're old enough to take care of themselves. This is about you, Shari. Your jealousy, your need for attention."

I felt a bubble of hysterical laughter rise in my throat. How could she twist this around, make it about me? But then, wasn't that always her way?

"This isn't about me," I said, my voice steadier than I felt. "It's about the safety of my siblings. It's about doing what's right."

Ruby's eyes flashed dangerously. "What's right? You have no idea what's right. You're just a child playing at being an adult. Your siblings are terrified of you now, for calling the police on them."

Ruby's face hardened, her lips twisting into a sneer. "One day, Shari, you'll come crawling back to me. Begging for my forgiveness. And it'll be hard for me to give it to you, but I'll be gracious."

"Forgiveness for what, Mom?"

"You're telling lies about me everywhere, and they're spreading like dandelion seeds across the field. The weeds are all going to pop up, and one day you'll have to go back and cut them all down and come apologize to me."

"I'm not going to apologize for telling the truth," I said, my voice quiet but firm.

"How dare you contact Chad and Kevin behind my back!" she hissed, spittle flying from her lips.

"They're my family, too. You don't get to dictate who I can and can't talk to." I could feel my anger rising, hot and fierce in my chest.

Ruby let out a harsh, mirthless laugh. "Family? Please. You've made it abundantly clear that you want nothing to do with this family. You're a traitor, Shari. A Judas in our midst."

I could feel the tears streaming down my face, hot and sticky on my cheeks.

"You've always hated me," she whispered. "Ever since you were five years old, I could see it in your eyes. The way you looked at me, the way you judged me. You've never appreciated anything I've done for you, all the sacrifices I've made."

"That's not true," I choked. "I never hated you, Mom. I was just scared of you."

Ruby shook her head. "You're like the Romans in the Bible," she said. "Feeding me vinegar when I'm dying of thirst, crucifying me for your own selfish gains."

I heard Mrs. Haymond mutter something under her breath, something that sounded suspiciously like "Oh, for goodness sake." But I was too focused on Ruby to pay much attention. I could feel a panic attack coming on, my chest tightening and my vision starting to blur.

Ruby wasn't finished. "When you're ready to apologize, really apologize, then maybe we can be a family again," she said to me. "But until then, don't contact me or Kevin or Chad or anyone else in our family. Because you won't get a response."

Mrs. Haymond stepped forward, her voice calm but firm.

"Ruby, I think it's time for you to give Shari her documents and let us be on our way."

For a moment, I thought Ruby might argue, might lash out with another barrage. But something in Mrs. Haymond's eyes, in the set of her jaw, must have given her pause.

Ruby thrust the papers into my hands, her fingers brushing against mine. "Here," she said, her voice cold and distant.

I clutched the documents to my chest.

"One last thing," Ruby said. "I saw your Instagram story. Can you promise to not talk about this anymore on social media?"

I waited until I had the papers safely in my bag before I responded, my voice shaking but clear. "No," I said.

And that was the last interaction I ever had with my mother.

Mrs. Haymond guided me back to the car, her arm wrapped securely around my waist as if she could sense the weakness in my legs.

As I collapsed into the passenger seat, the dam finally broke. My whole body shook, and I began gasping for air. Mrs. Haymond didn't say a word, just put the car in gear and drove, her hands white-knuckled on the steering wheel. The houses and trees and mailboxes blurred together in a haze.

I was excommunicated. Disowned. It was a pain beyond words, a loss so profound that it felt like a physical amputation, like a part of my very soul had been ripped away.

Mrs. Haymond's hand found mine across the center console, warm and reassuring. She didn't try to fill the silence with platitudes or empty reassurances. Didn't try to minimize the enormity of what had just happened. She just held my hand, a silent promise that she would be there, her fingers wound tight around mine.

PART FIVE

fall
of
the
damned

CHAPTER 38

the echo chamber

JOURNAL

I had a dream last night where I sat my youngest sister on my knee and explained why I couldn't talk with the family, for now. I told her I loved her and asked her to come find me one day. I woke up and had the feeling she had the same dream as me. I feel she's being guided.

Today also happens to be Dad's birthday. I sent him a text message and didn't expect a reply, but it still hurts that he didn't. I miss having someone to call Mom and Dad. It was endearing to my heart, and now all that's gone.

My Instagram story had set off a firestorm of gossip, with people from all corners chiming in with their opinions and theories.

I always knew there was something off about that family.

Poor Shari, I wonder what happened to make her turn her back on Ruby.

I read the comments, the DMs, the texts from well-meaning strangers. *If only they knew the full story of what's happened to my family*, I thought, heartbroken.

I took comfort in the sanctuary of the Haymonds' home. The Haymonds who had shown me a different way of being, a different kind of care than any I had ever known before. It was a care that didn't come with strings attached, that didn't require me to twist myself into knots trying to earn it. It was a care that was freely given, without reservation or expectation.

One day, I sat with the Haymonds in the cozy living room of their home, the words tumbling out of my mouth before I could stop them.

"May I call you Mom and Dad?" I asked, my cheeks burning.

Mrs. Haymond's face lit up like a Christmas tree, her eyes glistening. "Oh, sweetheart," she breathed, pulling me into a tight hug that nearly crushed my rib cage. "Of course you can. I would be honored for you to call me Mom."

I needed them, and the stability they represented. I needed people who behaved like real family, if I was ever going to get through this.

"Hello, everyone! I'm your host, Ruby Franke," my mother said brightly. "Welcome to another episode of the *ConneXions Podcast*, where we help you create joy in your life and relationships. Start your training today at ConneXionsclassroom.com. You can also follow us on Facebook and Instagram @ConneXionsCoaching, or join our private Facebook group, Moms of Truth with Jodi and Ruby."

Despite everything, Ruby and Jodi were pushing on with their obnoxious "Moms of Truth" crusade, seemingly oblivious to the fact that the whole world was turning against them.

To be accepted to the Moms of Truth Facebook group, you had to answer questions like "Are you willing to be grateful to receive parenting advice from experienced women?" Still, even with the screening, most of the women on that page were secret trolls, oddly fascinated by Ruby's narcissism and cruelty on 8 Passengers, curious to see what the hell she was up to now.

Pass the popcorn.

"A child is responsible for three things," Ruby preached. "A child needs to learn to manage their thoughts, their feelings, and their behaviors. And they need to learn to manage them in truth, which means they're going to be honest, they're going to be responsible, and they're going to be humble with all of that. And that is a lot of responsibility. . . ."

The sheer hypocrisy was staggering. Ruby and Jodi had crowned themselves the ultimate authorities on motherhood and family, yet their actions spoke volumes about their true nature. Jodi, estranged from both her son and daughter, had no contact with her own children. Ruby, who had cut me off entirely, was now hiding my siblings from the world, their lives shrouded in secrecy and isolation.

The internet was ablaze with reactions, particularly on Reddit, where former 8 Passengers fans expressed their shock and disgust at Ruby's trajectory:

> "These women are absolutely INSANE. The levels of absolute mental gymnastics they do is appalling."

> "Ruby gaslights SO much. Beyond sanctimonious."

But Ruby seemed oblivious to the outcry. She had retreated into an echo chamber of her own making, severing ties with everyone who might challenge her worldview. She had found her role as Jodi's devoted disciple, and it seemed nothing could shake her from it.

Jodi never explicitly declared herself a prophet or deity, but the implication hung heavy in every word and action. She had positioned herself as the chosen one, a savior sent to lead the faithful to enlightenment. Ruby, in turn, had become her most fervent follower. Together, they presented themselves as all-knowing and all-powerful, allowing no challenge to their authority.

My phone buzzed constantly with messages from concerned friends and even strangers:

"How are your siblings? Are they okay? Are you talking to them?"

I didn't know how to answer. My siblings, once so close, had become strangers to me. I had no idea about their well-being, their daily lives, or even their whereabouts. No one knew how they were doing—no one except Ruby. She was the gatekeeper, controlling all information about my siblings' lives.

I couldn't provide the answers people were looking for, and I couldn't ease their concerns—or my own. I had to face the reality of our situation: a family fractured, siblings hidden away, and a mother who had chosen delusion over her children's well-being.

CHAPTER 39

abandoned by justice

The knot in my stomach tightened with each passing day. I was back at school and couldn't stop pacing around my apartment, my thoughts spiraling with worry about my siblings. Everything was pointing to the fact that they were in serious trouble under Ruby's roof.

The phone startled me out of my frantic thoughts. I glanced at the caller ID—our neighbor, Mrs. Larsen. With a sense of dread, I answered.

"Shari, I thought you should know," Mrs. Larsen said, her voice heavy. "Ruby pulled all the kids out of school."

I felt like I'd been sucker punched.

"Oh no . . . thanks for letting me know," I managed, before hanging up.

I slumped into a chair, my head spinning. Then the phone rang again. This time it was the Gundersons from across the street.

"Shari . . . I hate to be the one to tell you this," Mr. Gunderson said apologetically. "But your mom got rid of Dwight."

"What? No!" I cried out. Our goofy, lovable Cavapoo. The kids were crazy about him. "Why would she do that?"

"I think . . ." Mr. Gunderson hesitated. "I think it's so the kids can't go out, you know, to walk him around the neighborhood. Seems like Ruby doesn't want them seeing anyone."

The question was, what else was she doing to them? The possibilities made my head spin. I had to do something, but what? Call the cops again? Barge over there and confront Ruby myself?

A crazy idea pushed its way into my head.

What if I went crawling back to Ruby? Pretended to apologize, play nice, so I could be around the kids again?

No. She wouldn't fall for it. I can't handle this on my own. I need backup, someone with real authority.

I grabbed my phone, scrolling until I found the entry for DCFS. Then punched the call button.

"DCFS, Kelly speaking."

"Hey, Kelly, it's Shari Franke. Remember me? We need to talk. I have new information on my siblings, and it's really bad. I need you to help us. Please. Before something awful happens."

The next few weeks were a blur of DCFS agents, lawyers—they even talked about bringing a forensic psychologist onboard. I recounted my own childhood abuse, every detail I could remember about my childhood with Ruby, my concerns that her cruel methods of psychological punishment and deprivation had worsened, and that the kids were now in significant danger. I talked until my throat was raw, begging them to step in before it was too late.

"The forensic psychologist believes there is significant evidence of emotional abuse," the DCFS caseworker told me, her voice reassuring. "We have no evidence of physical abuse. But we're going to do everything possible to get this in front of a judge and get those kids the hell out of there."

For the first time in forever, I felt a tiny spark of hope. Maybe, finally, someone with power would open their eyes and see what was happening. I prayed my heart out every day for those kids to hang on, until the right people could gather the evidence they needed and finally take action.

That little flicker of hope was snuffed out by a phone call I received about a month and a half later, on October 27, 2022.

"Shari . . . I'm so sorry." It was Kelly. She sounded upset. "We're closing the case. The DA claims there's not enough hard evidence. Without real concrete proof the abuse is happening . . . our hands are tied, it's all conjecture. It's this new law, it's making things so hard for us to investigate cases of neglect. I'm so sorry."

The phone fell from my hand, clattering to the floor. I collapsed against the wall as sobs overtook my body, sliding down until I was curled up on the floor. Hot tears streamed down my face.

"Heavenly Father," I pleaded desperately in between shuddering breaths. "Please help my family! Send us a lifeline in the form of Your light."

CHAPTER 40

mommy's mausoleum

> What is pain? Is it wrong? Is it something to be avoided? No. Pain is an opportunity for growth. It is a place where you can gain wisdom about your experience, and it is an opportunity to grow. Have you ever heard the saying "no pain, no gain" in the gym? That's what pain is for. It's an opportunity to develop, to stretch, to motivate yourself. Pain is a place where you can gain wisdom. So, the reality about pain is it's necessary. It is a gift.
> —JODI HILDEBRANDT, CONNEXIONS CLASSROOM

The crisp November air nipped at my cheeks as I walked on campus. Out of nowhere, a familiar face jumped out at me. Professor Kevin Franke. My father.

For the past year, he'd managed to steer clear of me, even though he was still teaching at BYU. We'd been like two ghosts, haunting the edges of each other's lives. But now, bam, there he was, right in front of me. I'd played out this moment in my head a million times, trying to predict how it would feel, but it still knocked the wind out of me.

Our eyes locked for a split second. He looked like hell warmed over. He shot me a strained, fake smile, then darted his gaze away, walking faster like he couldn't get away from me quick enough. Not a single word, just that pathetic little grimace.

I wanted to run after him, grab him by the shoulders, and yell in his face.

Are you blind? Where are your kids? Don't you care?

But I just stood there, frozen. Who was I kidding? He could barely keep himself afloat, let alone throw a lifeline to his drowning children.

Let it go, I thought. *He's not capable of helping.*

On December 5, my phone buzzed with a call from our neighbor. "Shari, I thought you should know," she said hesitantly. "Your mother is packing up the house. I think she's moving."

Dread clenched its fist around my heart. "What? Where? Did she say anything to you?"

"Well, she did ask about how much the HOA fees are, said she was thinking of renting out the house, or selling it. I know she's been putting belongings and furniture up online for sale."

I thanked her and hung up, my mind spinning. Was she moving her and the kids into Jodi's house in Ivins? I didn't know a soul in Jodi's neck of the woods. There'd be no one to keep an eye out, to pass on intel about how the kids were holding up. Or, even worse, what if they had something else in mind? What if they just up and vanished with the kids? Fell off the grid completely? Disappeared.

This can't be happening. I can't lose them. I CAN'T. My hands started shaking uncontrollably. I clenched them into fists, digging my nails into my palms, trying to ground myself. *Breathe, Shari. Just breathe.*

Panic rose in my throat. I felt like I needed to go to the house. I couldn't let her throw it all away. Everything from my childhood, every precious memento and keepsake, was still in that house. My tiny treasures from our family trips. The scriptures Ruby and Kevin had given me when I was baptized. Pieces of a life that had become a distant, rapidly fading dream. I couldn't let her erase me completely. I needed something, anything, to hold on to. Some scrap of proof that I'd existed.

I composed an email to Ruby, fighting to keep my tone neutral. I explained that I'd like to come retrieve a few of my things, if possible. I held my breath and hit send, hoping against hope for a civilized response.

The days ticked by with no reply. The silence was deafening, mocking. Of course. Why would Ruby make anything easy? Finally, I couldn't take it anymore.

"Dad, I need your help," I said to Mr. Haymond. "I have to go to the house in Springville and get a few of my things before it's too late. Will you come with me? I don't think I can do this alone."

"You aren't alone, Shari," he said. "I'll go with you, and we'll get your things."

The next day, we rolled up to the curb outside the house I'd grown up in. Ruby's car was MIA, thankfully. The place looked dead; all the curtains yanked shut. If the kids were home, I knew Ruby would have instructed them not answer to any knock at the door, which was locked. And I was sure they'd been told not to talk to me, especially. I was the bad guy.

So I marched around back. Dwight's old doggy door. It was a tight squeeze, but I managed to wriggle through, crash-landing on the kitchen floor in a graceless heap. *Ow. Okay. I'm in.*

I looked around. It seemed like nobody was home. A few boxes confirmed what Mrs. Gunderson had said, that Ruby was packing up. I ascended the stairs to my bedroom. The house was so quiet.

I grabbed as much as I could in just a few short minutes.

As I gathered my things, a random thought came. My parents'

wedding anniversary was just around the corner. It would have been twenty-two years.

As I sat there, clutching my measly little bag of memories, I wept. For the family I lost. For the black hole that had swallowed up my past.

Happy anniversary, Ruby and Kevin. Hope it was worth it.

CHAPTER 41

nobody's daughter

JOURNAL

I feel like an orphan. Like I'm nobody's daughter. But I know that I am His. I belong to Jesus Christ. Not even Jodi can change that.

In the midst of my sadness, a thought came to me: *Why not reach out to my aunts?* I'd never been especially close to any of them, but they were still family. And they'd never done anything bad to me.

As if the universe had heard my silent plea, that very day, my aunt Julie reached out to me on Instagram. Her message was simple, yet it felt like a lifeline.

"Hey, we just moved to Provo, not far from you. Just want you to know . . . we think about you all the time."

My heart raced as I read the rest of her message. She said she had heard about my situation, about how I'd been cut off, and she hoped I was okay. She asked if I would be interested in having dinner sometime.

I replied, my fingers shaking slightly as I typed. "I'd actually love to have dinner with you."

A flurry of activity followed. Julie told Bonnie and Ellie, and before I knew it, Ellie was driving the four hours up from St. George, where she lived, for a big dinner at Julie's house—Ruby's three sisters and me.

I approached Julie's house that evening, just two minutes away from my apartment, feeling a mix of excitement and apprehension. This dinner was . . . complicated. I hadn't seen them in years.

And yes, they had questions—so many questions. "What's going on with Ruby? What about Jodi? How are the kids?" It felt like I was being grilled, but I understood their desperate need for information. They, too, were estranged from Ruby at this point, caught in the same web of family dysfunction that had ensnared me.

The dinner, intense as it was, was also grounding. Here, finally, was some semblance of family. It wasn't perfect, it wasn't what I had lost, but it was something. A tether to my past, a possible bridge to my future.

In the weeks that followed, Aunt Julie and I grew closer. When I was around her, I felt some sense of peace wash over me, a new kind of kinship. One forged in shared pain, mutual understanding, and the tentative hope for healing. Sometimes, family isn't just what you're born into—it's also what you build in the aftermath of loss.

The glow of the television cast an eerie light across the darkened living room, the only sound the low murmur of the narrator's voice. I was curled up on the couch in my shared apartment, my eyes glued to the TV screen as another true-crime show played out before me and my roomies. Lately, I couldn't seem to watch anything else. It wasn't just morbid fascination; I think some part of me was searching for answers.

The story unfolding in front of me was chilling—a woman, trapped in a relationship with a controlling, obsessive man. As the narrator described the way he isolated her, stalked her, followed her every move, my skin crawled with a sickening sense of recognition.

I thought about the way Derek would look at me as he demanded to know where I'd been, who I'd been with. The constant barrage of texts and calls, the way he always guilt-tripped me over the smallest things. And then there were the strange, unsettling things he'd say to me.

Like that one thing he said that I couldn't get out of my head.

"You need to learn to defend yourself if ever you're in a bad situation, Shari. I'll teach you how."

A sense of unease settled in the pit of my stomach. "Really?"

A slow smile spread across his face.

"I'll just show up at your college campus, disguised, and I'll attack you. Just to see if you've been paying attention."

"*What?!*"

"Yeah! Just to make sure that you're prepared and know how to react."

He'd said it so nonchalantly. As though it wasn't a threat. But it was. I knew it was. It was him reminding me that at any given moment, he could . . . do whatever he wanted with me. And I'd be powerless to stop him.

My phone buzzed. I glanced down, my heart sinking as I saw the text from Derek.

"I know everyone in your life has let you down, Shari. You've been disappointed by a lot of people. Hurt. But I'm here for you. I am one of the few that actually cares."

I set my phone down and turned it to silent.

On the screen, the true-crime show was reaching its horrific climax—the ex-boyfriend, unable to accept that his love had moved on, had killed her. Police photos of the woman's lifeless body flashed across the screen, and suddenly I thought:

I need my father.

I wished I could have called Kevin, told him what was happening, asked for his help as my protector. He was right there, every day, teaching on the university campus. But it was as if I was invisible. My dad, still the man who had held me as a baby, who had taught me how to ride a bike and tie my shoes, could no longer see me.

He wasn't my protector anymore. He was just another person who had let me down, another person who had turned their back when I needed them most.

I glanced at the calendar on the wall, just two days until my birthday, circled in bright red marker. March 3. My birthday.

That night, as I lay in bed staring up at the ceiling, I prayed to God.

If I'm supposed to leave this situation, I need the clearest answer from you I've ever gotten in my life. I need you to help me know that I'm done with this. Please, God. Give me a sign.

The next morning, I woke with a start, tears streaming down my face. Three words rang through my mind, as clear as if they'd been spoken aloud.

It ends now.

And that was all I needed. With shaking hands, I grabbed my phone and started composing a message to my bishop. I knew what I had to do, knew what the church expected of me. But the thought of laying bare my deepest shame, my darkest secrets . . .

I closed my eyes, taking a deep breath. "Heavenly Father," I whispered, my voice cracking. "Please, give me strength. Give me courage." And then, I began to type.

"Bishop, I need to speak with you. I've done something bad, and I have to confess."

By the time I hit send, my face was streaked with tears. I was essentially sealing my fate.

I'm going to get kicked out of the church, I thought, my heart racing.

But I had to do this. I couldn't keep this inside anymore. I was willing to face whatever church discipline I needed, if it meant making things right and living my life with a clear conscience.

Next, I messaged my aunt Julie.

"Hey, I really need to talk to you guys about something."

Her response was immediate. "Sure, come over."

I left my phone at my apartment, not wanting to risk Derek seeing where I was going.

I found myself in my aunt and uncle's living room, my eyes fixed on the carpet as I tried to find the words to tell my story. It came out in bits and pieces. I didn't tell them all the details, but I think they understood.

"You poor thing," Julie said, pulling me into a tight hug. "I want you to know, we support you no matter what, Shari."

I went back to my apartment to pick up my phone, immediately returning to my aunt's house because I didn't want to be alone. I saw a barrage of texts from Derek, as usual. But that day, I couldn't bring myself to text him back right away. In fact, I waited as long as I could. The longest I'd ever gone without responding to him.

"Shari, what is going on, are you okay?" he wrote, in his hundredth text of the day. I caved and responded, just to shut him up.

"Nothing is wrong. I'm spending the day at my aunt's house," I replied.

"Which aunt?"

"My aunt Julie in Provo."

"But your phone showed you at your apartment all day."

"I forgot to bring it with me. That's why I didn't respond to you until now."

"You never leave your phone behind. You're upset about something. I can tell."

"Derek, I'm fine."

"You're sad because it's your birthday, aren't you? You're sad that you don't have your family to celebrate with. It's okay, I'm here, Shari. You won't be alone on your birthday. I'll make it special for you. I'll take you to dinner."

I couldn't bring myself to respond.

Less than thirty minutes later, I saw Derek's car pull into the street from my aunt's big living room window. I couldn't believe it—he'd used the location sharing function on my phone to track me down. I scrambled into the corner, trying to make myself as small as possible.

"He's here!" I gasped.

We all watched, frozen, as he pulled up next to my car, parked, and got out, his arms laden with gifts. He left them by my car before finally driving away, his expression dark.

Aunt Julie stared, aghast, at this nearly fifty-year-old man, acting like some love-sick Santa Claus.

"How dare he!" Julie whispered. "He's old enough to be your father! A married man, chasing after my niece!"

"I'm so sorry, I never meant to—"

Julie shook her head vehemently. "Shari, it's not your fault! That guy is completely nuts. Look at him! Do you want us to talk to him?"

"No," I said. "I'll end it myself. I'll message him later. It has to be me. Otherwise he won't believe it."

At night, I went back to my apartment and found myself on the living room couch, sobbing uncontrollably. I wasn't even trying to hide my distress from my roomies anymore.

"Shari, what happened?" asked my conservative roommate. I couldn't believe that this person, among the most religiously conforming girls I knew, was about to be the first person I'd ever fully confide in about this. But that's what happened. Through my tears, I told her everything. That there was a married man, much older than me. That I'd done things with him, very intimate things. Things I'd never wanted to do but did anyway. That I was a fornicator, an adulteress, a sinner. All the secrets I'd kept hidden for the past two years.

To my surprise, instead of judgment, I saw only compassion in her eyes. She hugged me tightly and said, "I'm so sorry this happened to you, Shari. I don't know who this man is, but he sounds . . . like a demon!"

"But I was complicit. I didn't stop it. I'm going to confess everything to my bishop."

I watched her eyes widen. "I'm probably going to get my temple recommend taken away," I added.

"No, Shari!" She shook her head, terrified.

A temple recommend is the document that certifies you're worthy to enter and participate in temple ceremonies. If you engage in serious sin, though, it can be revoked. It would be a source of great shame to me if that happened. It would distance me from God. It was the worst case scenario.

My roommate stood up and started pacing.

"No, you cannot lose your temple recommend. That wouldn't be right. This isn't your fault!"

My other roommate came in, and I explained what was going on.

"Shari, what are you going to do?" she asked, in shock.

"End it. But he's going to be very upset when I do. So from now on, we have to be extra cautious—we need to keep doors closed, blinds drawn, and everything locked."

They nodded, looking scared.

Then I took a deep breath and stood up, my phone in my hand.

"It's time. I'll do it in private, if that's okay."

I went into my bedroom and sat on the bed. With trembling fingers, I typed out the message, my heart pounding.

"Derek, I'm done. It's over. I want you to leave me alone. Forever."

My finger hovered over the send button, my heart pounding against my rib cage. He wouldn't let me go easily. But I couldn't keep living like this.

I hit send.

His response was swift, and cold.

"Wow, Shari. Well, I guess I was right. You never did care about me. You're a liar."

"That's not true. I did care. But this is wrong. And I'm just not okay with where this has ended up. It has to stop. Do not contact me ever again."

"Fine, Shari," he responded. "Have a good life."

I blocked his phone number and stared at my phone for what felt like hours before hearing a soft knock on the door.

"Can we come in?"

"Yes."

My roommates came in, and sat with me, quietly.

"Shari, isn't it your birthday?" one asked.

I nodded.

"Yeah."

"We should get stuff to make pizzas and watch a movie!" said the other, brightly. "No one should be allowed to ruin this day."

Their kindness and understanding meant more to me than they'll ever know.

The next day, my bishop and I had a Zoom call. I was going to confess.

The Zoom window flickered to life, revealing Bishop Johnson's concerned face. I took a deep breath, my hands shaking slightly as I adjusted my laptop screen.

"Shari, I'm glad you reached out. What's troubling you?" His voice was gentle, encouraging.

I swallowed hard. "I don't even know where to start."

"Take your time," he said softly. "Remember, we're here to help you find peace."

Tears welled up in my eyes as I struggled to find the words. "I got involved with someone . . . a married man. Derek. And things happened that shouldn't have. It's all my fault. I knew better, but I still . . ."

The bishop listened intently, his brow furrowed with concern. When I finished, he leaned closer to the camera. "Shari, I want you to listen to me very carefully. You were put in a situation no young person should have to face."

I burst into tears. For the first time, I felt a glimmer of understanding that maybe, just maybe, I wasn't entirely to blame.

Bishop Johnson's voice was gentle, but his eyes were serious. "Normally, in a situation like this, the minimum level of church discipline is losing your temple recommend," he said, his brow furrowed.

"I know. I'm ready to accept whatever punishment I deserve."

Bishop Johnson held up a hand, shaking his head. "Hold on, Shari. I'm not sure punishment is what you need right now."

"Thank you, Bishop, I know that."

"Ultimately, it's not up to me to decide what course of action the church wishes to take. I'll have to give the stake president a call and discuss these allegations."

The stake president was one level higher in the hierarchy and would give my bishop instructions on what to do.

A couple of days went by, each minute feeling like an eternity. When my phone finally rang, showing my bishop's number, I jumped, desperate to hear what he had to say.

"So, I talked it over with the stake president," he said, his tone measured. "He reminded me that we do have a responsibility to ensure that our members are living in accordance with God's laws. He thinks it's best if you take a break from the temple for a bit and hold off on taking the sacrament for a little while, while we investigate. I'm sorry, Shari."

"So I'm losing my temple recommend," I confirmed, a bitter taste in my mouth.

"For now, yes, I'm afraid so."

I felt a flicker of anger, hot and sharp in my chest. "And what about Derek? What's going to happen with him? Will he lose his temple recommend, too?"

"It's not up to me. I'm going to need his full name and address so that I can reach out to his bishop. I'll let you know what course of action they decide to take."

"I understand," I said.

"I'll pray for you, Shari."

"Thank you, Bishop."

There was nothing more I could say or do. The nightmare was over. At least, I thought it was, until the emails started.

"Shari, I'm so sorry, I've deeply hurt you."

"I hope you can forgive me someday."

"I'd just like things to end on a better note. We should talk."

I blocked Derek's email address, but he just created a new one, sending me more messages, begging to see me.

"Shari, you can't do this. I need you. And you need me."

"DON'T DO THIS."

Text messages started coming from his son's number—his son was on an LDS mission abroad at the time—an incessant, never-ending stream of manipulation and guilt-tripping.

One day, I saw his truck drive by my apartment building, circling the block, and that's when I got really scared. My roommates and I huddled in the living room, curtains drawn, one of them peeking out to make sure he was gone before any of us dared to leave the apartment.

Eventually, the texts, emails, and the drive-bys stopped, but I remained hypervigilant, always on high alert. Always looking over my shoulder, always double-checking the locks, worried he was going to show up and . . . take me.

Derek received no disciplinary action whatsoever—he denied everything, and his bishop believed him without question. He was high up in the church, after all. Who would take my word over his?

It didn't help that I'd deleted all his texts and emails—there was no proof. But still, it didn't make sense to me. If they really believed nothing had ever happened, why had they taken away my temple recommend? If I was a fornicator, then so was he. It takes two to tango, as they say.

After a month, the stake president agreed to give me my temple recommend back. But it still didn't undo the fact that I'd been made to feel like this was all my fault. My bishop advised me not to be upset, to just put it behind me. But how could I? I lost all trust and faith. Not in God, but in these men who, when faced with a young woman's pain, decided to brush it under the carpet and protect their friend.

In the end, I decided to change my ward, to start fresh with a new bishop and a new community. It would mean worshipping with a different congregation, with strangers. But that was okay. My Heavenly Father knew the depths of my heart and the strength of my spirit. From now on, in Him alone would I place my trust. And no one else.

CHAPTER 42

true crimes

In the spring of 2023, I finally broke the news to Kevin's parents about the family's disintegration. Grandpa Franke was in his late eighties, and Grandma Franke was nearing eighty, and they were woefully out of touch with the digital world, where much of our family drama played out. No social media, barely able to operate their iPhones; they were relics of a different era, and, until that day, blissfully unaware of the complexities of our modern family crisis.

Grandma greeted me at the door, her face lighting up. "Shari! What a lovely surprise. Come in, come in. You want some ice cream?"

As we sat around their worn kitchen table, the weight of what I had to say pressed down on me.

"So, how's everyone doing?" Grandma said, her eyes hopeful. "We haven't heard from Kevin in such a long while. He must be very busy with work."

I took a deep breath. "Well, that's why I'm here. There's something you need to know."

As I explained the situation—Kevin moving out, Ruby taking the kids, my estrangement—I watched their expressions shift from confusion to heartbreak.

Grandpa's weathered hand trembled as he set down his mug. "I don't understand. Kevin left Ruby?"

"She told him to leave."

Grandma's voice quavered. "And the children? Where are they?"

"I don't know, Grandma. No one's seen them for months. Ruby's gotten involved with this group. . . . They have some strange ideas about family and parenting. She's cut off contact with a lot of people, including me. And her parents and sisters."

"That doesn't sound like Ruby at all! She loves her mother!" Grandma protested weakly.

"Yeah, I guess she changed her mind."

The silence that followed was deafening.

"Don't worry, Grandma," I said. "I'm working with social services, and we're going to make sure the kids are okay. I'll keep you updated on things. I'm sure everything will get figured out soon."

"You're a good girl, Shari," said my grandfather, his voice wavering.

Weeks later, during another visit, Grandma cornered me in the kitchen, her voice hushed. "Shari, dear, have you heard anything from Kevin? Or any of the children? We're just so worried."

I felt a pang of frustration mixed with sympathy. "Grandma, I'm sorry. I don't know anything new. The second I find out anything, you'll be the first to know."

"But surely, there must be—"

I cut her off, as gently as I could. "Grandma, please. If I know anything, I promise I'll tell you. But asking all the time . . . it doesn't help. It just hurts us both."

She nodded, tears welling up. "I'm sorry, dear. I feel so helpless."

I hugged her then, feeling the fragility of her frame, the weight of her worry.

Throughout the spring and summer of 2023, I remained stuck in a nightmarish loop. My calls to the police and DCFS were getting us nowhere, thanks to Utah's "free-range parenting" law. Passed in 2018, the law was intended to protect parents who allow their children more independence—but it was absolutely sabotaging anyone's ability to protect my siblings.

On the surface, this legislation seemed like a breath of fresh air for parents who believe in fostering independence in their children. The law essentially redefined neglect, making it clear that allowing kids to engage in independent activities—like walking to school alone, playing outside unsupervised, or staying home by themselves—isn't inherently neglectful. But the law's vague language was open to interpretation that could potentially be exploited by those looking to justify genuine neglect, or even abuse.

Worst of all, it heavily impacted the ability of child-welfare agencies to respond to complaints of neglect. Faced with the fear of violating this new legislation, social workers and other professionals found that their hands were tied when asked to intervene in situations, even when it was clear that children were genuinely at risk, with potentially devastating consequences for vulnerable kids who desperately need help—like my siblings.

Even the disturbing videos Ruby and Jodi kept posting in their ConneXions Classroom weren't seen as cause enough to justify an intervention. They continued spouting their increasingly alarming ideas: that adults can force children to do whatever they want, that children have no right to privacy or autonomy, that medication is a sign of living in distortion. They railed against social media, claiming it was "corrupting" children and "turning them gay," while asserting that being gay was a sin and a choice. They argued that phones were more dangerous than guns and that school shootings were simply a result of people being "disconnected."

In just one episode, "Truthful Touch," Ruby unleashed a barrage of alarming statements, offering a disturbing window into her unhinged mindset. Most chillingly, she declared:

"If your child comes to you on fire, you don't pat them on the head and say, 'It's okay, I'll help you.' No, you beat them, and you kick them, and you hit them with a rod.

"You cannot put welts on your child's legs and then lovingly apply gauze and expect healing."

This statement sent shivers down my spine. *Welts?* Was this a hypothetical scenario? Or an admission? The casual way she spoke about inflicting harm on a child made my skin crawl. It wasn't just the words themselves, but the matter-of-fact tone, as if discussing something as mundane as making breakfast. I knew how harsh Ruby could be, when it came to child discipline. But this felt different. This felt like . . . sadism.

My mind raced down dark pathways. The image of my younger siblings, vulnerable and at the mercy of someone capable of such thoughts was haunting me, and every day that passed with Ruby having custody felt like watching a countdown to disaster. How long before her rhetoric might transform into irreparable harm—if it hadn't already?

Even with all of this disturbing content out there on the internet, accessible to anyone with a web browser, legally, there was nothing we could do to extract the children from her custody, thanks to that free-range-parenting law. The system designed to protect the vulnerable was failing spectacularly, leaving my siblings trapped in what I feared was a nightmare come to life. How could something so glaringly wrong be allowed to continue? And where the hell was Kevin?

In June 2023, news reached me that Kevin had abruptly abandoned his professor position at BYU. A pang of sadness hit me; his contributions in the field of geotechnical earthquake research could have saved countless lives in seismic zones around the world. But a bitter irony struck me—here was a man who'd dedicated his life to protecting people yet remained paralyzed in the face of the catastrophe unfolding in his own family.

What would it take for Kevin to redirect even a fraction of the energy he'd poured into his research toward safeguarding his own flesh and blood? I wished Kevin could somehow find the strength to stand up and fight against the real dangers that loomed over us—the most pressing being Ruby, the woman who had full, unchecked custody of my siblings. The same woman who brazenly discussed putting welts on kids' legs as if it were a normal parenting technique.

Forget earthquakes, Kevin. The ground beneath our feet was already crumbling.

JOURNAL

Tomorrow, it will have been a year since Dad was invited to leave. It also happens to be Pioneer Day. In a way, I feel like I'm a pioneer for myself and family. I'm breaking generations of abuse and evil. I will be better to my kids than my parents ever were to theirs.

On top of everything else that was happening, I was scrambling to find a place to live. The lease on my shared two-bedroom apartment was ending, and obviously I couldn't go back home to Springville. I'd lined up a one-bedroom apartment off-campus in Provo and was supposed to move in over the summer. Just me, all alone.

The problem was that Derek had cosigned the lease, months before I'd cut him out of my life. I didn't really get what cosigning meant back then. I had no credit or rental history, so when the landlord said I needed a cosigner, I was stuck. My parents weren't talking to me, so Derek had stepped in, offering to cosign. It felt like he was helping me out, but looking back, I can see it was just another way for him to maintain control over me.

After cutting things off with Derek, I knew I had to get out of that lease. I wanted—no, I needed—to go somewhere he wouldn't know about. Somewhere I could feel safe. I found myself on the phone with the landlord, trying to figure out how to cancel the contract. Luckily, he understood my situation and canceled the lease.

But that left me with a new problem: I had to find another place to live before my senior year started. It was stressful, searching for a new home with time running out. It wasn't until mid-August that I finally found a solution—some BYU students had an extra room in their apartment in Provo, and, thankfully, with days before the semester started, I moved myself and my few possessions in there.

As I unpacked my stuff in my new room, I felt both safe and unsure. Derek didn't know where I was now, which was a huge weight off my shoulders. But I also felt lost, drowning in the unending chaos of my life, facing the question of how to juggle a new semester of school with the ongoing drama in my family. The past year had tested me in ways I never imagined possible. I felt bent, nearly broken, by the forces tearing my family apart. And yet, here I was, still clinging to hope with a desperation that surprised even me.

Whatever was coming—good or bad, triumph or tragedy—I would face it head-on.

JOURNAL

I get the feeling something is going to happen with my family soon. I can't tell if it will be good or bad, but I feel it will be big. But I refuse to believe, after everything I've gone through in the past year, that I won't be given an opportunity to help my family be together again. I will do whatever God wants from me, in order to achieve that.

Shortly after moving into my new shared apartment, I sat with my new roommates in the living room, watching a true-crime documentary, *Sins of Our Mother*. It was about an LDS couple, Lori Vallow and Chad Daybell. They had gotten married super fast after both their spouses died under sketchy circumstances—Chad's former wife, Tammy Daybell, died in October 2019 under suspicious circumstances, and Lori's former husband, Charles Vallow, was shot and killed by Lori's brother in July 2019.

In September 2019, Lori's two children, Tylee Ryan, sixteen, and Joshua "JJ" Vallow, seven, were reported missing. Lori and Chad married in November 2019, just weeks after Tammy Daybell's death, and while their kids were still missing.

The couple were immersed in the same extreme religious beliefs and doomsday preparations as Jodi and Ruby, and the way this family spiraled into darkness felt horribly familiar: their intense belief in the Second Coming and their obsession with Thom Harrison's *Visions of Glory* prophecies. It was all the same stuff Ruby and Jodi were always going on about.

But it wasn't until watching that documentary that my hope faded into the darkest thoughts I'd had yet—Ruby and Jodi were just as unhinged as Chad and Lori, if not worse.

If we don't do something soon, my siblings are going to die.

Thank goodness for our Springville neighbors, my loyal allies in this fight. They were right there with me, leaving food on the doorstep of our house in case the kids were hungry, making call after call to DCFS, voicing their concerns about the kids being left alone for days on end when Ruby went to Ivins to see Jodi, leaving them without proper food or care.

But even as the hurdles kept piling up, I could feel a shift inside myself. Through therapy, meds, and a whole lot of hard work, I was getting stronger, better equipped to handle the emotional storms that had once threatened to drown me. Derek was no longer in my life. The fog of shame and self-blame was starting to lift, replaced by a new sense of clarity and purpose.

For years, I'd been pulled in two directions. One voice commanded me to be the perfect obedient daughter, putting my faith in supposed authorities. But another voice demanded that this time, I think for myself. That I had the courage to disobey anyone or anything that tried to dehumanize me or those I love.

Not mindless submission, but faithfulness to my own inner truth. Faithfulness to the divinity and sovereign worth of my God-given life on this earth.

Armed with this newfound strength, I doubled down on my efforts to come up with a plan to save my siblings. I'd be damned if I let them become another cautionary tale. I kept calling DCFS, kept studying the law surrounding child abuse, kept searching for legal avenues to save my siblings.

I kept trying until that phone call from my neighbor on August 23, 2023.

It was a Wednesday, and for as long as I live, I'll never forget hearing my neighbor's words.

"Shari, the police are at your mother's house!"

CHAPTER 43

the house of my mother

I stood paralyzed on the front lawn, my breath shallow, my hands shaking. The red and blue lights of the squad cars strobed as I stood in front of my house, frozen. Ruby's white 8 Passengers van sat in the driveway like a beached whale, gleaming under the pulsing lights.

Please God, let the children be okay, I prayed silently, my heart in my throat.

Crack! They slammed the battering ram into the door so hard I jumped. Wood splinters flew everywhere.

"Police! Everyone out, NOW!"

The team rushed inside, weapons drawn, voices booming off the walls. I felt like I couldn't breathe, couldn't think. This couldn't be real.

"Look everywhere! Any closet, any crawlspace, anywhere a child could hide!" an officer barked.

Half-packed boxes littered the floor. It was obvious that Ruby had been preparing to leave, before the world closed in.

But nobody was home.

Where are my siblings? I thought, desperate.

Later that day, I sat with a detective in a brightly lit room, my hands trembling as I tried to process the whirlwind of events that had shattered my world.

"So, Ruby had the youngest kids locked up at Jodi's house?" I asked, swallowing hard against the lump in my throat. "Why had they taken them there?"

The detective's eyes softened with sympathy, but his voice remained professional. "We're not sure; all I can tell you is that they're both safe now."

"And you've arrested both Jodi and my mother?" I asked, my voice cracking slightly.

"Yes," he confirmed, his tone grave. "Jodi first, then your mother upon her return to Jodi's property." He hesitated for a moment, as if weighing his words carefully. "Both women have been charged with multiple counts of aggravated child abuse, and they've been denied bail."

"What does that mean, aggravated?" I asked, my voice barely above a whisper, a part of me desperately wishing I could take back the question, to remain in ignorance for just a moment longer.

The detective leaned forward slightly, frowning. "Well," he began, his voice gentler now, "typically it involves repeated acts of abuse over time, showing a pattern of cruelty." He paused, gauging my reaction before continuing. "It can also include extreme neglect, confinement, or intentional infliction of serious physical harm on a child."

Each word was a dagger, twisting deeper into my heart.

"I'm so sorry, Shari," the detective added softly, and I nodded, numb, unable to form words, wondering what kind of a monster could ever inflict that kind of suffering on a child.

That night, alone in the silence of my room, I finally surrendered to the tsunami of emotions. Great, heaving sobs wracked my body, each one releasing years of pent-up fear, uncertainty, and anguish. *It's over,* I told myself, the words becoming a mantra in my mind. *Ruby will never touch them again. Jodi will never touch them again.* I repeated it over and over, willing myself to believe it, to internalize the truth of it.

I drifted into an exhausted sleep, my mind and body drained. I had been so focused on this moment for so long that I had no road map for what came next. Healing. Justice. Rebuilding. There was still a long road ahead, I knew that. But that night, for the first time in longer than I could remember, I could sleep in peace. My siblings were finally safe. For now, that was enough. For now, it was everything.

CHAPTER 44

rings of remembrance

DCFS had custody of all my siblings except Chad. I still didn't know exactly what Ruby and Jodi had done to the youngest ones. No one really did at that point. I focused on the now, and the knowledge that they were finally safe from harm. Far away from Ruby and Jodi.

When they were first taken into custody, both Ruby and Jodi played dumb, acting as though there must have been some terrible mistake. Ruby refused to speak during her first interview with police. Jodi, on the other hand, played the role of the traumatized victim with haunting precision. She sat in the interrogation room, her eyes wide and brimming with manufactured disbelief, gently insisting that there had been a terrible misunderstanding. Her act was as transparent as it was sickening.

After their initial processing, Ruby and Jodi were relocated together from St. George to Purgatory Correctional Facility in Hurricane, Utah. The irony of the name wasn't lost on me as I tried to imagine their journey. Ruby later told Kevin that the fifteen-minute drive was spent in silence, saying she couldn't bear to speak to or even look at Jodi. I can only imagine what thoughts might have been racing through Ruby's mind as she sat there, her hands cuffed, staring out the window. Did she think of her children, of the life she'd left behind? Or was she lost in the enormity of what she'd done, what she'd become? I can imagine the fear clawing at her insides, the desperation to wake up from this nightmare. But there was no waking up from this. This was Ruby's new reality. Our new reality.

Kevin was brought in for interrogation shortly after Ruby's arrest, as the police tried to determine the circumstances surrounding the chain of events. He seemed unaware of the situation, telling police Ruby had called him to pick up the kids the day she was arrested, but he wasn't sure why. When asked about his family, Kevin admitted, "I haven't seen them for over a year. I've been . . . separated from my wife and family. I have some problems."

He said that Jodi and Ruby shared a close relationship, that Jodi had recognized his need for help and that it was Ruby who had invited him to leave and take some space. Kevin said that he agreed with her decision, stating that the time apart had been exactly what he needed to confront his own "addictions."

"The space has been very, very good for me," he said, parroting Jodi and Ruby's manipulative rhetoric. The disconnect between Kevin's calm demeanor and the reality of what had happened was staggering. But he was still living in an alternate universe, one in which he'd been brainwashed into believing that abandoning his family was somehow therapeutic.

The police probed deeper, questioning Kevin's lack of knowledge about his children's living situation. He explained his role: "My job is to financially provide. I pay the bills with my job. I provide the money, which goes into a shared bank account." In the police raid on Jodi's home that led to her arrest, investigators had found a stash of $85,000 in cash hidden in the house—Ruby had cleaned out not only the joint accounts she shared with Kevin but also all her children's savings accounts, except mine. (I'd already moved my money to a separate account in my name only.)

Kevin said the last time he'd seen Ruby was five days prior. She'd told him in light of their separation, she was looking for ways to make money and asked him to sign over the titles to the cars she drove and wanted his permission for vague "investments" she refused to elaborate on. What he didn't know was that Ruby wanted to sell the house and couldn't because Kevin's name was on the mortgage. He confessed that he would have signed anything Ruby put in front of him, no questions asked. Luckily, Ruby's arrest happened before she had a chance to put any paperwork in front of him and strip away the family's assets.

Kevin still seemed confused as to why he had been called in for questioning until police painted a picture of what they suspected Ruby and Jodi had done to my youngest siblings, and the condition in which they had been found. Kevin was shocked, responding, "That sounds horrible. Disgusting. No human being should be treated like that."

The police informed Kevin that his children, aside from me and Chad, were now in the custody of DCFS and under a medical hold for seventy-two hours. Kevin became emotional, asking, "What's going to happen with my wife? I love my wife." He continued to express trust in Ruby, seemingly caught between loyalty to his wife and the shocking revelations about what she and Jodi had done to their children.

"I am completely misunderstood," Ruby said, in her first call to Kevin directly after her arrest, expressing no remorse. "That is the most horrible feeling. Like my own family misunderstands me, they misinterpret me, and poor Jodi, they misinterpret her, they misunderstand her."

She continued, her voice rising with emotion, "I mean, it is just horrendous. But you know what, like Joseph Smith, every wonderful man of God has been misunderstood. I'm going to get out of this. Who knows, maybe in ten days I'll get out of this."

Her words came faster now, as if she was caught up in a vision. "God spoke to me when I was driving, before I called you. The Spirit said, *Your children are going to be removed.*"

A long pause.

"I'm committed to our family," Kevin said. "I'm committed to you and our marriage, no matter what happened."

"Well, thank you for stepping up," was Ruby's reply.

Amazingly, Ruby had expressed confusion as to why anyone would be concerned about the shocking state her youngest kids had been found in. "I don't understand why they're in the hospital; they're perfectly fine," she declared.

The children were not *fine*. I knew that much. So did everyone who'd seen them. Paramedics. Police. Witnesses to the outcome of Jodi's and my mother's acts of extraordinary cruelty.

I asked the police if I could go into my house to gather some personal items that had not been confiscated as evidence: journals, tablets, cell phones, and passports. And trinkets that I wanted to make sure were safe, like the little brooch Kevin got me when he went to Italy, which I wanted to give to one of my kids one day.

I walked in, accompanied by an officer, and looked around. I found one of Ruby's laptops and easily figured out her password to her Apple iCloud account. I read some text messages, emails, and journal entries in the Notes app that confirmed for me the truth about the nature of her relationship with Jodi and how it had spilled over into the physical. Ruby, expressing her frustration about having to cater to Jodi's needs for physical affection without getting anything in return. My mother, servicing someone else? First time for everything.

I didn't read on. What happened between them, romantically, was none of my business. I didn't care to know nor think about it any further.

My eyes fixed on the door to the master bedroom—Ruby and Kevin's room. Before I could second-guess myself, I walked over and pushed the door open. It looked so normal, so unchanged, that for a moment I could almost pretend that nothing had happened. That any minute, Ruby would walk in, complaining about the mess or lecturing about the importance of making beds.

My eyes landed on Ruby's ornate jewelry box atop the dresser. Inside, nestled on velvet, lay the rings—beautiful, sparkling testaments to the milestones of Ruby and Kevin's relationship. Anniversary gifts, birthday presents, spontaneous tokens of affection. Each one carefully chosen by Kevin, each one a symbol of his love and commitment.

I saw the first engagement ring he got her, from the days when my parents were young and money was tight. It was very simple, a modest band with a tiny diamond. A few years ago, Kevin had surprised Ruby with an upgrade—a huge, glittering diamond surrounded by two thick silver bands. A gesture of his unconditional love for the wife he thought he knew.

Was it possible that all the love, all the attraction had been one-sided? A current flowing from Kevin to Ruby, never quite making the return journey? If Ruby had never truly loved Kevin, what did that make me? The product of a false love, a union where Ruby saw in Kevin not a partner to cherish but a means to an end? A sperm donor and a sidekick in her grand plans?

Almost without thinking, I slid both bands onto my own fingers. Ruby didn't deserve those rings. Not after what she'd done.

I stared at my hand, making a silent vow of eternal remembrance. *I will never forget what you did, Ruby*, I promised myself, staring hard at the bands on my fingers.

I understand the fickle nature of memory—how our minds can sometimes erase the most painful experiences, leaving behind a sanitized version of the past. But I couldn't afford that luxury. I needed to remember, to hold onto the harsh reality of what happened, of what she did to our family. Those rings weren't just jewelry; they were anchors, tethering me to a past I couldn't allow myself to forget.

When I slip those rings onto my finger, it's not out of nostalgia or lingering affection for Ruby. They're not mementos of happier times or symbols of a mother's love. No, these rings serve a far more crucial purpose. They're a contract I've made with myself, a constant reminder cast in metal. With those rings, I bind myself to the truth.

CHAPTER 45

evidence in plain sight

Kevin was furious when he found out that I'd gone home and taken those journals, tablets, cell phones, and everyone's passports from the house, even though I was accompanied by the police. He was still so ill, so brainwashed, back then, still loyal to Ruby and Jodi above all.

Kevin told the cops they should charge me with burglary, and they pretty much laughed in his face, pointing out that I had just as much right to retrieve items from the family home as he did.

"Kevin was displeased with this answer and advised we would be hearing from his attorney," an officer wrote in his report.

I felt sorry for Kevin, more than anything.

I gave the items back to the cops, and they returned everything to Kevin. I didn't focus on it too much, at the time. For now, there were more pressing issues at hand—ensuring that justice would be served.

At first, Ruby spoke out in Jodi's defense, but that loyalty quickly dissolved when she realized she could improve her own situation by turning against her friend. By pleading guilty and agreeing to testify against Jodi, Ruby could paint herself as a victim of Jodi's manipulative influence during the abuse of my siblings. With Utah's current push for justice reform emphasizing rehabilitation over punishment, Ruby's strategy was clear: show remorse, keep a low profile, and hope for an early release on good behavior.

Ruby's guilty plea to four counts of aggravated child abuse with consecutive sentencing meant a maximum of thirty years under Utah law, and possibly as little as four years. Adding more charges wouldn't have increased her potential sentence. It was infuriating to think that Ruby's manipulative tactics could lead to a shortened sentence, despite the unimaginable suffering she'd inflicted on my siblings.

After Ruby's arrest, an unexpected emotional storm hit me. At first, I couldn't make sense of it. It wasn't until I sat down with Dana, my therapist, that I began to unravel the complex emotions I was experiencing. Alongside the horror I felt toward my mother's actions, I found myself drowning in a tidal wave of guilt and self-loathing—all stemming from what had happened with Derek. The sense that I was a homewrecker, a fundamentally bad person, overwhelmed me to the point where I questioned my will to live.

"Why am I thinking about Derek now?" I asked Dana, tears streaming down my face. "It's over, it's been over for months. I don't know what to do! I can't handle these feelings, not on top of everything else."

Ruby had implanted in me very effective mechanisms for intense guilt, shame, and self-loathing. The situation with Derek was the first real-world instance where I faced the repercussions of this conditioning. Understanding this connection was crucial. My experience with Derek was the first example of how my inner critic could lead me to a dangerous mental state, fraught with anxiety, panic attacks, and self-blame—a state that, for many, can lead to suicidal thoughts.

As Dana and I peeled back the layers, we realized that addressing what had happened with Derek was crucial before we could even begin to unpack the complex layers of my upbringing with Ruby. How could I hope to understand twenty years of Ruby's influence if I couldn't make sense of what had happened over the past two years with Derek? The guilt I felt was so intense, so all-encompassing, that it was becoming a barrier to addressing anything else.

I had once believed that as soon as Ruby was out of my life, the negative voices in my head would eventually disappear. But they were still steering the ship. I was overwhelmed and unable to process what was happening. I would need to learn new tools to recognize and manage my intense emotions if I ever hoped to truly reclaim my narrative, and my life.

In early December 2023, Ruby called Chad from prison. As fate would have it, I was with him at the time. With a grim nod, he answered and put the call on speakerphone, allowing me to bear witness. Ruby's voice, once commanding and self-assured, now came through in hushed, almost reverent tones. She spoke of her recent deep dives into scripture, desperately searching for meaning in her current circumstances.

"I was reading in Doctrine and Covenants," she said, referencing one of our church's foundational text, "Christ had a bitter cup he didn't want to drink, but he did, because that was his mission. I'm drinking my bitter cup now."

There she was again—Ruby, fallen family vlogger, comparing herself to Christ on the cross. And in her narrative, the rest of the world was cast as the Romans, cruel persecutors forcing her to drink vinegar. Chad and I locked eyes, mine wide with disbelief, his dark with disgust. The delusion was breathtaking. Comparing her suffering to that of the Savior? It was a breathtaking display of narcissism, a twisting of faith so profound it bordered on blasphemy.

Publicly, though, Ruby's narrative had shifted dramatically, to one of humility and contrition. Likely on the advice of her legal team, she began describing her arrest as "the strangest and most miraculous intervention." She claimed that being separated from Jodi had brought her clarity: "I'm not hearing her. And I think not hearing her has cleared a lot of things up for me." Ruby started emphasizing her own susceptibility to Jodi's influence: "How gullible was I? Oh my gosh, how much power I gave this person. And I didn't see it."

However, Ruby had already pleaded guilty to severely abusing the children by this point. Her claims of being under Jodi's spell could only explain so much of her actions. The truth remained that she had actively participated in the abuse of my siblings, and no amount of revisionist history could erase that fact. Ruby should not be allowed to manipulate the legal system into an early release and paint herself as solely a victim of Jodi's manipulation. She was a malignant narcissist who needed proper psychological help and rehabilitation if she was ever going to be able to safely reenter society.

The evidence of her preexisting abuse was already out there, online, in the form of thirteen hundred 8 Passengers videos she'd made during her seven years of vlogging. Alongside all the other evidence, those videos would surely provide proof that Ruby had utilized harsh and excessive discipline against her children, long before Jodi came on the scene. I took it upon myself to create a compendium of those videos, so that the prosecution could more fully understand the person they were dealing with. That, for me, Ruby had always been an abuser.

The thought of going through more than a thousand videos was overwhelming, so I posted a story on Instagram, inviting people to DM me questionable or concerning clips from Ruby's old videos. The response was immediate, supportive, and enthusiastic, so much so I started a Google Doc where people could post links. I felt stronger, knowing I wasn't in this alone. Within about six hours, the Google Doc was filled with dozens of links to video footage showing Ruby being Ruby.

Showing her taking away the kids' bedrooms, withholding food as punishment, canceling Christmas for the youngest kids for being "selfish." What an ironic reversal—the woman obsessed with sharing her most intimate family moments online in exchange for fame and money was about to be exposed by those same videos; evidence of her sins, proof of her mean and bizarre parenting philosophies.

And then, of course, there was the ConneXions Classroom: hours upon hours of footage showcasing Ruby and Jodi preaching their dangerous ideology. Their obsession with pain, their vitriol against children and those struggling with mental health issues. Their strange and unyielding manifesto was laid bare, word for word, straight from the source.

The harsh reality of her situation was finally sinking in for Ruby. Even in a prison population filled with women accused of heinous crimes like murder and assault, Ruby quickly realized that convicted child abusers were considered the lowest of the low. In a letter to Kevin, her fear was palpable. She confessed her terror of being attacked, writing that she was constantly on edge, afraid she might be shanked at any moment. Ruby described a delicate balancing act: learning to keep her head down while not allowing herself to be perceived as weak or vulnerable.

As I read about her struggles, I felt a confusing mix of emotions. Part of me couldn't help but worry for her safety, despite everything she had done. The thought of anyone, even Ruby, living in constant fear was unsettling. But another part of me, the part still raw from the pain she had inflicted on our family, whispered a harsh truth:

Ruby, you did this to yourself.

CHAPTER 46

home sweet home

Kevin had moved back into our house permanently. Every night, he slept alone in his too-big bed in his too-quiet house, haunted by "if onlys," caught in an endless feedback loop of his own failures, the warning signs he overlooked, the moments he could have been braver, stronger, better. But the past can't be unwritten. It can only be reckoned with, learned from, one brutal day at a time. He had been making huge strides, mentally, and was in therapy, as was I, as we learned to stand side by side again as imperfect partners in recovery from what happened.

I could tell he was trying to make things better, to repair his relationship with his kids, to prepare the home for the kids' eventual return. He'd have to prove to the authorities, of course, that he was responsible enough to be their father again, and that would take time. For now, he was trying his best to turn Ruby's house into a home.

The first thing he did was get two new puppies—a Cavapoo named Ren and a Bernedoodle called Stimpy. He'd emptied out

Ruby's pantry, keeping only the freeze-dried food, buckets of flour, and rice. All the canned goods got donated. Except for the cans expired by five years (we had fun trashing those). "As long as we have enough to feed us for a few months, that's all we need," he said. "The rest is just . . . clutter."

As he cleansed the house of its past under Ruby's dominion, he told us that once everyone was home again, we could decorate our rooms however we want. "I don't care anymore, make it your own space," he said. "And hey, you know what, you can all have TVs in your rooms, too."

Sure, the house was messier, but it felt lived-in. Shoes in the house? No problem. Animals on the couch? Kevin didn't bat an eye.

I was living in my own one-bedroom apartment near campus—no roomies this time—completing my final year of school. I'd begun to push back against that ingrained minimalism taught to me by Ruby. A few carefully selected photos—my senior portraits—were taped to the walls, tentative steps toward self-expression, toward making my space truly my own and inhabiting my world on my own terms.

Still, until the kids were back home, there was no way I could even begin to relax.

That Christmas of 2023, it was just Kevin and me in the house, both of us feeling depressed that the seven of us couldn't be together as a family for the holidays. Not yet.

We were sitting on the couch when he suddenly turned to me.

"You know, I've always wanted to get a cat," he mused.

I perked up. "Really? Me too!"

Before I knew it, we were in the car, heading to look at some kittens from a local ad. That's how we ended up with Katniss, Kevin's cat, and Muppet, who would be mine, my son in cat form.

I brought him home and settled into life with my chaotic little tornado of mayhem. Muppet was literally bouncing off the walls 24/7, landing on my head during Zoom calls, climbing my hair, only to pass out on my computer keyboard, purring, as soon as it was time for me to do homework.

Now that I was a parent (albeit to a feline), I found it even more impossible to understand what Ruby and Jodi meant about the hardships of motherhood, the dangers of putting the needs of a little bundle of joy above your own.

The thing I liked most about Muppet was that he, like all cats, is utterly immune to any form of discipline. Obedience? Forget about it. I could only imagine trying to explain to Muppet that his lust for Cheez-Its was distorted and that he was going to be damned.

No, my furball was on his own unique life path, and I was honored to witness him and his frankly bizarre and mystifying choices, and provide whatever snacks he needs along the way. One thing is for sure; I had no intention of putting him on YouTube and monetizing our little party of two. Nope, Shari and Muppet's special moments would be just for us, and us alone.

CHAPTER 47

judgment day

JOURNAL

As much as I don't love the woman, Ruby is my mother and deserves a free and fair trial. I'm devastated I don't get privacy in any of this, but that's been my life for a long time.

On Tuesday, February 20, 2024, the day of my mother's sentencing, I found myself waking up in St. George, having made the four-hour journey down with Kevin and Chad the previous day.

As the miles stretched out before us, Kevin and I engaged in an intense discussion about the current legal situation, while Chad remained engrossed in his phone in the back seat. Some things never change.

Conversation focused on what the next steps would be for getting restitution from Jodi. We had learned that she had listed her house on the market for $5.3 million, and we were convinced that she was attempting to dispose of her assets in a desperate bid to prevent them from being seized by the courts. The thought of Jodi evading financial responsibility for the harm she had inflicted on the children was unthinkable, and our lawyer was working to secure a restraining order that would prevent her from liquidating her assets until a fair and just allocation of restitution and reparations could be made for the children, providing the necessary resources for their ongoing mental health treatment and support.

We arrived in St. George and had a strangely normal evening, the three of us getting Indian food and watching basketball. It was almost like old times. A fleeting glimpse of the life we once knew, a reminder that beneath the pain and trauma, the bonds that connected us were still there. Kevin wasn't a pod person anymore. There was a lot more work to do, a lot more healing to happen for all of us, but for now, we were united in the same cause. Making sure justice was served and the children's futures protected.

The next morning, we met up with the prosecutor and a victim's advocate, who walked us through what to expect in court. The judge was almost certain to hand down the agreed-upon sentence, but still, my stomach churned as we made our way to the courthouse, slipping in a side door to avoid the media. I kept my head down and put one foot in front of the other, willing myself not to trip. I couldn't wait for the day there weren't cameras in my face, capturing my worst and most tender moments. To my relief, the media presence outside the courthouse was mercifully minimal. Thank goodness. A reprieve from the circus.

When Chad, Kevin, and I walked into the courtroom, I immediately realized why there had been no media outside—they were all in *there*, waiting for us. Every head in the room swiveled in our direction, a sea of curious eyes fixed upon us.

We took our seats in the front row, the leather creaking beneath us as we settled in, waiting for the proceedings to begin.

"All rise for the honorable judge," the bailiff's voice rang out as the judge entered the courtroom.

Moments later, Ruby was led in, her wrists and ankles shackled. Her prison jumpsuit seemed to hang off her frame. I couldn't bear to look at her. My heart was hard. I was filled with disgust. I fixed my gaze upon the judge.

Ruby delivered her statement, painting herself as the ultimate victim, how she'd been "deceived for so long," almost as if she had been an unwitting participant in the abuse. Then, in a tone better suited to a Grammy acceptance speech, she launched into a laundry list of thank-yous to every officer, lawyer, and judge who had "snatched her out of a hell she didn't know how to get out of."

Are you sure, Ruby? I silently questioned. The preposterous notion that she had been trapped, helpless to escape the nightmare she had willingly perpetuated, was an insult to the court, and to the world.

Ruby declared that the moment of her arrest was the moment she gained her freedom. Then she turned her attention to Kevin. "You're the love of my life," she said, and I watched as Kevin bowed his head, his shoulders shaking with the weight of emotions he could not hold back.

After thanking everyone and their dog, Ruby finally turned her attention to me and my siblings. She didn't use our names, instead referring to us as her "six little chicks" and herself as our "mama duck" who had been "dragged into a current" while trying to lead us to safety. Not once did she acknowledge having been anything less than mother of the year before Jodi entered our lives. There would be no apology for the years of torment and exploitation that preceded Jodi. Listening to her hollow words, I wondered if, in her narcissistic mind, Ruby would ever fully comprehend the gravity of her actions or experience genuine remorse.

A memory popped into my head from when I was twelve years old, right before Ruby launched 8 Passengers. I had forced Ruby and Kevin to endure my three-hour stage adaptation of *Frozen*, starring myself and my siblings, written and directed by me, in our living room. The part of me that was still that little girl longing for her mom's love and approval, suddenly wondered if maybe Ruby, like Elsa, the ice queen, could travel up the mountain of the Utah prison system for a few years and up there, just . . . let it go.

Let go of the curse of control. Let go of coldness. Let go of lies.

Let it all go, until one day she would come down the mountain a different person. One who understood the meaning of love.

Reality quickly snapped me back to the present. I was no longer a little girl, and Ruby was no Disney princess. She was an adult who had made a conscious choice to inflict unspeakable harm upon those she was meant to protect. And now, she would face the consequences of her actions. Four sentences of four to fifteen years, to be served consecutively, as delivered by the court.

As Ruby was led away, I realized I, too, would have to learn to "let it go." That wouldn't mean forgetting or excusing what had happened. It would mean allowing myself to feel, to be imperfect, to love myself and others without judgment. It would mean breaking the cycles of fear and control that had been passed down to me. It would mean recognizing my power, facing my fears, and always choosing love over fear, again and again.

I reached out and grabbed Kevin's hand. Having sought guidance from Jesus, forgiving him had emerged as the right choice. I would never forget the pain he had caused, ignored, and enabled. He had not been absolved. But I had chosen to release the burden of resentment I held against him. In extending a hand of compassion and understanding, I was granting myself the freedom to heal.

Next, Jodi was escorted into the courtroom. I chose to look

directly at her face. Gone was the meticulously coiffed hair that had once been her signature; it now hung limp and greasy, framing her ashen skin. She kept her gaze resolutely trained ahead, never once making eye contact with anyone in the room, as if by avoiding our eyes, she could somehow escape the weight of her actions. As the judge rehashed the plea agreement, Jodi's lawyer tried to argue that there were "two sides to every story," prompting the judge, clearly incensed by the audacity of the statement, to demand what "other side" there could possibly be to the torture of children.

Jodi had been making phone calls from jail to her followers, painting herself as a prophet wrongly persecuted, God's messenger behind bars, comparing herself to Joseph Smith, the founder of my faith, saying things like "God speaks directly to me." The sheer arrogance and delusion of her statements left me in no doubt: Jodi was entirely unrepentant.

I had assumed that Jodi would remain silent, but to my surprise, she stood up to deliver a statement, only a few brief sentences. "I loved those children," she began, and as soon as the words left her mouth, Chad and I locked eyes, a shared sense of incredulity passing between us. Then she wished the children "beautiful, happy lives," showing zero remorse or accountability.

The judge, however, was not swayed by Jodi's empty words. He hadn't made any comment before passing sentence on Ruby, but he did this time, speaking of how adults, especially those with specialized training, have a sacred duty to protect vulnerable children, and that Jodi had done the opposite, terrorizing those in her care. He deemed her "so far detached from reality, common sense, and decency" that consecutive sentences were the only appropriate response. It was validating, hearing the disdain in his voice, the confirmation that Jodi was no innocent bystander but an active perpetrator of unspeakable horrors. She got four to thirty years, the same as Ruby.

As Jodi was led out in cuffs, reality sank in. We had won. The monsters had been caged. For how long, who knew—that would be up to the parole board. But at the very minimum, they would be inside for four years.

As soon as the gavel banged, Chad, Kevin, and I bolted for the side exit, desperate to avoid the inevitable onslaught of cameras and reporters. Our hopes were dashed as soon as we pushed open the heavy metal door and stepped out into the sunlight. A pack of reporters lay in wait, their hungry eyes fixed upon us, their cameras and microphones at the ready. They descended upon us like vultures, shouting questions that echoed across the manicured lawn as we made a mad dash for the parking lot.

"Shari, do you have a comment?" one reporter called out, thrusting a microphone in my direction.

"No comment," I replied, quickening my pace.

The reporter persisted, undeterred by my curt response. "Kevin, did you know this abuse was happening?"

"No comment," Kevin echoed, his jaw clenched.

"I understand," the reporter continued, her tone dripping with false empathy. "Chad, any remarks?"

Chad, his patience wearing thin, turned to face the reporter, and threw her one of his famously withering stares.

"I don't think you understand any of this at all, do you?" he said.

And with that, she finally shut up.

Shell-shocked and emotionally spent, we climbed into the car, each of us lost in our own thoughts as we drove through the streets of St. George. Then we did the only thing we could think to do. We drove to Cafe Rio in St. George, ordered three burritos with a side of guacamole, and talked about nothing in particular.

CHAPTER 48

ruby's journal

All I had wanted for so long was for the world to just sit up and listen, to understand that Ruby and Jodi needed to be stopped. But once they did, it seemed like people couldn't get enough. Again, thanks to Ruby, our lives were no longer our own.

Media outlets in the United States and all over the world immediately picked up the story of the holier-than-thou YouTube mommy blogger who'd been arrested on charges of child abuse alongside her best friend. The story had all the ingredients—a beautiful God-fearing American family, turning their rags into riches on YouTube, only to be wrenched apart in a dramatic turn of events featuring demon possession, doomsday-prepper cults, with lesbian undertones.

Those who had been following our family for years felt vindicated as the rest of the known universe finally woke up to what had been happening behind Ruby's white picket fence. In a way, we represented the first true, damning proof of how badly things can go wrong in a social media–driven world where kids are content and content is king.

A few weeks after Ruby's sentencing, the Washington County Attorney's Office released the evidence to the public, and with that, my nightmare was about to worsen. Because amid the photographs, documents, and digital files were my mother's handwritten journals, documenting in cold and horrible detail what had happened when she'd taken my two youngest siblings from our Springville house to live with Jodi, leaving my middle sisters behind. How for those three months, Ruby and Jodi had been putting my youngest siblings through a twisted training program, in the name of purging the evil from them, through a system of daily punishments.

Without reading them, I knew those sickening journals chronicled, right there in my mother's cursive, exactly how Ruby and Jodi had morphed into the very demons they claimed to be purging from my siblings' souls, twisted fiends who tortured little children, like something out of a grotesque Hieronymus Bosch painting.

I never wanted to read it. I never wanted to know the details. And when the authorities released my mother's journal, my world stopped spinning for a moment.

There it was, laid bare for all to see. Sixty pages of horror, and I refused to look. I knew it was bad. My imagination was filling in the gaps, and sometimes that's worse than knowing. But I couldn't . . . I wouldn't read those pages. I didn't need to read it to know what had happened.

I'm sorry, I thought, imagining my youngest siblings, trapped in that nightmare. *I'm so, so sorry. I wish I could have done more. I wish I could have taken away your pain. And everyone else: Please, just stop. Let them heal in peace. Let us all heal.*

But everyone was talking about it. The news, social media, even people on the street. Dissecting every detail, feeding this . . . this true-crime circus. Didn't they understand? These are children. My siblings. Real people who have suffered unimaginable horrors. It's not entertainment. It's not a story to be picked apart and analyzed. I wanted to scream at them all to stop. To leave it alone. Some things should remain unspoken. Some horrors should be left in the dark where they belong. This was one of them.

The day after the release of the evidence, I sat with Kevin and Chad, cameras pointed at us. We were about to watch the *20/20* episode called "Ruby Franke: From Momfluencer to Felon." Surreally, we were watching it in front of a documentary crew that was filming us, making their own film about our family. I hated this—cameras, on us again. But we'd all agreed that we had to take control of the narrative somehow, and that's why we'd decided to allow these highly reputable filmmakers in, if only to help us set the story straight, before moving on with our lives.

As the *20/20* episode began, I felt a knot form in my stomach. The room fell silent as images flashed across the screen. Suddenly, without warning, pictures of the kids' injuries appeared. I felt the air leave my lungs.

None of us had seen the photos yet.

Kevin reached out, squeezing my hand. Chad stared at the floor. I couldn't stand it.

Jodi's face appeared on-screen, and I felt a wave of disgust wash over me. Seeing Ruby's face, I felt numb. I didn't know who this person was anymore.

I hated *20/20*'s approach. It didn't feel emotionally sensitive, or appropriate in tone. I didn't think they had any other motive rather than to make a popular documentary and capitalize on a shocking news story. I wondered how the public's consumption of others' pain and suffering cross the line from empathy to voyeurism? How quickly have we, as a society, become numb to the struggles of others, our capacity for compassion eroded by the sheer volume of human drama we're exposed to daily? We were just characters in a soap opera now, except the drama was real and the consequences permanent. Our grief had been reduced to a mere commodity, packaged and sold, consumed and discarded.

For content creators, news outlets, and true-crime documentarians alike, the rewards of this emotional economy can be seductive. And the digital and media landscape remains vast and full of promise—but it is also a wilderness, and I fear we have lost our way.

I knew I had to make a stand, somehow. Part of that would be saying no to the world's desire for me to talk about my siblings, anywhere. Even in the pages of my own book. It is up to my brothers and sisters if they wish to share their story one day. But I'd be no better than Ruby if I detailed their experiences without their consent. They deserve to be given back the choice that had been stolen from them for so long.

I don't want to be anything like her, I thought. *I won't exploit them the way she did.*

CHAPTER 49

it ends here

In August 2024, I received a letter from Ruby in prison. Her lawyer passed it on to me, explaining that Ruby had written it months before, in February, but it had gotten lost in the shuffle of legal paperwork.

Reading my mother's words brought on a strange mix of emotions. It was five pages long, but its length didn't equate to substance. Two entire pages, for instance, were devoted to describing my nursery. Ruby waxed poetic about the excitement of preparing for her firstborn, the care she took in choosing colors and decorations. She spoke of me as her baby, her words dripping with nostalgia for a time long past. But reading it felt like looking through a stranger's photo album. I recognized the characters, but I couldn't connect with the emotions being described.

The letter did contain an apology. Not for any of the things I might have expected or hoped for. She didn't say sorry for the pain she'd caused us, nor did she acknowledge the reason she was in prison. Instead, Ruby expressed regret for not spending more time with me before I moved out before college. It felt like such a small thing to fixate upon, in the grand scheme of our history.

As I read, I found myself growing increasingly detached. The Ruby who wrote this letter seemed to exist in a delusional reality—one where our relationship could be mended with reminiscences about baby blankets and wall colors. She appeared to be reaching back to a time before the hurt, before the cameras, before everything went wrong. But she was still sidestepping the very real and painful issues that had driven us apart.

In the end, the letter merely reinforced my opinion of Ruby. Even now, behind bars, she still couldn't—or wouldn't—acknowledge the deeper wounds, the years of emotional manipulation, the public exploitation of our family life, the shocking harm inflicted on my youngest siblings.

The question was, why?

"Narcissism" has become somewhat of a buzzword lately. Got a self-centered boss? Narcissist. That friend who always makes it about them? Narcissist. That relative who dominates every family gathering? Narcissist. But not every self-centered act is a sign of a personality disorder. Sometimes, people are just having a bad day—or maybe they're just garden-variety jerks.

True Narcissistic Personality Disorder (NPD) is a complex and serious condition that goes far beyond being self-centered or difficult. It's a pervasive pattern of grandiosity, need for admiration, and lack of empathy that can cause significant problems in many areas of the disordered person's life.

In the world of someone with Narcissistic Personality Disorder (NPD), the universe doesn't just revolve around you—you *are* the universe. It's not a conscious choice, but rather the only way your psyche can function. Your mind is a fortress built to protect an incredibly fragile sense of self. For Ruby, narcissism wasn't a choice; it was survival, as instinctive and necessary as breathing. Just as my fawning response was my shield against the world, her grandiosity was her armor. Two different strategies, both born from the same soil of trauma and insecurity.

Imagine, if you will, the exhausting mental gymnastics going on inside the mind of someone with NPD. It's a relentless, contradictory monologue:

"I'm special. I'm the best. But why doesn't everyone see it? They must be jealous or stupid. I need to show them how amazing I am. But what if they see through me? No, that's impossible. I'm perfect. Aren't I? Of course I am. I have to be."

This isn't just ego or self-centeredness. It's a desperate, all-consuming need to maintain an image of perfection, both to the world and to oneself. Any crack in this facade isn't just uncomfortable—it's existentially threatening.

Understanding this doesn't excuse the behavior, but it does shed light on the profound suffering at its core. Extreme narcissistic behavior isn't about asserting superiority; it's about compensating for the fact that you feel fundamentally flawed and completely empty inside.

Why some people develop these behaviors while others don't, I'm not sure. Ruby might have learned as a kid that being "good" and "perfect" was the only way to be loved. "But I'm a good girl," she cried to Kevin, in the one and only phone call he had with her after her arrest.

Whatever the cause, narcissism develops as a shield—a way to protect yourself from feelings of inadequacy or harm. The cruel irony is that this very shield, meant to safeguard the self, ultimately becomes a barrier to genuine connection and fulfillment. It's a fortress that keeps others out, but also traps the narcissist within.

As for social media—for narcissists, it's like throwing gasoline on an already raging fire. Every like, share, and comment becomes a hit of validation, a momentary salve for that deep-seated insecurity. It's easy to see how it can become an all-consuming obsession, a digital stage for their never-ending performance of perfection.

Learning about narcissism has helped me process the impact Ruby's had on my life. It doesn't excuse what she did, not by a long shot. But it reminds me that behind all that manipulation lay a deeply wounded person who never learned how to connect with others in a healthy way.

Realizing your own mother was incapable of truly seeing you—of loving you for who you are rather than as an extension of herself—is a bitter pill to swallow. It's the death of a fundamental childhood hope, the one where if you just try hard enough, Mommy will love you unconditionally.

But in a strange way, this understanding has also been incredibly liberating. I now know that I could never have been "good" enough or "perfect" enough to make Ruby truly happy or proud. The insatiable void I was trying to fill wasn't created by me, and it wasn't mine to fix. That realization, as painful as it is, is the first step on the path to healing—for me, if not for her.

Sometimes I find myself tumbling down the rabbit hole of "what-ifs." What if Ruby hadn't felt like motherhood was the only path to fulfillment? What if she'd been encouraged to explore all facets of herself, beyond what her family told her was "right" for someone born a woman? Maybe if she'd had the chance to pour herself into a high-powered career in banking or physics—fields where empathy isn't exactly a priority—she wouldn't have seen her kids as employees and extensions of herself. Or maybe she wouldn't have had kids at all. It's impossible to know.

But this mental gymnastics is crazy-making, and probably just another manifestation of my fawning nature. Always trying to solve the Ruby puzzle, searching for that magic key that would've made her happy and kind. The truth is, there probably isn't a magic key. Narcissism isn't a choice; it's a deep-rooted defense mechanism. And while it can be treated, it requires extensive and dedicated effort on the part of the narcissist themselves.

There are a few "self-aware narcissists" out there on social media, and listening to them describe their true experience of the world is both fascinating and chilling. Their accounts of their feelings—or lack thereof—when it comes to the well-being of others are a stark reminder of the fundamental disconnect at the heart of this disorder.

So where does that leave us? How do we deal with the Rubys of the world? How do we balance empathy for the wounded person behind the narcissistic mask while protecting ourselves and others from the damage they can cause? I don't have all the answers, but I do know that awareness is a start. Understanding that narcissism is a complex disorder, not just a label for selfish people, is crucial. And recognizing fawning as a trauma response, not just people-pleasing, is equally important. And while all that is happening, protecting the children; regulating or outright banning family vlogging for the questionable exploitative practice that it is would be a great start.

For me, understanding the patterns has been both heartbreaking and liberating. Seeing the pattern means you can break it. It's not easy, and some days, it feels like I'm fighting against my own instincts. That urge to fawn, to sacrifice my well-being on the altar of others' comfort, still lurks in the shadows of my psyche. But every time I speak up instead of staying silent, every time I honor my own needs instead of burying them, every time I allow someone else to sit with their discomfort instead of rushing to smooth things over—I'm severing another link in that chain of generational trauma, that toxic relay race passing the baton of pain from one generation to the next.

It must end here. It's not just about healing myself anymore. It's about creating a new legacy, a new pattern for the generations that come after me and my family. I am proud of my ancestors, and I want the generations that come to be proud of me, too. That way, when we run into each other in heaven, we can look at one another and smile. (And yes, I did consult my bishop about the possibility of encountering Ruby in the celestial afterlife, should she make it there, somehow. He assured me I'm under no obligation to acknowledge or engage with her whatsoever. Small mercies, indeed.)

In the letters Ruby wrote to Kevin—letters that will forever go unanswered—she described sitting in her cell, crying the days away. And there have been moments, like on her birthday or Mother's Day, when the image of Ruby alone in her cell floods my mind and a wave of sadness washes over me. I do not wish suffering upon her; rather, I desperately hope for her to find some kind of path toward redemption, if that's even possible.

I heard she was trying to get a degree through the prison system, which is a positive step. She never finished college, after all, dropping out as soon as she married Kevin. She'll need to prepare herself, because the reality is that when she's released—whether that's in ten years or when she's much older—she'll need to support herself. I don't have a desire to see her destitute. My hope is that she can use this time to educate herself, so that upon release, she can find a way to survive. Have a small house and a quiet life. Far away from me.

Perhaps, by then, she will have found the courage to truly look within herself and begin the arduous journey of inner change. However, change was never something that came easily to my mother, if at all. At forty-three years old, when she was arrested, she was still convinced that the world revolved around her. Now, with the facades stripped away, she's left with only the truth—the raw, unfiltered truth—as her sole companion. Could she possess the strength to confront her own reflection? To see herself for who she truly is? I hope so.

As for Jodi, I'll leave her diagnosis to the experts. And the fate of her soul to God.

EPILOGUE

seven passengers

One year later

One Sunday morning, I kissed Muppet goodbye as he lounged on my bed, his newly acquired collar glinting in the sunlight streaming through the window. He looked up at me with those big, innocent eyes, and I scratched behind his ears, my heart swelling with love for this zany little creature who had become my anchor in the chaos.

As I stepped out into the crisp Utah air, a flutter of nerves danced in my stomach, but this time, they were the good kind. The kind that comes with anticipation, with the promise of something beautiful on the horizon—I was headed to a family dinner. No cameras rolling. No one telling us what to do or what to feel. Just us, together again.

I slid into the driver's seat of my Ford Focus, the engine humming to life, and navigated the well-worn path to Springville. The gridded streets, the patches of green parks, so small against the backdrop of the mountains and the vast sky above—no matter where life took me, I knew a part of me would always belong to this little town nestled at the foot of the mountains.

As I came off the highway into town, my phone buzzed with an incoming text. It was from my new bishop, the one who had become such a beacon of support since I'd left my old ward behind. He said Derek was being brought before a formal disciplinary council, his calling stripped away. A small victory, but not enough.

Derek had never lost his temple recommend, like I had. And the experience had taught me a vital lesson: that just because a church leader says something, doesn't mean they're right. Doesn't mean it's necessarily coming from God. With everything I'd gone through, I'd realized that what a human being says holds less value to me than my personal conversations with God. Those, now, are my North Star.

I turned onto my street and saw the sprawling silhouette of my home. Sitting in the driveway, rusting away, our old Chevy van—Kevin had long ago removed the 8PSNGRS license plate and the sticker. He wanted to sell it and get a truck, for when the kids came back. We really didn't have a need for such a large vehicle anymore.

I parked and walked toward the house, detecting the distinct smell of melted cheese and pepperoni as I reached for the doorknob. Was this really still my home, after everything that had happened? I wasn't sure. But hearing the sound of laughter, I knew one thing with a fierce and sudden certainty. We were together, and that was the only place I wanted to be.

I used to believe that every good thing I had in my life was thanks to Ruby. There are certainly some positive traits that stem from her. My fierce loyalty to my convictions. My knack for cleaning a bathroom until it sparkles. Yes, that's all Ruby, the echoes of her presence within me. But as I've gotten older, I've realized that the life I've created for myself and the person I've blossomed into are not *because* of Ruby but *in spite* of her.

For the first time in my life, I am genuinely happy. I've emerged from the cocoon of my past and somehow found the light. With the help of my community, endless therapy, and the healing power of mini corn dogs and powdered donettes, I'm slowly stitching my psyche back together, teaching my nervous system that it's safe to feel again, safe to rest. I'm learning to honor the grief, the rage, the riotous joy of reclaiming the autonomy stolen from that little girl forced to smile emptily for a camera she never asked to be in front of.

Yes, I still deal with the mental health consequences of my upbringing and all that's happened, but I can't help feeling proud of myself when I think about the strange odyssey I've been on in my short time on this earth. With each breath I take, I am reminded that I am alive, that I survived, and that I have the power to create a legacy of my own—without YouTube. (Oh, I took down my own channel, and made all those years of content private, just for me and my family to enjoy. I felt no emotion, no sense of loss in doing that. In fact, it felt right.)

My focus is now turned toward the future. A blank canvas waiting to be painted. But this, I know: I will break the cycle. I will trust the children. The child within me, and the children I will one day nurture.

I will trust in their resilience, their wisdom, their limitless imagination, and their innate capacity for love.

I will guide them, but I will also learn from them and allow their innocence and wonder to heal the wounded parts of my soul. Together, we will create a new story.

Now that I have peace, this is my promise. Now that I have happiness, this is my purpose.

Finally.

ACKNOWLEDGMENTS

I'm filled with gratitude for those who've helped bring this story to light. First and foremost, I'd like to thank Simon & Schuster for providing me the platform to share my truth, and my editor Natasha Simons, whose thoughtfulness and understanding helped me navigate my fears and doubts throughout this difficult process.

I'm forever grateful to Caroline Ryder, my writing collaborator, for putting to words the raw emotions and dialogue I've held close to my heart for years.

This book also wouldn't have been possible without Larry Shapiro, my manager and friend. Your unwavering support has been my anchor in turbulent times.

I'm profoundly grateful for the love and encouragement given to me by Mom and Dad and all my other chosen family. Your support has been a beacon of hope, reminding me that family can be more than just blood.

And last of all, I couldn't have written this book without the courage of my siblings and my father, Kevin; thank you for your pure hearts and love. This book is a testament to our shared resilience and the unbreakable bonds between us—now and for eternity.